THEORY AND PRACTICE IN THE STUDY
OF ADULT EDUCATION

RADICAL FORUM ON ADULT EDUCATION SERIES
Edited by Jo Campling, Series Consultant: Colin
Griffin

Theory and Practice in the Study of Adult Education

The Epistemological Debate

Edited by
BARRY P. BRIGHT

ROUTLEDGE
London and New York

First published 1989
by Routledge
11 New Fetter Lane, London EC4P 4EE
29 West 35th Street, New York, NY 10001

© 1989 Barry P. Bright

Printed in Great Britain by
Richard Clay Ltd, Bungay, Suffolk

British Library Cataloguing in Publication Data

Theory and practice in the study of adult education: the
    epistomological debate. – (Radical forum
    on adult education series)
    1. Adult education
    I. Bright, Barry II. Series
    374

    ISBN 0-415-03909-6 (pbk)
        0-415-02446-3 (csd)

*Library of Congress Cataloging in Publication Data
is available on request*

This book is dedicated to the efforts
and wisdom of its contributors:

Paul F. Armstrong
Stephen D. Brookfield
Colin Griffin
R.W.K. Paterson
and Robin S. Usher

CONTENTS

CONTRIBUTORS

Paul F. Armstrong Research Evaluation Officer, London Borough of Haringey, Education Service; formerly Lecturer in Adult Education and Sociology, School of Adult and Continuing Education, University of Hull. Recently completed two years' secondment as Research Officer with Further Education Unit, London. Author of many articles and chapters in journals and edited books in adult education.

Barry P. Bright Lecturer in Psychology and Adult Education, School of Adult and Continuing Education, University of Hull; author of a monograph on adult learning and development, an article on adult education epistemology; contributor to several national and international conferences in adult education.

Stephen D. Brookfield Professor of Higher and Adult Education, Teachers' College, University of Columbia, New York City. Serves on editorial boards of Adult Education Quarterly (USA), Studies in Continuing Education (Australia), and the Canadian Journal for Studies in Adult Education. His books include Adult Learners, Adult Education and the Community, Understanding and Facilitating Adult Learning, Learning Democracy, Developing Critical Thinkers and Training Educators of Adults.

Colin Griffin Tutor at Hillcroft College, Surrey; part-time tutor at the University of London Extra-mural Department; Associate Lecturer in the Department of Educational Studies, University of Surrey. Author of Curriculum Theory in Adult and Lifelong Education (Croom Helm, 1983) and Adult Education as Social Policy (Croom Helm, 1987).

Ronald W.K. Paterson Senior Lecturer in Philosophy, School of Adult and Continuing Education, University of Hull. Author of Values, Education and the Adult (Routledge, 1979) and several articles in adult education journals.

Robin S. Usher Senior Lecturer in Adult Education, University of Southampton. Author and co-author of several articles in adult education journals, and co-author with I.Bryant of The Captive Triangle: Theory, Practice, and Research for Adult Education (Routledge, 1988).

Chapter one

INTRODUCTION: THE EPISTEMOLOGICAL IMPERATIVE

Barry P. Bright

BACKGROUND TO THE BOOK: A PERSONAL ANECDOTE

The idea of this book first occurred to me at about 3.30 a.m. in the back of a motor home when travelling overland between Texas and Syracuse, New York State, in May 1986. I was part of the second contingent of British adult educators who were visiting America within the Kellogg UK-USA Adult Education Exchange programme. Having completed the first stage of my visit as the guest of Texas A and M University, I, and several colleagues from that university, were travelling to the Adult Education Research Conference in Syracuse. The overland trip, which took forty-eight hours' non-stop travelling, offered me a golden opportunity to experience American culture and landscape on a scale not available to most of the exchange fellows. Because of the richness of this experience, and the geographical vastness of America, I found myself unable to sleep and consequently began to muse upon my position in adult education in Britain, in comparison to that of my American counterparts. I was also worrying about the paper I was due to give at the Syracuse conference, which was concerned with the epistemological relationship between adult education and psychology. This paper was based on an earlier paper which had been published in 1985 and which was my first published paper in adult education. As a result of my limited exposure to American adult education, it did not appear that my American colleagues were very concerned with or interested in such epistemological issues in their teaching or research, hence my worries about the kind of reception my conference paper would get. On reflection, it also appeared that my colleagues in British

1

adult education were not really interested in these kinds of issues either, although frequent informal discussion and comments did indicate an awareness of these problems and their impact upon professional activities. From these thoughts emerged the idea of an edited book on the epistemological status and nature of adult education. On my return to Britain I discussed the idea with Paul Armstrong, Ronald Paterson, and Colin Griffin, all of whom strongly supported it, and all agreed to contribute a chapter. Following this I approached Stephen Brookfield and Robin Usher, who also warmly welcomed the book and agreed to write a chapter each.

This, of course, is to summarize heavily a relatively drawn out process which involved many doubts and uncertainties over a protracted period of time. It may be pertinent to dwell on the real origin of the book, which lay in the circumstances surrounding the writing of my first published paper in adult education (Bright, 1985). The reason for this is that it may indicate in detailed professional terms the kind of problems I was experiencing within adult education, and how these came to be recognized as epistemological in character. These problems also forced me to question the true nature and definition of adult education.

I entered adult education more by accident than by intention. Having recently finished a degree in psychology as an adult student in 1981, I was unable to obtain a full-time teaching post or a funded research position, and consequently offered my services to Hull University's Department of Adult Education as an extra-mural part-time tutor, doing courses in developmental psychology. Shortly after this, in 1982, a full-time post for a psychologist became available. I applied, although, since I did not possess a PhD at that time and my experience of adult education was very limited, I doubted that I would be asked to attend for interview. However, because I had an academic inter-disciplinary background (degrees in economics, psychology, and a postgraduate degree in town and country planning), and nearly ten years of professional experience in local government, and had demonstrated some degree of commitment and interest in adult education, I was deemed suitable and was offered the post. The duties, in addition to extra-mural work, included teaching on postgraduate courses in the study of adult education, and, more particularly, courses oriented to teaching and learning in the adult context, about which I knew very little in the academic, formal sense. This is possibly a typical experience in Britain, since there are no undergraduate degree courses in the study of adult education.

My first two years (1982-4) studying and teaching adult education as a subject were profoundly frustrating both to myself and, I suspect, to my students. I read a representative sample of the relevant literature (e.g. Knowles, Knox, Brookfield and many others) in the teaching and learning of adults but quickly came to approach such reading with an apprehension that bordered on dread. The material seemed superficial in the welter of insignificant and marginal detail and, in other instances, the gross over-simplification of complex theories and perspectives. This superficiality was in stark contrast to what I had come to recognize in psychology as deep and thoroughly investigated knowledge, even accepting its limitations. In my teaching I adopted an orientation which was rooted in mainstream psychology and its theories, but used the literature within adult education as examples of the adult context for these theories. There appeared no other option, since all the literature seemed to indicate a thinly disguised - indeed, palpably obvious - adoption of a similar approach, but one which flattened and reduced the richness and highly textured quality of psychological knowledge. The students, although very hard-working and conscientious, often found great difficulty in grasping basic psychological concepts and issues and their relevance to adult education. Even allowing for the fact that none of the students possessed a degree in a social science subject, I was perplexed, since I had taken great care to pitch my teaching at a very broad and relatively simple level, using many examples from everyday life.

At this point I decided that there was a need to deepen adult education's understanding of psychological knowledge. However, I recognized that the only way this could be done was by offering a broader level and a more general frame of reference within which psychological theories and concepts could be located and interpreted, rather than by focusing upon some highly specific theory or concept. Again, the reason for this was the literature within adult education, which seemed to avoid the detail of psychological theories but, on the basic principles of those theories, produced an alarming and largely vacuous plethora of supposedly distinct adult educational tenets or applications, which often contradicted the principles of the original theories. What

3

appeared to be needed was a clear statement of those original principles. I began working on a paper which was an attempt to locate theories of adult learning and development within the metaphysical models of mechanism and organicism, the two major models within psychology. After several months of attempting, but always failing, to find an appropriate form in which these models could be readily described and comprehended, I came to the conclusion that the problems experienced by students in relation to taught psychological knowledge would also be experienced by the teachers of adult education, including those who possessed a psychology degree. Respectable psychological knowledge would not fit into the simplified and readily digestible but superficial form common in adult education, and I was intuitively certain that colleagues, divorced from this level of complexity, would not find it readable or understandable. Imagine my frustration at recognizing the obvious but ignored and highly distorted dependence of adult education upon psychology, and my inability to remedy this (to some small extent) in a direct manner with respect to either students or their educators. A further source of exasperation was the fact that the study of adult education in Britain takes place within universities, the archetypal institutions of academic learning and scholarship.

At this point I was forced to abandon my original intention for the paper and was thrown into an intense period of re-evaluation in which the epistemological relationship between adult education and psychology was fundamentally questioned, which, in turn, led me to question the nature and status of adult education itself. The overwhelming conclusion appeared to be that adult education could not be regarded as epistemologically distinct from psychology and the major social science disciplines, and that attempts to render it as distinct in theoretical knowledge terms were bound to fail, and, indeed, had already failed. I therefore suggested that, although its epistemological base, as far as 'theoretical' knowledge was concerned, had to be regarded as residing within the major disciplines, adult education could define itself in 'practical' terms which would bestow a degree of distinctiveness upon its activity and study.

From the original position of intending to write a paper concerning substantive psychological knowledge, I was forced to write a paper which was effectively concerned with epistemology and the epistemological structure, status and definition of adult education. This was a direct result of my earlier teaching and research efforts and their attendant failure. Although my relative lack of experience within adult education (at that time two years) was a cause for considerable hesitancy on my part in writing and submitting the final paper for publication, it was probably an advantage, since I had not become socialized into the normally accepted epistemological chaos and confusion represented by adult education. Also, having recently finished a degree in a major discipline (psychology), my expectations were, and still are, very much influenced by what I regarded as a more fundamental and intrinsic approach to the definition and discovery of knowledge.

THE EPISTEMOLOGICAL IMPERATIVE

The point of referring to this anecdote in some detail is that it does demonstrate the epistemological conflict, in practical and professional terms, between adult education and its source disciplines and, more important, suggests an imperative need for educators to be explicitly aware of the knowledge base they are using. This awareness may not take the form of a rigid acceptance of one particular view of knowledge or epistemological definition of adult education. On the contrary, the first academically legitimate step in approaching this awareness is the recognition that epistemology itself is eclectic and contains many views and definitions of knowledge and their consequent definitions of education and adult education. For example, my 1985 paper was not categorically stating that adult education should be defined in either a 'theoretical' or a 'practical' manner, but was, rather, drawing attention to these as possible alternatives with consequent epistemological implications and problems, which it is the professional responsibility of adult education to recognize and determine with respect to itself. A 'blind' commitment to any one view or perspective is itself antithetical to a meaningful commitment, which can be defined by informed awareness. This seemed especially relevant in respect to university-level adult education and its educators, who, presumably and reasonably, can be expected to demonstrate an informed and critical perspective. Indeed, this suggestion can be applied to all 'educators', in that whatever view of knowledge is encapsulated and assumed within, and thereby determines, their professional activities, it demands an informed recognition. Too often, perhaps, educators make the false distinction between epistemological issues and the knowledge they use in their work. Emphasizing the relevance of the latter and the irrelevance of the former amounts to a tacit acceptance of one view of knowledge to the total exclusion of other views. The earlier anecdote draws attention to the logical impossibility of this position in adult education, and the consequent necessity of recognizing the direct link between epistemology and the professional activity of educators. Alternative views of knowledge entail alternative definitions of educational practice, and thus have a direct bearing on the detailed structure and objective of professional practice.

This is, of course, precisely the objective and purpose of the present book, which attempts to offer a variety of perspectives concerning the definition of knowledge and their consequent definitions of education and adult education, in both epistemological and their associated professional terms. Whilst some may view this debate with apprehension, suspicion, or even derision, an additional objective of the book is the further development of adult education, which, it is suggested, cannot proceed in the absence of such a debate. Indeed, all the contributors to the book suggest, from their different positions and perspectives, that the absence of this debate has produced the unfortunate situation adult education now represents. More of the same is regarded as regressive, ill-advised and unprofessional. It is only by engaging with, and considering, the views presented in this volume that a deeper and more fundamental understanding of adult education, its epistemology, and professional activity will be achieved. This is a necessary requisite for the suggested need for an improvement in, or redefinition of, the activity represented by adult education.

Of course, such engagement with and consideration of these differing views may not occur easily. Epistemology is complex and often abstract. This is especially the case with an interdisciplinary area such as adult education, which has hitherto assumed and therefore avoided, rather than examined, the nature of its complex epistemology. In addition, the very existence of the epistemological problems, as outlined by each of the contributors and the manner with which these relate to professional practice, prevent or obscure recognition of those problems. In this sense, the problems take on a self-fulfilling and stubborn character, which requires a considerable degree of re-evaluation, often at a personal professional level, in order to penetrate the comfortable, but misplaced, sense of professional security and identity.

As indicated, the book focuses upon the study of adult education as a subject in which university postgraduate degrees are awarded. Although not receiving formal professional recognition and certification in Britain, such courses typically involve teaching the teachers of adults in a multitude of institutional and vocationally oriented settings. As a subject adult education typically offers courses in the teaching and learning of adults, the organization and management of adult educational institutions and providing agencies, the history of adult education, community adult education, adult education and social change, the philosophy of adult education, continuing professional and in-service education, the nature of the curriculum and the developing curricula within adult education, and adult education in developing countries. Adult education as a subject must not be confused with extra-mural adult education, which comprises day and evening courses for the general public in a variety of social science, humanities, and natural science subjects. Extra-mural adult education could form a specialized topic within the study of adult education and, indeed, the study of adult education could be used as the content of an extra-mural course. However, the two are not synonymous. Adult education does, however, bear an obviously close relationship to the subject of education itself, and as several of the following chapters indicate (e.g. Paterson, Armstrong, Usher), all the issues discussed have a direct relevance for interdisciplinary educational areas and activity. In this sense, the present book has greater significance and relevance than its declared focus upon the study of adult education would indicate.

STRUCTURE OF THE BOOK

The structure of the book and the sequencing of chapters are based on an attempt to provide the reader with a logical progression through the differing views of the contributors. Although difficult and fraught with exceptions and qualifications, the underlying rationale governing their arrangement was a perceived continuum, from those views suggesting a close and logically necessary relationship between adult education and the major disciplines, to those which suggested the opposite of this, the two ends of this continuum being represented by Paterson (chapter two) and Griffin (chapter six) respectively. Brookfield (chapter seven) represents a problem in this respect, since, although he adopts a position close to that of Paterson, his major focus is upon cross-cultural, transatlantic issues. The impact and relevance of these issues were regarded as better maximized if Brookfield's chapter was read in the context of the other contributors' views, which suggested its location subsequent to them.

Another structural theme within the book, and one which is largely but not totally achieved within its present form, is the distinction between a specific discipline focus and a general focus upon the social sciences. Thus Paterson, Bright, and Armstrong consider epistemological issues in the study of adult education from the perspective of individual disciplines (i.e. philosophy (chapter two), psychology (chapter three), and sociology (chapter five), respectively), whilst Usher, Brookfield, and Griffin adopt a more general epistemological remit and perspective. The only exceptions to this theme in the structure of the book are Armstrong's and Usher's chapters. Because Armstrong, in contrast to Usher, agrees with Griffin's ideological criticism of the conventional disciplines and thus adopts a more negative view of them within adult education, it was felt that his chapter should follow Usher's, in conformity with the previously mentioned objective of placing the chapters in order of disagreement with the role and status of the discipline model of knowledge within adult education.

SUMMARY OF CHAPTERS

Chapter two (Paterson) considers the current and suggested future relationship between adult eduction and the discipline of philosophy. It represents a cogent and tightly argued analysis in which it is suggested that adult education and many of its concepts and statements stand in need of logical criticism. Some of the concepts (e.g. 'praxis', the social construction theory of knowledge) that are criticized in this chapter represent the interpretive basis and framework of other chapters (e.g. Griffin, Armstrong, and Usher). The logical necessity of adult education's dependence upon

philosophy and the latter's major contribution to epistemological validity in terms of logical criticism are strongly
evident. Adult education's current lack of adherence to this
epistemological method poses major questions concerning
the legitimacy of its activity as a branch of education and
the status of adult educators as 'educated'. The chapter
concludes with an outline suggestion of six models which
prescribe adult education's relationship to philosophy
consistent with the approach adopted.

Bright's chapter (chapter three) adopts a somewhat
similar approach but in the context of adult education's
relationship to psychology. The chapter examines the issues
of the origin, selection, and status of psychological
knowledge within adult education, and suggests that the
latter is guilty of epistemological vandalism with respect
to all three issues. It is suggested that adult education
effectively ignores the psychological origin of much of the
knowledge it draws upon and its vandalism (e.g. false
dichotomies, high levels of abbreviation, conceptual
inaccuracies) of this knowledge. Similarly, adult education
ignores the selection problem created by the high degree of
epistemological overlap between psychology and adult
education. A further theme within the chapter is the view
that adult education exploits its dependence upon
psychology in the manner of legitimizing its own existence
whilst simultaneously reneging upon the epistemological
imperatives of this dependence. This is also the case, it is
suggested, with respect to all of its source disciplines.
Although accepting this view within a 'theoretical' definition
of adult education, Bright also suggests that a 'practical'
definition is possible and that this does not necessarily
contradict the use of theoretical knowledge. Whether a
theoretical or practical definition of adult education is
adopted, Bright suggests the inevitable use of theoretical,
discipline-based knowledge and the epistemological responsibilities this entails. Within a practical approach, this
knowledge would be complemented by informal theory
residing at the practitioner level. Bright also draws
attention to the epistemologically and professionally contradictory position in which the subject specialist in adult
education is currently placed.

The theme of informal practitioner knowledge is taken
up and discussed in more detail by Usher (chapter four). The
coventional discipline model is regarded as inappropriate for
education, since the latter is essentially concerned with

9

localized practice involving heterogeneous situations and contexts, which contain value judgements and operational differences. The conventional discipline model is criticized on the grounds of its claim to objectivity and its generalized and universal character, which cannot be directly 'applied' to any particular situation. Other problems include inter- and intradisciplinary eclecticism, which render impossible the selection of any one theoretical approach. Praxis is suggested as the only realistic approach to education, this involving the dialectical relationship between situated practice and informal theory. Formal theoretical knowledge is also regarded in this dialectical manner such that it, too, can be regarded as occurring within localized contexts and their moral value and methodological assumptions. Within this 'praxical' definition of education, a role for formal discipline-based knowledge is accepted as both a source of metaphor and sensitizing concepts for the interpretation of informal knowledge and as an example of the dialectical relationship between theory and practice.

Chapter five (Armstrong) focuses upon the relationship between adult education and sociology. Within this, Armstrong discusses the problematical history of professional education courses. Although emphasizing generic teacher education, its relevance and applicability to adult education are obvious. Armstrong examines the related issue of whether sociology is relevant within education and, if so, which sociology should be included. The latter invokes the interdisciplinary eclecticism within sociology and the question of left-wing bias in some of its theories. Within this approach the relevance of sociology is referred to as offering a useful perspective on the activity of educators. However, doubts are also raised concerning the possibility of teaching a complex subject at a lower level to students inexperienced in relation to social science subjects. Similarly, the possibility of sociology being reduced to a technical educational instrument within a given social system, rather than it raising questions about that system and thereby contradicting the objectives of sociology, is also suggested. In addition, Armstrong quotes one view which suggests the incompatibility between a critical thinking mode and the requirements and operations of practical teaching. The question of left-wing bias within sociology Armstrong regards as due to the false perception of sociologists and educators, suggesting that sociology can be better regarded as right-wing rather than left-wing. Claims for a humble eclecticism (whether or not they exclude supposedly left-wing sociological theories) he regards as fundamentally dishonest. The chapter concludes with the view that the questions of whether to include, and if so, which, sociology, can be regarded as 'red herrings' which, although raising important and interesting issues, essentially lie outside the practical nature of education. Like Usher, Armstrong suggests the need for a 'praxical' approach which includes a role for conventional discipline-based knowledge but which will 'cut across' the disciplines. Although Armstrong does not discuss this in detail, he does refer to the ideological nature of conventional knowledge and the manner in which it maintains unequal social and economic relations in society.

Griffin (chapter six) invokes critical theory as the interpretive basis for his claim that adult education directly reflects the ideological assumptions, methods, and content of the conventional disciplines. Like Usher, Griffin defines knowledge in a context-dependent and dialectical manner. However, unlike Usher, he extends this context to the cultural and political level. The chapter suggests that conventional knowledge, as represented by the disciplines, conveys a fundamentally unreal and deceptive perception of knowledge in its divorce from ideological content, as manifested in the false divisions between objectivity/ subjectivity, fact/value, theory/practice, pure/applied, and instrumental/intrinsic dimensions. All knowledge is regarded as a function of the political context within which it occurs, and whose social and economic relations it legitimizes, maintains, and perpetuates. Griffin suggests the adoption of a 'praxical' dialectical approach to adult education in which current concepts and theories within it would be subject to ideological scrutiny, to discover the particular professional manifestation of the deeper social and economic interests they serve.

Chapter seven (Brookfield) comprises a cross-cultural analysis of the epistemology of adult education in Britain and the United States. The chapter suggests that, although there is historical evidence indicating the previously strong presence of political and philosophical debate within American adult education, currently this debate is present only within British adult education. Brookfield places this conclusion within a comparative cultural perspective which includes the greater American emphasis upon pragmatism and consensus relative to Britain. The latter is regarded as possessing a much greater cultural acceptance of political and philosophical dissent and an awareness of history, which is reflected within British adult education curricula and academic debate. The lack of this debate within current American adult education is attributed to its definition in technicist professional terms, which largely eschews such debate, and which is infused with a capitalist political ethos resulting in a consumer-oriented approach to adult education and education generally. In addition, this pragmatic, technicist tendency betokens a professional insecurity which is manifested in the questionable validity of the epistemological and methodological distinctiveness of adult education. Brookfield suggests the need to reintroduce political and philosophical debate within American adult education as an educational, not a political, objective, and also suggests the need to recognize its epistemological dependence on conventional knowledge.

Bright (chapter eight) attempts to offer an interpretive framework within which the views presented in the earlier chapters may be located or better understood. Within this he suggests the presence of three alternative positions in relation to the view adopted of the role of the conventional disciplines within adult education. He further suggests that these views are related to different definitions of knowledge and the nature of logic itself as a method of defining knowledge.

The final chapter (chapter nine) comprises further thoughts and elaboration by several of the contributors as a postscript to Bright's overview and conclusions (chapter eight). All the contributors were offered the opportunity of commenting upon that chapter and suggesting alternative interpretations and/or further thoughts and observations. Griffin and Brookfield, although critical in some respects, were happy with it; however, Armstrong, Usher, and Paterson took the opportunity of responding to particular aspects.

REFERENCE

Bright, B.P. (1985) 'The content-method relationship in the study of adult education', Studies in the Education of Adults 17: 168-83.

Chapter two

PHILOSOPHY AND ADULT EDUCATION

R. W. K. Paterson

Each of us operates with some kind of map or overall picture of the world, tucked away somewhere in our minds, by conscious or unconscious reference to which we try to make some sense, however rough-and-ready, of our daily experience. The structure and contents of our world-pictures are selected and shaped partly by adventitious features of our personal lives; partly by various general truths and forms of understanding discovered and developed by whatever branches of scientific or other public rational inquiry have happened to impinge on our awareness; partly by 'common sense', that is, by the largely uncriticized beliefs widely held among those with whom we habitually associate; and partly by the influence upon us of some favoured belief-package which for one reason or another we may find unusually convincing - for example, reductionist materialism, Christianity, or Marxism. The more reflective we are, the more strenuously we try to fit new experiences into our overall cognitive map, and to test the accuracy of our map against the challenge of new experiences. But some kind of map is there, even when it is left for the most part unexamined.

There are many good reasons for attempting to state our overall world-picture clearly and systematically. (For instance, this exercise may reveal that it contains serious gaps or, worse, serious inconsistencies.) And when we do attempt to state our most fundamental beliefs about the world comprehensively and coherently, we shall typically find that our general statement is made up of propositions which belong to several quite different logical kinds. There will be empirical propositions, which may be more or less wide-ranging in their subject-matter: for example, 'All human beings die', 'The human race has evolved from more primitive life-forms', 'The Earth is a planet revolving around one of the ten thousand million stars in one galaxy of perhaps a hundred thousand million galaxies in the Universe'. There will be <u>value judgements</u>: for example, 'The quality of an individual's life ultimately resolves into the happiness he succeeds in generating for himself and others', 'It is unfair that anyone should have a better or worse life than anyone else'. There will be sets of propositions which enshrine <u>arguments, inferences, chains of reasoning</u>: for example, 'Since language is essential to our humanity, and since language is a social institution, human nature is inextricably social', 'Because our mental processes replicate the workings of ultra-sophisticated computers, human choices do not arise from any kind of freewill but are always the outcome of a complex type of programming'. And there will be non-empirical or trans-empirical propositions which make higher-order, <u>metaphysical assertions</u> about the overarching constitution of the world: for example, 'Nothing can exist which is not a physical object or force, existing or operating in space', 'The Universe is the creation of a purposive Intelligence', 'All events result from antecedent conditions in complete accordance with natural laws'.

Now, what special contribution can be made by philosophy, as a distinctive branch of inquiry, to the formation and assessment of the world-pictures into which we fit our experiences and from the standpoint of which we make our personal responses and take our social initiatives?

It must be said at the outset that there are certain tasks which philosophy <u>cannot</u> be called upon to perform. Although philosophy is a study of beliefs, it needs to be distinguished from the psychological, sociological, or historical study of beliefs. The psychologist may trace the ways in which, for instance, religious beliefs reflect the psychological characteristics of those who hold them; the sociologist may illuminate the part which, for instance, beliefs about male superiority tend to play in the economic functioning of various kinds of society; the historian may show us how this or that system of beliefs has in fact emerged - how, for instance, the rise of Protestantism accompanied the growth of capitalist property institutions. The philosopher does not <u>qua</u> philosopher study the empirical origins, accompaniments, or consequences of human beliefs, past or present. Like scientists, philosophers are concerned with the <u>grounds</u> for our beliefs and the <u>logical implications</u> of our beliefs (what other beliefs follow from the beliefs being examined), not with their psychological, social, or historical contexts. Like scientists, philosophers are interested in which of our beliefs are actually true.

However, unlike scientists, philosophers do not devise or conduct experiments or construct and test empirical generalizations based upon a range of carefully noted observations. Philosophy is esentially an a priori inquiry, and thus philosophers have no professional competence to pronounce upon the truth or falsehood, the probability or improbability, of the empirical assertions made by scientists (or indeed by psychologists, sociologists, or historians). Such pronouncements must be left to the appropriate specialists.

Nor can philosophers qua philosophers propound value judgements or lay down moral principles. Although there is indeed an area of philosophical inquiry which we designate as 'moral philosophy', the moral philosopher is not the custodian of a body of moral truths or insights in the way that a geologist is the possessor of a body of truths about the strata of the Earth's crust.

Yet undoubtedly philosophy does have an important part to play in our pursuit of moral truths, of surer moral perspectives and nicer moral distinctions; and it even has a significant, if lesser, part to play in our scientific pursuits. Our debates about the morality of this or that type and degree of punishment, about abortion, euthanasia, war and peace, or the fair distribution of wealth, all involve patterns of reasoning which may be in different measure valid or invalid, perhaps to some extent depending on logical ambiguities, fallacies, or concealed premises; and they will necessarily involve the use of moral concepts like 'desert', 'obligation', 'entitlement', and so on, which may be used with great consistency and clarity, or with some inconsistency and logical muddle; and on these aspects of our moral discussions a philosopher is professionally competent to make judgements. Likewise, the natural and social sciences have philosophical aspects. Questions about the nature of 'proof' in the physical sciences, the logical problems of induction, the logical status of postulated entities, the concept of 'explanation' in the human sciences, deterministic presuppositions in psychology and sociology - these are merely a few examples of issues in which philosophers of science and of the social sciences have a distinctive professional interest. And of course the very claim that 'moral' principles are under discussion, or that an activity is 'scientific', embodies a claim about types of epistemological status, to which contemporary philosophers have given more detailed attention than perhaps ever before.

Philosophy is often thought of as being mainly if not exclusively concerned with the kinds of non-empirical or trans-empirical propositions which I referred to earlier as 'metaphysical assertions'. Discussions as to whether everything that exists is physical, or whether there is a God, or whether every event has a determining cause, are often regarded as belonging essentially to the province of philosophy. However, although traditionally such questions have tended to be left to philosophers (or appropriated by philosophers as their specific concerns), strictly speaking they are interdisciplinary questions, to which admittedly philosophy can make a central and sometimes decisive contribution. Much of the reverence which philosophy as a subject has enjoyed, and from which it has also suffered, has arisen from the undoubtedly true belief that the answers to our metaphysical questions will have the profoundest significance for any world-picture or map of experience which we may try to construct, and from the false belief that it is to philosophy alone that we can look for these answers. The universality of determining causation is a question to which certain discoveries and theories in physics and astronomy are plainly relevant; a reasoned belief in a God cannot ignore the testimony of religious experience and of revelation, and here philosophy must be partnered by theology and perhaps also science; the truth or falsity of physicalist monism will partly depend on data from physics, biochemistry, neuropsychology, and even linguistics, as well as on philosophical analysis.

Nevertheless, although philosophy is not uniquely concerned with these overarching metaphysical questions, which have such constitutive importance for our overall cognitive maps or world-pictures, it is fair to say that philosophy does have a special interest in them. There are four reasons why this is always likely to be so.

In the first place, metaphysical issues are never resolvable solely by utilizing the techniques or data which fall within the province of a single specialist discipline. This is partly because they often arise at the intersection of two or more disciplines, which may tend to overlap or seemingly conflict, and thus at points of common interest where there are no clear boundary demarcations. The precise nature of the relationship between mental states and physical brain states, for example, cannot be established either by brain scientists or by psychologists, working separately or even together, since this issue is largely about possible logical relationships between data of radically different kinds. To clarify this central human and intellectual issue it is necessary to examine various logical models - such as dualistic, epiphenomenalist, or identity theories - the development and analysis of which is a distinctively philosophical task. Philosophical analysis is by no means sufficient, but it is indispensably necessary as part of our attack on the mind-brain problem.

Secondly, the concepts around which metaphysical issues revolve are public concepts, rather than technical concepts which are used in accordance with strict definitions laid down by some specialist discipline. Concepts like 'space', 'time', 'move', 'cause', 'result', 'think', or 'remember', are quite different from such concepts as 'integral', 'gravity', 'radioactivity' , 'photosynthesis', 'cyto-plasm', or 'synapse', which are relatively uncontentious because their use is tightly governed by rules which are generally agreed within the disciplines in which they figure. There are no generally agreed rules governing the use of concepts like 'free', 'choose', or 'act', which everyone uses almost from the earliest beginnings of speech, and which are of key importance in our discussion of whether there is such a thing as a 'free choice' or a 'free act'. The issue of freewill and determinism is greatly illuminated by psychological, neurophysiological, and other empirical discoveries, but it cannot be fully clarified without the contribution made by philosophical analysis of the many public concepts which are centrally at stake and of the logical relationships which may hold or fail to hold among them.

Thirdly, metaphysical issues tend to occur at an unusually high level of abstractness, and their connection with concrete empirical facts tends to be methodologically remote. The work of physicists and chemists can proceed satisfactorily without these specialists bothering too much about whether they are investigating 'ultimate reality'. Nevertheless this remains a perfectly relevant human question. Are sense data, which arguably could not exist in the absence of sentient beings, the ultimate constituents of knowable reality? Is the physical world a logical construction from sense data? Or are sense data merely the representations, to beings equipped with a sensory apparatus, of an underlying, non-sensible, colourless, odourless, soundless physical substance or force? How, then, can the physical world be truly knowable as it is 'in itself'? From ancient times, and in modern times from Descartes through Kant to Russell up to the present day, this has been seen as a prime example of a small number of fundamental questions which are <u>exclusively</u> philosophical in character, because no accumulation of new truths about the observable world could possibly resolve an issue which puts the ultimate status of these truths themselves in question.

Fourthly, metaphysical issues loom large in those <u>belief-packages</u> which are on more or less permanent offer to the believing public - neo-Darwinism, Marxism, Christianity, reductionist materialism, and so on - and which make competitive bids for our intellectual assent and often practical loyalties. Such belief-packages may be high in empirical content, with abundant references to genetic mutations, animal behaviour, class conflict, computer functionings, or whatever. However, they also depend on sundry views about the logical nature of knowledge, and they lay claim to internal logical consistency as well as explanatory comprehensiveness. They therefore cry out for searching logical analysis. Thus Popper has argued, for example, that reductionist materialism, while of course claiming to be rational, undermines the very concept of 'rationality'; that Marxism, whatever else it may be, is certainly not a 'scientific' theory because it does not lend itself to falsification; and that Darwinism should be regarded as a 'metaphysical research programme', that is, not as a testable scientific theory but rather as a possible framework for testable scientific theories. Perhaps he is wrong in each of these conclusions. But the point is that questions about the epistemological status of belief-packages do need to be asked, and it is the business of philosophy to ask them and try to answer them.

From everything I have said it should now be evident that philosophy, as a distinctive academic discipline, is essentially an activity of logical criticism. Criticism of beliefs, both prevailing beliefs and (equally) proffered alternative beliefs, has always been at the centre of serious philosophy. Socrates was distinguished, not by his knowledge, but by knowing that he did not know, and the name of Descartes is almost synonymous with systematic rational doubt. Philosophy is the criticism of beliefs from a logical standpoint. This form of criticism is not an optional extra, which we may adopt or leave alone according to circumstances or our personal or social preferences, since someone who states a 'belief' which is logically incoherent has in fact simply failed to state a belief. A self-contradictory 'belief', for example, simply annuls itself. Similarly, a logically invalid 'argument' is not a weak, or idiosyncratic, or ingeniously novel type of argument. It is not an argument at all. We do not need to observe the requirements of logic if we confine our mental lives to blind feeling and our physical and social lives to mindless reactions. But if we wish to entertain thoughts, to communicate them, and to reason, either by ourselves or with others, we must at least meet the demands of logical consistency. As the theory and practice of logic, it is the task of philosophy to ensure that this absolutely necessary condition of all thinking, discourse, and reasoning is satisfied in the main areas of serious human concern.

Philosophy, then, is not a body of knowledge but a form of activity, of critical inquiry. Of course all academic disciplines involve distinctive forms of critical inquiry. However, other academic disciplines seek also to establish a body of ascertained truths on which they can build a greater and better structured body of truths, even if they of course recognize that the claimed truths which they have at present assembled are always open to subsequent revision or even complete rejection. It is sometimes objected against philosophy that it 'never achieves definite results'. This is wholly to misunderstand what philosophy essentially is. Certainly it does not of itself discover new truths about the universe, man, or society. Its function is to exercise ceaseless vigilance over the ways in which we pursue and proclaim new truths, lest these be contaminated by any of the numerous forms of logical ineptitude or improbity to which our intellectual endeavours are always vulnerable. It also exercises this function upon itself, for clearly the work of monitoring needs to be itself ceaselessly monitored, and much of the history of philosophy (as with any academic discipline) consists in the detection and amendment of previous philosophical errors. To be effectively critical, philosophy has to be continuously self-critical, examining and re-examining its own practices, approaches, and techniques. It accepts no limits whatever to rational criticism. Thus its chief intellectual instrument - logic itself - is constantly under debate and review by its specialist logicians. Alone of all academic disciplines, philosophy is totally presuppositionless. And if the identification of unavowed assumptions, the exposure of fallacies in inference, and the elucidation of vitiating ambiguities in the use of key concepts, are a vitally necessary task, not only for the progress of the physical and human sciences but also in the fields of morality and social action, I think it can be claimed that philosophy has produced 'results' in perhaps dismaying abundance. And if these are not 'definite' in the sense of final and unalterable, this is because finality is not to be attained in the sphere of human understanding.

We can be sure that anyone working in adult education -as teacher, organizer, planner, or theoretician - will, like everyone else, perceive his distinctive activity as 'situated' somewhere on the overall cognitive map on which, consciously or unconsciously, he fits each of his experiences, beliefs, and practical commitments. Each day, each week, he will see his work as figuring somehow in a complex pattern of human relationships and social processes which take place against some background of meaning to which they can be referred. A professional educator is, we may suppose, more likely than a professional accountant or engineer to strive consciously to understand the ultimate point of his activities, since as an educator he will consider himself to be specially concerned with enterprises centring on knowledge and understanding as worthwhile attainments. We can at least say that educators, of all people, ought to have a clear idea of the significance and ultimate justification of what they are engaged in doing.

I shall allude to five areas of belief which, separately and together, are bound to give decisive shape to the kinds of map which adult educators will tend to use when interpreting and 'situating' their distinctive professional activities. First, there are beliefs about the nature of reality, its grounding structures, its origins and directions, and its surmisable meaning, if any. Secondly, there are beliefs about the nature of knowledge, about rationality, proof, and the possibility of objective inquiry. Thirdly, there are beliefs about human nature, for example about the status of consciousness, about creativity, conditioning, and the extent of human potentialities. Fourthly, there are beliefs about the nature of society, government, authority, the forms of social progress, and the requirements of personal freedom. Lastly, there are beliefs about values, about what things are worth having and what activities are worth pursuing for their own sakes, and why.

I should guess that the (largely unformulated) metaphysical assumptions on which the majority of Western adult educators base their perceptions of human life are overwhelmingly naturalistic and positivistic in character. The physical world is the whole of reality, although among its contents there are human beings with experiences who are born, grow up, think, act, desire, aspire, love, hate, enjoy happiness, suffer, die, and are replaced by others who proceed through essentially similar sequences. Our lives are governed by extremely complex natural laws which can, however, be in some measure understood by us; by increasing our understanding we can take steps to better our condition, sometimes by altering our desires and shaping our aspirations in more rational and harmonious ways; and educational activity, including adult education, can and should make an important contribution to these endeavours. Probably to most contemporary adult educators in the West some version of this scenario seems self-evident. Of course there are Marxists, who may reject the positivistic elements, but who are no less naturalistic and humanistic in their general outlook. The world of material, social, and economic interactions is 'the very world, which is the world of all of us - the place where in the end we find our happiness, or not at all'. The transcendent, the daemonic, the numinous, the immeasurable, the mysterium tremendum et fascinans, the sense of possible realities beyond this-world observation and computation, and essentially different in kind and ultimate importance - these tend to be ruled out of our standard picture of how things are.

Fortunately, there exist adult educators who work within quite different metaphysical schemata. In Europe and America there are Christians of many kinds. And the most complacent Western humanist can nowadays hardly ignore the radically different perspectives from which Sikh, Hindu, Jewish, and Islamic educators view and judge the quality of our consciousness and culture. Adult educators working in Africa and Latin America are frequently confronted by patterns of belief about the world, animistic or spiritistic, attitudes to life, and forms of traditional wisdom, which challenge the frameworks of understanding they may have learned from their European or North American counterparts, and with which they have to come to terms. The mere existence of such diversity, and sometimes conflict, should act as a douche to our ideological self-righteousness. But how much better it is when adult educators, from their own intellectual resources and a recognized duty to be

21

critically open-minded about the most fundamental questions, are willing to review their most deeply held convictions about the nature of things and if necessary revise their beliefs about the background of constitutive meaning against which they conduct their educational activities. Here surely is a contribution which philosophy can and ought to make to the education of adult educators. Philosophy can and should impel adult educators to think again and again about the overarching meaning of the whole drama within which human life is set and in which they believe themselves called upon to play a creative part. Roles are always enacted within a context, and our interpretation of the context largely shapes our interpretation of our roles. The wider the perceived and understood context, the clearer and truer will be the interpretation we place upon our roles.

Although they should always be willing to reconsider their world-pictures and should be on their guard against mistaking a cosily familiar outlook on life for a demonstrably true outlook on life, I am not suggesting that adult educators should be perpetually and on principle agnostic. After all, many famous philosophers, despite everything I have said about philosophy as an activity of limitless criticism, have felt entitled to propound definite and distinctive systems of metaphysical beliefs, and have claimed them to be essentially true. A study of the history of philosophy - of the elaborate metaphysical edifices constructed by the Platos, Spinozas, Hegels, Bergsons, and Whiteheads - will show adult educators the immense range of options which have been devised and for each of which closely reasoned, if inconclusive, arguments can be persuasively advanced. Obviously it is perfectly justifiable, and in any case unavoidable, that an adult educator should work within that framework of stabilizing meaning which he finds, after due reflection, to offer the most satisfying account of our overall condition. But he can do this undogmatically, preserving a real imaginative sympathy and sensitivity towards the very different frameworks of world-meaning within which other adult educators claim to discern the significance of their work. If creeds can collide, they can also communicate with one another, and an understanding both of the metaphysical questions which unite, and of the metaphysical answers which divide, can facilitate communication between adult educators who are working within differently orienting visions.

Another major contribution which, I suggest, some acquaintance with philosophical thinking can make to the mind of every adult educator is in the field of epistemology. In thinking about curricula, teaching and learning, and the cultural context of adult education programmes, adult educators inevitably find themselves confronted by questions about the nature of knowledge and inquiry, rationality, and conceptualization. However, when these topics are treated in the professional literature, the questions focused on tend mainly to be sociological or psychological in character, and the underlying logical questions too often get overlooked. Take the currently fashionable notion of 'praxis' (which in fact has a long and controversial history). It is sometimes used as if the social consequences to which a theory leads furnish the necessary and sufficient criteria of the truth of the theory. Naturally the exemplifying theories are nearly always political, economic, or otherwise social in content, since this general claim about truth-criteria is much less plausible when applied to the physical sciences or mathematics. But there remain grave logical difficulties even when it is a social theory which is under examination. After all, social praxis is supposed to be crucially different from mere social prediction. Ceteris paribus, a theory which predicted a widening gap between rich and poor would be verified if the gap between rich and poor widened. This is relatively unproblematic. But if the test is that of praxis, a theory will be deemed true if and only if it helps to bring about a narrowing of the gap between rich and poor. Some obvious logical questions are these. How do we pick out those social consequences (e.g. greater equality?), which count as verifying a theory in terms of praxis, from those (e.g. less equality?) which count as falsifying it? Intuitive desirability? Are we really entitled to assume that the truth is invariably benign? Or are we being told to forget about what is true and think only of what is benign, assigning this the name 'true' as an honorific title? And what about theories, e.g. the claimed heritability of intelligence, which advocates of praxis regard as malign, but which can lead to benign results, e.g. when believers in heritability champion policies of compensatory education to negate the inequalities which they believe that Nature tends to produce?

A huge body of work has been done by philosophers on the concepts of 'truth' and 'knowledge'. Yet in contemporary educational debates we find a continual blurring of the fundamental distinction between 'knowledge' and 'belief'. Thus if an educator argues that education should be concerned primarily with the transmission of knowledge, he is liable to meet the allegation that the knowledge which is transmitted necessarily reflects the structure of the society which transmits it and that there is therefore no such thing as objective knowledge which adult educators could teach in a socially neutral way. But clearly what this allegation amounts to is really that social systems tend to propagate sets of beliefs many of which are false and backed up by highly selective and therefore largely spurious 'evidence'. Whether this allegation is itself true, and to what degree, is obviously an empirical question in sociology. However, it is logically quite irrelevant to the argument that education should be concerned with the transmission of knowledge, since by 'knowledge' here is meant beliefs which are true, reasonably representative, and validly based on adequate grounds. There is much more than a merely linguistic point at stake in this conflict. When the distinction between knowledge and belief gets eroded, standards of evidence and argumentation can come to be regarded with indifference or even hostility, and the way is open for a flood of indiscriminately semi-rational and irrational teaching flimsily based on sacrosanct myths, fashionable dogmas, and uncriticized emotion. The least baneful outcome, when rational educators are forced to retreat, is that adult education becomes a playground of popular whims and instant fancies on the part of transient pseudo-students, whose haphazard flounderings are blasphemously but unctuously styled 'creativity' and 'self-expression'. The most probable eventual outcome is that whole areas of adult education get taken over by the indoctrinators.

The keeping of the flame of rationality is, then, one of the major contributions which philosophers (along with other serious and responsible intellectuals) can make to the education of adult educators. Another sphere of traditional philosophical concern is the encouragement of thinking about the nature and status of the human person. It clearly matters greatly whether adult education professionals are taught to see their prospective clients as computers which need to be programmed, as sets of reaction-patterns which can be reinforced or modified by behavioural engineering, as evolutionarily selected lords and masters of Nature, as free if wilful children of a single loving Father, or as private centres of consciousness and aspiration each uniquely individual. Advances in artificial intelligence and socio-biology, the testimonies of religious faiths, and the insights of humanistic psychology may seem to favour now this, now that, perception of our human identity. At no other time has there been such a plethora of miscellaneous data from which we can seek to build a fuller image of what we essentially are. The difficulty is to bring the many different types of data into logical coherence with one another, avoiding a shallow eclecticism, and to identify those questions which scientists in particular too often beg - conceptual questions about freewill and determinism, for example, or problems about the disparate logics of physical and psychological propositions - but to which philosophers ought by their training and special interests to be professionally alert. The subject is too vast to go into here. But I hope it is obvious that no theory of human nature can be complete or consistent without a closely argued philosophical under-pinning. And given that this is so, it follows that the education of adult educators needs to include some treatment of philosophical psychology and philosophical anthropology so that they shall at least be aware of the pitfalls awaiting those who embrace stereotyped versions of what it is to be a living, choosing human being.

Next, there is the whole area of social philosophy. Here I shall confine myself to one example. Students who are being prepared to become professional adult educators are frequently taught that adult education is, can be, or ought to be a powerful instrument of 'social change'. Now, the concept of 'social change' is so nebulous as to be almost worthless. It cries out for analysis and elaboration. Manifestly it does not mean 'change towards greater social equality' any more than it means 'change towards a greater recognition of differential social contributions'. In Great Britain adult educators who wanted social change of the former kind have, since 1979, been forced to witness social change of (it is claimed) the latter kind. In any case changes in relative social equalities are far from being the only kinds of significant social change. There are also changes in the degree and forms of social control and personal liberty, in the dissemination and quality of cultural achievements, and in the levels of individual and overall material prosperity. And in all these cases the call for 'social change' presupposes value judgements about the worthwhileness, the tolerability, or intolerability, of existing conditions. Adult

25

educators, of all people, cannot ignore these controversial issues. They can hardly be deemed to have had an appropriate professional preparation if they have not been induced to identify and confront such issues and subject them to rational examination. Adult educators also need to ask questions about the social <u>legitimacy</u> of their role as putative reformers. Are we specifically licensed by society to initiate a reform of its institutions and practices? What other professional groups could rightfully claim to be so licensed? Medical practitioners, bureaucrats, the military, the police? Can adult educators rightfully claim a special social role on the ground that they possess special social insights? If so, how generally are these ostensible insights in fact agreed among adult educators? Before a licence to promote social and political criticism can be construed as a licence to promote specific forms of social and political change, valid arguments need to be produced and a wide variety of germane concepts ('democracy', 'freedom', 'responsibility', and 'rights', for example, as well as 'education' and 'indoctrination') need to be brought under searching logical analysis.

Finally I should like to allude to the crucial domain of value judgements. Although value judgements (including negative value judgements) obviously pervade and shape all our thinking about the distinctiveness (or lack of distinctiveness) of our identity as human persons and play a central part in our conceptions of the social role appropriate to adult education, here again I shall confine myself to one example. Decisions about the structure and contents of a <u>worthwhile curriculum</u> cannot be made without the making of many quite complex value judgements. No doubt the curricula of vocational courses are largely dictated by the requirements which govern successful practice in the professional spheres for which vocational students are being prepared. Determined by more or less strict utilitarian considerations, the curriculum of an in-service or 'updating' course for cost accountants, hospital administrators, or water engineers will inevitably reflect the changing needs of these professions. The course content will be highly specific to the contemporary needs of the profession, and will seldom give rise to fundamental issues of general curricular principle, except perhaps when there are serious disputes within the profession concerned (to which adult educators, <u>qua</u> educators, will normally be unable to make any very significant contribution). But the picture is quite

different when we are contemplating a curriculum intended
to meet the general <u>educational</u> needs of adults, viewed as
free human intelligences, not just as relatively limited
functionaries and employees. How important is it that
mature men and women should be equipped with a balanced
historical perspective and a critical understanding of the
history of their country and of other countries? Is this more,
or less, important than helping people to acquire a better
grasp of scientific principles and of the methods used by
modern scientists in unlocking the secrets of nature? What
degree of priority ought to be given to the nurturing of
aesthetic sensibilities, to the developing of students'
capacities to make perceptive judgements of quality and to
respond meaningfully to human achievements across a wide
range of different art forms?

Adult educators sometimes appear to be embarrassed
by such questions, perhaps because they feel that there can
be no rational and objective answers to questions about
comparative intrinsic value. This may be why we tend to
leave curricular choices to the students themselves.
(Another, perfectly legitimate reason is, of course, a just
respect for the educational autonomy of men and women
whom we must regard as mature choosers.) However,
curricular permissiveness does not make the questions go
away. It merely devolves the responsibility for answering
them on to the students, and clearly individuals can
themselves make mistakes about what it would be most
educationally worthwhile for them to study. Everyone has
a right to decide for himself what is in his own best
interests, but it is mere superstition to suppose that
everyone's decisions about his own educational well-being
will invariably be absolutely correct. Hence the need
for counselling, which once again requires the professional
educator to make value judgements about the comparative
worthwhileness of different kinds of educational attainment.
Now, the philosophical study of value judgements cannot of
itself provide adult educators with quick and reliable
answers. But it can at least help adult educators to draw a
large number of relevant distinctions, which too easily get
ignored in our polemics - for example, the distinction
between 'absolute' value, which admits of no degrees and
therefore no comparisons, and merely 'objective' (i.e. real,
true) value, which of course is a matter of degree and
therefore solicits comparative judgements and the establishment of valid priorities, or the distinction between the

claim that the value of a given study topic is 'relative' to the circumstances and needs of a given student, in a completely objective sense which calls out for rational investigation and discussion, and the claim that its value is 'relative' to the value placed upon it by the student, his peer group, or the social system, in a destructively subjective sense which would make all rational evaluation futile. Clearly the accuracy and pertinence of such distinctions need to be argued about. But if they are altogether ignored, those who are responsible for preparing adult educators for their future work will be placing themselves in the position of the blind leading the blind.

We are now in a position to ask questions about the epistemological and pedagogical relationships between philosophy as an academic discipline and the study of adult education as a field of concerned action. Such answers as are available may (or may not) be transferable to the cases of other academic disciplines on which the study of adult education also typically draws. Neat formulae based upon blanket distinctions of 'theory' and 'practice', and representing the fundamental academic disciplines as storehouses of 'pure' knowledge from which adult educators can borrow items to be 'applied' to the contingent circumstances of their practical needs, must, I think, be regarded as huge over-simplifications. Certainly adult education is an arena of human activity, while philosophy, psychology, sociology, economics, and history are branches of knowledge. However, here we are considering the academic study of adult education, and the study of adult education is a study. History, economics, and sociology also study arenas of human activity.

Let us begin by accepting the immense difference in cognitive status between the great disciplines like philosophy, psychology, physics, and so on, on the one hand, and such inherently limited, derivative, and socially contingent subjects as adult education studies, marketing studies, or insurance studies, on the other. We must accept that there is an immense difference in scale of subject-matter: contrast the scope of the subject-matter studied and taught by historians of adult education with the subject-matter of history as an academic discipline, which is as wide as human life itself. We must accept that the key concepts developed and the central questions addressed by the great academic disciplines have formative importance for all serious thinking on all topics by which our minds can be engaged, whereas - compared, for example, with philosophy or psychology as irreducibly fundamental forms of knowledge - any work done in the philosophy of adult education or the psychology of adult learning will be massively dependent on the achievements of their parent disciplines and will be unlikely to have very great significance or novelty for the work of students and researchers in domains other than adult education itself. And we must accept that, while the characteristic problems studied by, say, sociology or biology are intrinsically of universal and enduring intellectual interest, the themes and topics to which students of adult education give their minds are unlikely to grip many people who do not already happen to have some close practical involvement with adult education as an activity.

Although organizational changes can and do from time to time take place within and across the major academic disciplines, the cognitive and educational primacy of the great disciplines, when viewed in their fullness as mankind's most deep-questing forms of knowledge and understanding, is, I submit, permanent and unshakeable. Of architectonic significance for all knowledge and inquiry of all kinds, they constitute our most profound and complete ways of receiving and interpreting human experience. Hence they must be recognized as having epistemological sovereignty over all other, lesser, localized bodies of knowledge. What kinds of epistemological and pedagogical relationships can subsist, then, between a logically primordial form of knowledge and inquiry such as philosophy and a contingent ensemble of cognitively localized themes and topics such as adult education studies? I shall suggest six conceptual models of possible relationships. I am far from claiming that this is an exhaustive list, and it will be quickly evident that the different models are by no means mutually exclusive. Nevertheless the exercise may serve as a stimulus to further thought on this controversial question. In considering these models, everything I have said in the bulk of this chapter about the uses of some acquaintance with philosophy for students of adult education should of course be borne in mind.

1.   A deductive model. Philosophical propositions of a very general kind might be conjoined with more specific propositions about processes or situations in adult education, to yield new propositions which will illuminate theoretical

or practical problems faced by adult educators (in something like the way that a conclusion logically follows from the conjunction of a major premise with a minor premise in standard deductive inference). Thus from the twin premises, 'Autonomy is a necessary condition of moral agency' and 'Adult education can help to create morally better human beings', a conclusion seems to follow, viz. 'Adult education can help to foster people's moral autonomy'.

There are obvious difficulties in this model. First, it greatly oversimplifies the problems involved in educational reasoning. This is not just an accident of my necessarily abbreviated example. To any serious problem in adult education there will be a host of different principles, facts, and also other problems which are relevant in a host of different ways and which therefore demand fluid procedures of analysis defying such straightforward formalization. Secondly - and connected with this first difficulty - we shall commonly find that the 'minor premise' is itself riddled with philosophical issues. For instance, it could be that adult education can help to create morally better human beings, but only if they are already autonomous - in which case it would not follow that adult education can help to foster people's moral autonomy. Thirdly, I am not at all sure that there is a fund of 'philosophical propositions' which can be used as premises in educational arguments. It may be that there are only philosophical issues, questions, or tasks, which adult educators should confront, and philosophical skills for tackling these, which adult educators can master.

2. A reciprocity model. There are, it is often claimed, many types of research directed primarily to highly specific, concrete, practical goals which incidentally result in discoveries or insights of great value to the fundamental research being done in mainstream academic disciplines. If certain kinds of military, industrial, medical, or space research, which draw heavily on the knowledge of physicists or biochemists, can have a 'spin-off' which enriches our academic knowledge of physics or biochemistry, the work done in adult education studies might sometimes have the result of initiating new developments in philosophy, psychology, sociology, and the associated disciplines from which it begins by drawing. However, whether mutual fructification of this kind actually occurs is largely an empirical question in the history of ideas. My own impression is that the traffic is overwhelmingly one-way, and that any contribution to philosophy, for example, by

thinking about the philosophy of adult education, will always be minuscule. The analysis of 'adulthood' and 'maturity', and certain implications of adult education for concepts of 'citizenship', may be of some relevance to some questions in moral and social philosophy, but it seems improbable that the philosophy of adult education will ever have very much to offer philosophy in general.

3. A focusing-and-illustrating model. Philosophy addresses extremely general questions at a very high level of abstraction. By focusing on the ways in which such questions arise in concrete situations involving real human interaction, the force (and perhaps even the meaning) of some philosophical questions can be more vividly seen. Discussions of the 'social purpose' of adult education can highlight some of the strengths and weaknesses of utilitarianism as an ethical theory, and debates about the content of a worthwhile curriculum for free adult human beings can help bring to life traditional philosophical questions about the nature of intrinsic value and its complex relationships to human choice. But of course this benefit will accrue only to those philosophers who interest themselves in the problems of adult education. And it seems clear that the vast majority of philosophers will continue to seek illustrative workings-out of their theories in areas of human life which they understandably regard as more central and important, such as politics, economics, science, medicine, and law.

4. A guidance model. Although we probably cannot deduce lessons for adult education from any claimed 'findings' in philosophy, it may be that the work done by some philosophers can pertinently influence our thinking about adult education in a somewhat looser and more general way. It may help us to reach a clearer overall understanding. Overviews of adult education are of course provided, ready-made and conveniently thought out on our behalf, by the vendors of the popular belief-packages. A Marxist perspective on adult education, for example, is available (in several different versions) and many adult educators rely on it to guide their judgements and responses to the problems they encounter in their professional work. An overview can sharpen our perceptions, stabilize our judgements, and bring consistency to our attitudes. But we do not need to go to a standardized belief-package for these benefits. We can seek a wider orienting vision of our work by actively exploring for ourselves its meaning, context, and implications. And in so

doing we can give close consideration to the work done by academic philosophers, including philosophers of education, on those issues - liberty, justice, personhood, values, and so on - which are bound to figure prominently on any landscape of adult education we can try to map. If philosophy cannot of itself instal us in an eagle's eye view, it can at least help us to fly more like eagles.

5.   A critical model. There should be no need to say very much about this. We have seen that philosophy is an activity of limitless logical criticism. Adult educators use concepts, such as 'creativity', 'dialogue', and 'education' itself, which need thorough logical analysis as a condition of their responsible use; there are logical assumptions and value judgements which need to be plainly identified and convincingly defended; and adult education policies are usually supported by forms of reasoning which need to be subjected to careful logical scrutiny. Self-evidently, a branch of study which hopes to make rational progress must continually test its own assertions to ensure that they fulfil the requirements of rationality.

6.   An educative model. Philosophy is not only a technical instrument which can be used by professionals to further their specialist inquiries. It is also a major dimension of human thought and understanding, and as such it ought to be part of the mental possessions of any educated person. Now if adult educators are not themselves well educated persons, they have no right to put themselves forward as the educators of others. We can speak of the training of adult educators, or of the education of adult educators, but if we speak of the latter we must take the term 'education' seriously.   An educated person needs to be in adequate measure conversant with the issues, procedures, and achievements of most if not all of the great forms of knowledge, understanding, and human awareness. Philosophy, we have seen, along with many of the other arts and sciences, especially the social sciences, can help to equip adult educators for their professional role. But it can also help to entitle them to occupy that distinctive role.

The above six models manifestly stand in need of much greater elaboration before they can be tightened up for serious critical evaluation. They are starting points for, not termini of, systematic thinking about the relations between the mainstream forms of human knowledge and the study of adult education. Other models are readily conceivable (e.g. models based on the macro-problem/micro-problem relationship, or on a homogeneity/heterogeneity contrast). However, it may be well to emphasize here that all such models would be examples of epistemological models, embodying possible forms of cognitive relationship between adult education studies and other branches of knowledge. They would revolve around logical links or divergences between different kinds of knowledge in their character as knowledge. In addition to epistemological models of adult education studies, there are of course psychological, political, sociological, cultural, and economic models. It cannot be too strongly emphasized that these are each utterly different in their nature and purpose from logical, cognitive, or epistemological models. Thus there can be no possible 'rivalry' between, say, sociological models and epistemological models of adult education, for they are trying to do entirely different things. Any rivalry is internal to the different exercises, various epistemological models 'competing' with one another, and various sociological models competing with one another, for rational appraisal and acceptance, rejection, or modification.

Ultimately the most important contribution which philosophy, psychology, history, sociology, and the other great academic disciplines can make to the study of adult education, in their own essentially different ways, is no doubt their contribution to our building-up of an overall map of human experience on which we can locate, and therefore better understand, the many processes involved in the education of adults. Epistemologically this would seem to point to a Guidance Model as having special relevance. Yet, when we remember that we are seeking to understand adult education, with the implications of that concept for the distinctive characteristics of those who purport to be 'adult educators', an Educative Model would seem to be at least an indispensable component. And when we are thinking of the contribution which philosophy, as a separate form of under-standing and inquiry with its own special procedures and objectives, can make to the study of adult education, a Critical Model may then seem to be by far the most apt. It is significant that, in the earlier sections of this chapter, philosophy emerged as above all an activity of limitless logical criticism. Clearly, there is no opportunity to examine these questions in greater detail here. But they are, I submit, among the questions that we need to go on thinking about. And, of course, we also need to go on asking whether the questions have been properly put.

Chapter three

EPISTEMOLOGICAL VANDALISM: PSYCHOLOGY IN THE STUDY OF ADULT EDUCATION

Barry P. Bright

The present chapter is concerned with the epistemological relationship between the study of adult education as a university postgraduate subject in the UK and the discipline of psychology as one of the former's source disciplines. More particularly, the chapter will suggest an interpretation of this relationship which supports the assertion that it involves a degree of avoidable epistemological vandalism. This is alleged both in terms of the psychological knowledge the study of adult education utilizes and in terms of the manner in which adult education ignores the nature of its own activity and unique knowledge content. Stated simply, the study of adult education bastardizes its derived knowledge content in a manner which simultaneously assumes but ignores this knowledge and its vandalism by adult education, and which also enables adult education to ignore the nature of its own activity and content.

In order to elaborate the nature of this relationship it will be necessary to consider the meaning of the term 'vandalism'. Similarly, some understanding of the conventional epistemological relationship between psychology and the study of adult education will be necessary. Following this, detailed consideration will be given to several problem areas within adult education as examples of the problematical nature of its relationship with psychology. The final section of the chapter will attempt to suggest an alternative approach to this relationship which avoids some of its current epistemological problems.

It must be noted that reference to 'conventional epistemology' is taken to refer to the vertical segregation of intrinsic disciplines (e.g. Hirst, 1974). Although the current analysis is almost totally within the framework represented by this approach, the author does not preclude the existence and logic of opposing approaches which may have different implications for the analysis of the study of adult education.

THE MEANING OF VANDALISM

For the purpose of the present analysis, 'vandalism' is held to refer to the three major characteristics of deviance, damage, and deliberateness. Deviance obviously involves the notion of a departure from or transgression of accepted norms, methods or behaviours in some regard. The study of adult education, like all interdisciplinary 'fields' of knowledge, does represent a fundamentally different epistemological enterprise compared to the intrinsic, intra-disciplinary disciplines. However, it is suggested that the study of adult education attempts the impossible by over-identifying with the academic, theoretical model of the intrinsic disciplines. In doing this it ignores its own legitimate difference from them. The attempt to conform to an inappropriate model itself represents a deviance from a natural and essential difference between it and its source disciplines. The damage notion involved in the concept of vandalism refers to the defacement of public property, and in respect to the study of adult education this 'public property' corresponds to the knowledge and professional activity of its source disciplines and that of itself. It is suggested that adult education is irresponsible and engages in the defacement and disfigurement of its source discipline knowledge and avoids the elaboration and differentiation of its own activity, content, and purpose. The final defining characteristic of vandalism is the notion that such deviance and damage are commissioned deliberately by the vandal-izing agent. This also involves the related notions of rebellion, revolt, and iconoclasm. Unfortunately, this particular characteristic is not true of the study of adult education. Indeed, were such epistemological damage and deviance the result of rational, structured, deliberate, commissioned activity by adult education, it could be regarded as a healthy sign of a developing epistemological persona. However, the contrary would appear to be the case, since adult education attempts (or feigns) conformity with the intrinsic discipline, academic, theoretical model. The epistemological damage it wreaks upon itself and its source disciplines is due to errors of omission rather than commission. In this manner, and at a professional body level, it avoids the cognitive dissonance (and the need to resolve this) arising from the mutual contradiction of itself and its source disciplines whilst simultaneously proclaiming the legitimacy of both.

Although no doubt an exaggeration, adult education can be likened to an adolescent in Erikson's Psycho-Social Theory of Development (Erikson, 1974) who has reached the identity versus identity confusion ego crisis. Adult education represents the latter developmental option in that, because of its confusion, it has over-identified with an inappropriate role model (i.e. academic, theoretical, intrinsic disciplines) which it cannot live up to, and the reality of which it remains ignorant in the manner of ego defence. Similarly, in these terms, adult education has not clearly established the terms and domain of its epistemological boundary and independence within the wider context of its dependent relations with the intrinsic disciplines.

EPISTEMOLOGICAL BACKGROUND

A previous analysis (Bright, 1985) of the epistemological relationship between the study of adult education and the conventionally regarded 'intrinsic' disciplines in the social sciences, philosophy, and history (Hirst, 1974) concluded that this relationship was characterized by a dependence of the former upon the latter. Within the terms of such an approach, adult education can be regarded only as a 'field' of study in contrast to these intrinsic 'forms' of knowledge, and does, therefore, represent a derived, interdisciplinary and eclectic knowledge content. Metaphorically, adult education (like all fields of knowledge) is spread horizontally across the vertically segregated and independent disciplines, and represents an accumulation and collection of the epistemological content of these (see fig.3.1). By virtue of this relationship, and as a further elaboration of it, adult education possesses contradictory characteristics compared to those of the intrinsic disciplines. Whereas the latter are strongly independent of each other, adult education is dependent upon all its source disciplines, a characteristic which further bestows a marked interdisciplinary (between-disciplines) orientation, in contrast to that of the intrinsic disciplines, which is intradisciplinary (within-discipline). Distinct methodological, evaluative, logical and conceptual

Fig 3.1: Schematic relationship between adult education and its source disciplines

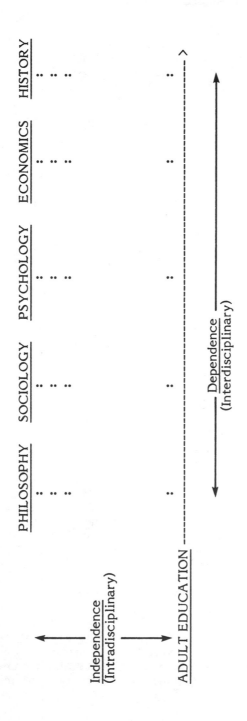

modes are held to support the independence and intra-disciplinary orientation of the intrinsic disciplines and 'forms' of knowledge (Hirst, 1974).

Unlike the intrinsic 'forms' of knowledge, fields are extrinsic, derivative and virtually limitless in number (potentially so) and can represent any combination of the independent disciplines and their dependent 'fields' (e.g. civil engineering includes physics, chemistry, geology, geography, urban design, economics, psychology). Fields are regarded as socio-culturally defined and are relative to different social needs as these emerge historically within a given social system, or as these mutually coexist between different systems. The rationale and purpose of fields are the focusing and organization of intrinsic discipline knowledge around a particular theoretical or practical pursuit. This is in contrast to forms of knowledge whose rationale is the elaboration of their distinctive and independent epistemological domains from which, by definition, knowledge and understanding about the world within these forms will also be elaborated and forthcoming. Forms of knowledge, because of their alleged idiomorphic and naturally occurring nature, are held to exist in their own right and are thus self-validating, but fields of knowledge are secondary, derived, extrinsic, instrumental, and relative to the forms of knowledge, whose epistemological content is focused and centred upon localized and socially defined theoretical or practical interests.

In pursuit and realization of their organizing and focusing function, fields of knowledge are required to discriminate, contextualize, interrelate, integrate, synthesize and co-ordinate the epistemological sources they draw upon in terms of the particular focus of interest which defines them. To justify the logic and existence of their declared focus of interest they must do more than merely regurgitate, in a relatively undigested form, the knowledge sources they draw upon. It is suggested (Bright 1985) that adult education does not satisfy this requirement and that it effectively mimics the content and methods of its source disciplines in a literal rather than derived manner. In these terms, adult education is regarded as seeking academic legitimation by its over-identification with the theoretical, academic model so characteristic of intrinsic disciplines and the structure of British universities. At the same time, this legitimation removes the need for adult education to consider its epistemological relationship with intrinsic disciplines and the content and method of its own activity,¹ with the latter simply being assumed to be identical to the former. Apart from identifying the source disciplines it is dependent upon and their necessary inclusion within its curricula, adult education would not appear to engage in delineating its content in any more detailed or specific form, and therefore fails to define the epistemological enterprise it can or should represent. It emphasizes the subject specialists who operate within it, yet simultaneously isolates these from their first discipline and any coherent and compelling account of adult education, thereby placing them in an epistemologically contradictory position. This perspective also has considerable implications for the academic status of adult education, since, if it cannot be regarded as a legitimate and distinctive epistemological subject, postgraduate academic awards in this non-existent subject become meaningless.

Similarly, this view has implications in epistemological terms, since the essential nature of adult education would appear to be contradictory to that of its source disciplines. Assuming that both content and method are logically inextricable and mutually define each other, the knowledge base represented by the intrinsic disciplines is defined by methods and an epistemological typology unique to them but fundamentally different from the nature of adult education. This can reasonably be expected to produce epistemological problems in terms of academic and theoretical rigour relative to the status and validity of knowledge within (intra-) a given intrinsic discipline, and in the relationship between (inter-) disciplines. The latter, by conventional definitions (e.g. Hirst, 1974), does not exist, owing to their epistemological independence of each other, while the former represents divorcing intrinsic discipline content from the epistemological context within which it can only be interpreted and from which it derives its meaning. The occurrence of such problems is not axiomatic, since 'fields' such as medicine and civil engineering simply cannot afford, on public policy and professional responsibility grounds, to distort or deface the knowledge content of their source disciplines. Because of this, such fields appear to recognize their epistemological dependence and remain faithful to its academic origins yet place it within the context of their particular area of practical interest. Rather than vandalizing their knowledge base they define the appropriate level and types of knowledge within these that meet their professional requirements and particular applied context. In doing this they recognize their dependence but simultaneously delineate their epistemological and applied uniqueness by synthesizing, interrelating and contextualizing the knowledge that they use. Of course, it can be argued that such fields involve 'hard' facts in contrast to 'soft' interpretive and theoretical areas such as adult education, and that building a suspension bridge or diagnosing an illness is not the same as educating teachers. Yet the above arguments can also be held to apply to the theoretical, 'soft', interpretive fields. Indeed, it could be argued that precisely because a field is theoretical (the current assumption within UK adult education) and because its knowledge base is also, by definition, theoretical, the requirement of academic and theoretical authenticity is stronger and extends to a deeper level of detail and analysis compared to practical fields.

The study of adult education would not appear to recognize this type of issue or its implications, although several researchers, within the context of a professional conference (SCUTREA, 1986), have drawn attention to the general problem of its epistemological identity (Bright, 1985, 1986b,c; Usher, 1986; Squires, 1986; Griffin, 1986). Its explicit emphasis upon specialist subjects and subject specialists appears paradoxically to lead to a legitimation of ignorance concerning these issues, and acceptance of a pseudo-imitation of the theoretical, academic model of the intrinsic disciplines as a defining epistemological identity and niche. Such epistemological pseudo-imitation is deceptive, and the vandalism it represents is fundamentally destructive of adult education itself and of the knowledge it utilizes.

EPISTEMOLOGICAL PROBLEMS IN THE STUDY OF ADULT EDUCATION AND ITS RELATIONSHIP TO PSYCHOLOGY

Essentially there are three major issues involved in the question of adult education's epistemology and its relation to psychology (and its source disciplines generally). These issues can be summarized under the interrelated headings of origin, selection, and status. The origin issue refers to the question of the sources of the epistemological content of adult education. This has implications for status, since, if adult education is using knowledge from a source other than itself, epistemological and academic rigour would suggest the need to respect and reflect the contextual constraints and defining properties of this knowledge that its origin invokes. Whilst such knowledge may be further contextualized within a given theoretical or practical area of interest, it is not acceptable for such knowledge to be epistemologically decontextualized from its source. This, of course, raises further issues concerning the definition of epistemological contextualization and decontextualization.

The issue of selection assumes the logical distinction between an identified body of knowledge, which may have origins in one or many sources, and the activity and process by which some or all of this knowledge is incorporated within curricula or utilized within research by an academic group or 'field'. This process can be formal or informal, intentional or unintentional, and can occur at a professional group or individual level, but amounts to an epistemological definition and delineation of the subject domain of the field. The latter can comprise any combination of knowledge from a variety of intrinsic disciplines (e.g. psychology), other fields (e.g. education), and knowledge it has generated itself, either independently of its sources or dependently as a result of its prior incorporation of source content. However, the essential point is the process and content of this selection. The content of selection also refers to the earlier issue of epistemological origin.

The status issue implies a treatment of source discipline knowledge at the hands of the field of interest and invokes the distinction between selection of source material and the way it is used (i.e. teaching and research) by the given field. The latter question involves three further issues concerning the validity of the knowledge as it is treated by the given field. These questions involve intradisciplinary concerns (e.g. Is its origin clearly stated? Is its epistemological validity and character retained and represented?), interdisciplinary concerns (e.g. Is knowledge from different sources interrelated? Is a coherent epistemological map of the field's subject domain being created?), and intrafield concerns (e.g. Does all this knowledge and the way it is represented and treated represent a distinct and valid epistemological, professional, and academic activity and definition of itself as a field?). This is to state no more than that derived, composite, and interdisciplinary fields such as the study of adult education have three types of epistemological concerns or criteria for authenticity and validity. They must pay attention to the intradisciplinary nature of the knowledge they are using from the perspective of each of the intrinsic disciplines they draw upon. They must adequately represent this knowledge and the inter-disciplinary relations between them. And they must evaluate their selection and treatment of all this knowledge from the intrafield perspective they represent, to assess whether it displays sufficient distinctiveness and validity to justify the declaration of themselves as differentiated fields. It is suggested that in terms of adult education's relationship to psychology, it demonstrates none of these concerns.

Origin issue: psychology and adult education

In one sense the origin issue is obvious, since, by definition, all fields are characterized by an epistemological depen-dence upon the intrinsic 'forms' of knowledge or other fields. Yet the obviousness of this dependence often produces a failure to recognize it explicitly. Indeed, the very conventionality and institutionalization of the vertical segregation of knowledge tends to lead to an assumption of it and a failure to recognize its problems and implications. By the law of inclusion, any epistemological activity (such as the study of adult education) which is consistent with this traditional approach to the structure of knowledge is assumed to be valid without further consideration of its nature and the validity of its products in its own terms. This tends to be more the case at a professional group level than at an individual level, since, although individuals are much more prepared to recognize this type of problem, professional-level recognition is the more difficult yet more important. A possible reason for this, and other examples of epistemological narrow-mindedness and defacement, is adult education's need for professional identity (Brookfield, 1985, 1986; Usher, 1986; Bright, 1986b,c).

In addition to the need for explicit recognition of its epistemological dependence upon all its source disciplines, adult education also needs to recognize the degree of this dependence, especially with regard to psychology. This implies a distinction between a dependent relationship and the strength, level or degree of dependence. In terms of its epistemological impact upon the study of adult education, it is the degree of dependence that is the more important, since this logically, and initially, determines the dependent/independent boundary between the field of adult education and its source disciplines. It is the beginning of the distinction between a valid, unique epistemological field and an invalid, indistinct one, and has direct implications for professional identity. Precisely because of this, it is suggested, it is the issue that receives the most superficial attention, or is simply ignored or assumed in order to avoid it. Of course, even if a field is strongly dependent upon its source disciplines, this does not preclude its possessing, or coming to possess, a complementary degree of independence relative to that dependence. This will be determined by the distinctive and authentic manner in which a field combines, integrates, and treats its derived knowledge.

In the case of psychology it is suggested that adult education is strongly dependent and that this arises from the very high level of epistemological overlap from the former to the latter. This can be seen in several ways. First, there is the problematical definition of 'adult' in relation to the discipline of psychology. With obvious and explicit exceptions (e.g. childhood development, juvenile psychiatry), it can be argued that the content of the discipline of psychology is predicated upon the assumption of a population of adults, variously defined and categorized within the terms and variables of a complex set of theories and concepts. From this perspective, every major area within psychology has relevance for the theoretical understanding of adults. Thus all psychological modes of functioning (e.g. personality, intelligence, motivation, perception, cognition, learning, memory, etc.), types of psychology (e.g. developmental, social, abnormal, physiological, occupational, environmental, educational, sociobiological, etc.), together with the various sub-groups of each of these, and the major interpretive paradigms within psychology (e.g. behaviouristic, cognitive, psychoanalytic, humanistic, gene-environment interactive, statistical, etc.), represent the theoretical formulation of adult experience. Resolution of this epistemological imperative is not achieved by claiming the pre-eminence of learning to adult education and the restricted focus and epistemology this represents in relation to psychology. Learning itself is regarded as a central concept within psychology and one which affects and is affected by every other branch and type of psychology. Similarly, claims that 'education' focuses and restricts adult education's epistemological remit from psychology also falls upon unproductive ground for this reason. And adult education's frequent claim that 'adult education', as distinct from pre-adult education, must be defined in a fundamentally wider and experiential manner (i.e. the familiar equation 'adult education' = 'the education of adults'), necessarily involves admitting the influence upon adult learning of a heterogeneous multitude of factors and variables.

It is not being suggested that psychology's account of adult experience and phenomena is veridical. Indeed, within psychology, there would appear to be some difference of opinion in terms of the definition and orientation that psychology should represent (Westland, 1978; Heather, 1976; Shotter, 1975). One of the major claims is that the intra-disciplinary structure of psychology is identical to that of the conventional structure of knowledge itself, i.e.vertical and segregated, and is, therefore, logically reductionistic, piecemeal, and incomplete. However, if the discipline of psychology represents the theoretical and academic account of adult experience, and if the study of adult education defines itself as an academic and theoretical activity concerned with adult learning, the heavy epistemological dependence of the latter upon the former would appear inevitable. To this extent, adult education is epistemo-logically compelled to recognize and utilize the knowledge residing within psychology. In a later section it is suggested that this is precisely what adult education does at a formal, institutional level in order to legitimize its status, but that the extent and epistemological implications of this position are not fully recognized or dealt with.

A further illustration of the epistemological overlap between psychology and the study of adult education is the manner in which many psychologists contribute to adult education. This is often a logical necessity stemming from the nature of psychological theory and its subject matter. Thus, for example, Piaget's theory of cognitive development (1972) is commonly and correctly regarded as a theory pertaining to childhood development. However, and to the extent that the theory can be accepted (e.g. Riegel, 1976), it can also be regarded as specifying the adult form of cognitive functioning (i.e. formal operational stage). This involves regarding the same theory as developmental in childhood but specifying cognitive process continuity in adulthood. Theories which recognize but differ from Piaget's view of adult cognitive functioning invariably reside within the discipline of psychology. Labouvie-Vief's theory of adaptive cognitive functioning in adulthood (1980) and

Riegel's theory of dialectical operations as a fifth stage of development occurring within adulthood (1976, 1979), for example, are both within psychology. Similarly, andragogy, the jewel in American adult education's crown, is firmly based on Rogerian and humanistic psychology principles. Other examples readily spring to mind and are easily identified (e.g. Cattell, 1963: theory of adult intelligence; Maslow, 1973: theory of adult motivation; Rotter, 1966: theory of adult attribution; Schaie, 1965: theory of method in studying age, cohort and historical time effects in ageing). Finally, the emergence of life-span-developmental psychology (e.g. Baltes et al., 1980) clearly illustrates psychology's explicit recognition of and activity in adult phenomena.

Of course, this is very obvious and itself represents a truism, which may render the present chapter a victim of the very processes it is attempting to draw attention to (e.g. poor academic status). However, despite the apparent simplicity of the argument, it is essential to put it forward, since it has serious theoretical and practical implications. In addition, although the argument appears simplistic (which it is not) in connection with adult education's relation to a single discipline, the epistemological complexity and its attendant problems take on a geometric progression when the interdisciplinary nature of adult education is taken into account. The high level of epistemological overlap between adult education and psychology, it is suggested, is equally true for all its dependent source disciplines, since all of these similarly predicate their knowledge content on the basis of an adult population and adult experience.

Selection issue: psychology and adult education

As stated previously, there is a distinction between recognizing the origin and existence of a body of knowledge and selecting that content which is deemed more appropriate and relevant to a derived and secondary interest. This selection process corresponds to the formulation and design of teaching and research content and itself represents an implicit, if not explicit, definition of the derived field itself. Similarly, it also involves acting upon and dealing with those epistemological sources. This process offers the possibility of vandalism in terms of the manner in which it is executed (formal/informal; explicit/implicit;

professional group/individual level) and in terms of the potential knowledge it fails to draw upon through ignorance or negligence. Research and teaching in the study of adult education would appear to be guilty of the latter type of vandalism, since they do not explicity represent the conceptual and theoretical eclecticism, at a detailed level, found within psychology itself. At a general level they do, but, of course, this is a necessary corollary of the origin issue and argument presented earlier, in that, given the strong degree of epistemological overlap between psychology and adult education, it could reasonably be expected that this overlap should be apparent within adult education itself. However, although the intradisciplinary eclecticism of psychology is reflected in adult education in general germs, the real epistemological problems occur in the lack of detailed treatment such diverse and theoretical bodies of knowledge receive at the hands of adult education.

In terms of the manner in which selection takes place, it is suggested that adult education adopts an informal, implicit, and individual approach, and that this represents a form of epistemological vandalism. As indicated earlier, apart from specifying the major disciplines it is dependent upon, it would appear to allow curriculum selection to occur at the individual subject specialist level. Apart from recent and tentative moves in this direction, as a national, professional body, no indication or consideration is given to the areas and types of psychological content that the study of adult education should comprise. In a manner very reminiscent of traditional liberal, extra-mural adult education, the emphasis is upon the individual tutor/lecturer in selecting the content of courses. To this extent, adult education would appear not to possess a professional definition of its epistemology. Indeed, it would be a healthy sign if adult education was prepared to accept this at a professional level, but this, of course, would be a very unprofessional course of action to take. From this perspective adult education would appear to place its subject specialists in a contradictory position, since it does not specify its epistemological content in relation to psychology, which simultaneously does not specify the epistemological nature and definition of adult education. This situation also coexists within an ethos of stressing and emphasizing the importance of the subject specialist whilst systematically undermining his/her professional identity and practice. For reasons to be discussed in the following sub-section, adult education turns its subject specialists into generalists and divorces them from their first discipline. What this also means is that, given that it is these individuals who select the content of adult education, and that they have 'lost touch' with psychology, their knowledge of that subject is outdated and general, which influences their ability to select accurately from currently available psychological knowledge and perspectives. In addition, and as discussed in the previous sub-section, it is the very multiplicity and richness of psychological concepts appropriate to adult education which further exacerbates the problem of selection and which suggests the need for it to be formal, explicit, and at a professional, group level. Presumably, artistic licence and the need to ensure innovative flexibility could be invoked to support the current approach to the curriculum. However, these may not have to be surrendered in the establishment of a more formal and explicit curriculum, which does not have to be rigid and absolute. Within psychology, for example, different academic institutions offer degree courses with different emphases, but this degree of variability is relative and exists within the framework of a well accepted and professionally validated broad curriculum base. Finally, it may not be possible to establish an approach to the curriculum in adult education in this manner, since it is an extremely difficult and complex issue. However, the important point is that an attempt be made and that discussion concerning it be initiated and sustained.

It must also be noted that the selection issue is linked and has connections with the status issue. If the selection process can be regarded as relatively random, disorganized, invalid, and implicit, the treatment and status of the knowledge selected by this process can reasonably be expected to possess similar unprofessional (in the epistemological sense) characteristics.

Status issue: psychology and adult education

As suggested above, the status issue refers to the treatment and utilization by adult education of its source discipline knowledge and the epistemological effects of this, all of which can be held to define logically the nature and status of its own activity as an epistemological enterprise. This issue can be considered in terms of specific problems which, it is suggested, are created by adult education's manner of incorporating psychological knowledge within its teaching and research. Such problems also relate directly to the intradisciplinary, interdisciplinary, and intrafield status dimensions referred to earlier. All the problems can be regarded as examples, or effects, of epistemological vandalism.

The problem of abbreviation

It is a truism that derived 'fields' of knowledge cannot be expected to incorporate all of a source discipline's knowledge content, since this would amount to plagiarism and would render the field indistinct from its source discipline. It was suggested earlier that, owing to the epistemological eclecticism in terms of defining the term 'adult', the large degree of epistemological overlap between adult education and all its source disciplines represents a serious content selection and identity problem for adult education. These problems are, of course, logically connected in the manner of an approach-avoidance conflict, since too little or too much incorporation of source discipline content threatens identity and external and internal validity respectively. One response of adult education to this dilemma has been an over-general and superficial eclecticism in which a large variety of psychological concepts, theories, and paradigms are drawn upon but in a heavily abbreviated and consequently disjointed manner. Works such as Osborn et al. (1981) and Child (1981), for example, typically represent a 'cafeteria' approach to psychology in which subject-matter is heavily compartmentalized and treated in a brief and artificial manner in comparison to the much greater detail and conceptual sophistication with which these subjects are discussed and elaborated within psychology itself. Squires's contingency model (1982) refers to several psychological dimensions (e.g. personality, intelligence, motivation, cognitive style) within which contingent individual differences of the participants in learning may be characterized. However, very little reference is made to the large number of different and conflicting theories residing within each of these. In a more selective form of eclecticism, Mackie (1981) and Okum and Dubin (1973), for example, investigate the worthy topic of the application of learning theory to the teaching of adults. However, Mackie describes three types of learning theory in half a page, devoting one short, notational sentence to each, and concludes his entire analysis (including bibliography, annoted references and notes) in a mere nineteen pages. Okum and Dubin achieve a higher level of abbreviation by investigating eight theories of learning and their implications within seventeen pages. Squires (1982) similarly treats four theories of learning in a heavily summarized and abbreviated manner. Bright (1986a) offers a further example of heavy summarization of learning theories and adult development theories, which, although at a deeper level of analysis, does reflect the 'cafeteria epistemology' approach. Of course, there are other works (e.g. Knox, 1977; Cross, 1981) which enter into more detailed consideration of psychological theories. However, these may also be criticized, since they tend to confuse breadth of coverage of psychological content with intellectual depth. Whilst such works seriously attempt to construct their psychological material in a distinctively 'adult' manner, they are subject to the problematical nature of the psychological definition of that term and represent thinly disguised litanies of psychological theories and unexamined concepts. A similar response, it is also suggested, exists in terms of adult education's teaching, since a course such as 'The Psychology of Adult Learning and Development' often represents a hurried, brief, and inadequate 'guided tour' through a collage of theories and perspectives.

If it is assumed that the epistemology of adult education is (or should be) different from, rather than identical to, its source disciplines, the problem of abbreviation can be regarded as inevitable, and one that does not, in principle, threaten its status as an academic and theoretical field. In these terms a theoretical inter-disciplinary 'topping up' course for existing practitioners is legitimate. However, it is suggested that the problem of abbreviation resolves into a selection and academic standards problem and that this involves selection of appropriate academic level rather than (as discussed earlier) selection of content themes/topics. In this regard it is suggested that the academic legitimacy of adult education's level of incorporation of psychological knowledge needs to be made explicit. What level of abbreviation of source discipline knowledge is acceptable and authentic? Indeed, what academic criteria and definition of 'acceptable knowledge' can adult education offer in contrast to that which exists within its source disciplines? If adult education regards itself as a theoretical, academic field, it can reasonably be expected to possess the epistemological awareness and justificatory criteria for defining the nature and status of its own epistemology, in contrast to its source disciplines, which also define themselves as academic and theoretical. This imperative suggests itself as a result of the 'introductory' level of psychological knowledge currently achieved by adult education and the potential conflict between this and the postgraduate level of most of its courses, and its claim to be a university level subject.

The problem of 'bad' eclecticism

The eclectic response of adult education to its need to incorporate source discipline material whilst maintaining its own independence is also manifested in the breaking of epistemological rules in the manner in which it ignores philosophical and paradigm assumptions concerning major categories of that knowledge. Both Mackie (1981) and Squires (1982), for example, suggest that the main learning principles from major schools of learning theory (behaviourism, cognitive, humanistic, information processing) can be combined or used discriminately in an applied sense, depending upon the local teaching and learning context that teachers of adults face. This, it is suggested, is an example of 'bad eclecticism' (Reese and Overton, 1970) since it involves the mixing of paradigm metaphors at a meta-model level. Although these learning theories may be regrouped into two main categories of metaphysical models, i.e. organicism and mechanism (Bright, 1986a; Reese and Overton, 1970; Pepper, 1942), they contain contradictory philosophical assumptions concerning reality and phenomena, and cannot be mixed in this manner. Individually they represent 'world paradigms' (Pepper, 1942) and can explain all events without reference to the other. Youngman (1986) also recognizes the epistemological problem caused by this approach within adult education and refers to it as 'naive' eclecticism. He also notes its atheoretical, pragmatic orientation.

Bright (1986a) draws attention to this problem and attempts to identify the philosophical assumptions of each of these metaphysical models and the manner in which they relate to the different learning theories. Theories of adult development were also analysed in this manner with the intention of providing a more fundamental understanding of the epistemological and philosophical axioms underlying them. However, whilst accepting the earlier view of Reese and Overton (1970) that the organismic and mechanistic models are the major paradigms within psychology, Bright (1986a) fails to include the paradigm of interactionism, which is also prevalent within psychology and which is regarded as representing a superordinate model which could encompass both the previous views (e.g. Anastasi, 1958; Bell, 1968; Sameroff, 1975; Lerner, 1976; Hultsch and Hickey, 1978; Riegel, 1979). Despite the dated nature of Bright (1986a), it was written to fill a perceived gap in philosophical and epistemological understanding of major psychological theories referred to in adult education. Current models within psychology were not drawn upon, owing to a suspicion that adult educators would not be familiar with or interested in them.

The epistemological vandalism represented by 'bad eclecticism' is dependent upon the definition of adult education as an academic and theoretical enterprise, which entails the reasonable assumption that such an enterprise obeys the rules and constraints governing the formulation of theories, and theories about other theories (i.e. epistemology). In this regard, adult education would not appear to conform to such rules and is therefore unacademic in the decontextualization of theories from their philosophical frameworks and assumptions. Indeed, it could be suggested that most adult educators are apparently not aware of such rules, since very few make reference to them or their implications. More significantly, adult education would not appear to offer a rationale or opposing theoretical position within which such 'bad eclecticism' may be comprehensible or justified.

The problem of false dichotomies

Another and opposite type of response, relative to broad eclecticism, of adult education to the problem represented by its source discipline knowledge is that of specialization. From the perspective of the present chapter, this involves two processes. The first is an undeniably high degree of dependence upon one particular theory within psychology. The second comprises an insistence upon the uniqueness of this theory in its application to adult learning and development. The best, if not the only, example of this response is the concept and practice of andragogy (Knowles,

1984a, b), in contrast to pedagogy, which defines the nature of pre-adult learning and teaching. Andragogy is claimed to represent the principles and practice of adult learning and has its psychological roots clearly and firmly within humanistic, and more particularly Rogerian, approaches to individual and group psycho-dynamics. Its emphasis upon the necessary importance of subjective experience and the consequent imperative of self-direction and discovery in learning, and the development of individual potential, are very familiar notions within this area of psychology. Similarly, the facilitative and non-directive role of a professional therapist in assisting the 'client' in formulating and fulfilling his/her own subjective learning and developmental needs is a well known psychological concept.

In the application of this approach to adult education, it is suggested that there are two false dichotomies. The first concerns the degree of epistemological overlap between andragogy and humanistic psychology. Although the psychological roots of andragogy are explicitly referred to (e.g. Knowles, 1984a,b) this is done in a minimal sense. It is suggested that despite the numerous books and articles on andragogy (see Brookfield, 1986) these represent obvious variations upon and marginal differences between the major themes rather than the edifice of a massive new intellectual and practical approach to adult learning. Although the practical application of these principles may demonstrate a breadth and variety (Knowles, 1984b) which is impressive, their substantive content remains the same and resides firmly within mainstream psychology.

The second false dichotomy within andragogy refers to the criteria which Knowles (1984a) and others (e.g. Allman, 1983) utilize in justifying the distinctive and fundamentally different nature of 'adults' as opposed to children. Humanistic psychology, although more concerned with adult experience and problems, does not make this distinction and would theoretically apply its principles to all humans. In order to establish a distinctively 'adult' paradigm of learning and development, adherents of andragogy were led to formulate criteria and dimensions of adult experience which did not apply to children. This, it is suggested, represents a false dichotomy in that it artificially creates two sub-groups within the population by invoking criteria which do not apply in the distinctive manner claimed.

The four well known features of adults which Knowles (1980) identified as characteristic of adults (i.e. self-directedness, possession of rich experience, specific learning needs, competence and applied learning based) can all be applied, in different ways, to children. Knowles himself (1980, 1984a,b) has recognized that children outside formal educational situations may display self-direction. However, this is insufficient, since it can be argued that this criterion (as does the second criterion, experience) smacks of the traditional and outdated 'passive-active' dimension in terms of which children and adults were respectively interpreted. Modern developmental psychology and humanistic psychology itself regard all individual humans as interacting with and influencing their environment in a reciprocal and dynamic manner (Lerner, 1976, 1978; Sameroff, 1975; Lerner and Busch-Rossnagel, 1981; Baltes et al., 1980; Lerner and Spanier, 1978; Schaffer, 1976; Danziger, 1978; Bell, 1968; Anastasi, 1958; Clarke and Clarke, 1977). Lerner and Spanier (1978), for example, offer numerous instances of the effect upon the family of a young child or fetus. Similarly Sameroff (1975) indicates the self-selecting manner in which a young infant can contribute to its own physical maltreatment by a caregiver experiencing psycho-social adversity. The concept of the self-selection and creation of environments is a frequent theme in this research. Knowles could argue that some types of self-selection and direction are of an automatic, rather than conscious, nature, but this is a far more complex concept than simply stating self-direction as a fundamental criterion for the definition of adults and their learning. Allman (1983) makes the same mistake of blandly categorizing adults as active and children as passive.

Knowles's second criterion of experience can be subjected to the same type of argument, since it implicitly assumes that children either do not have valid experience or that such experience cannot be regarded as a rich resource in learning situations. The nature of childhood experience may be different from that of adult experience, but its complexity and sophistication cannot be doubted, if the scale of childhood development and the incredible achievements that a child typically accomplishes in terms of linguistic, cognitive, moral, emotional, social, cultural, and physical development and skills is recognized. Indeed, it could be argued that Knowles's criterion of experience smacks of arrogance and age discrimination. It is also inconsistent with one view of the nature of thinking which has been invoked as supporting the andragogical approach.

Riegel's theory of dialectical thinking is frequently referred to as the fifth stage of cognitive development occurring in and characteristic of adulthood (Allman, 1983). Yet Riegel (1979) explicitly states that dialectical thinking is developmentally superior to formal thinking and exists in all humans at birth. (Novack, 1978, suggests that, philosophically, dialectical logic pre-dates and is superior to formal logic.) Riegel's point is that the intrinsic dialectical mode of thinking is suppressed by formal, compulsory education and its encapsulation of formal logic as an epistemological method. Following the end of compulsory education and entrance into adulthood, the individual's natural dialectical mode of thinking returns. Also, of course, in terms of an approach to formal childhood education, Bruner (1974) recognizes and invokes the use of the experiential and discovery method, although this is within the context of an other-directed educational programme.

Similarly, the third and fourth criteria of adults suggested by Knowles (i.e. specific learning needs generated by real-life problems and the competence-based approach) can also be applied to children - witness the persistent and tenacious efforts of children to master a variety of skills, from the art of tying shoelaces, jumping in at the deep end of a swimming pool, or riding a bicycle to acquiring the sematic difference between 'feline' and 'feminine', learning to play the guitar, or acquiring the concept of a planetary system and the location of the planets within it. Given the large number of tasks that development in childhood comprises, and the active, highly motivated and voluntary manner with which children seek competence in them, to state that adults are characterized by specific learning needs and a desire or necessity to be competent borders on the banal and simplistic. Of course, it could be argued that what Knowles and others are referring to is not the nature of adults or children, but the manner in which children are taught and educated, which is a different issue. Similarly, whilst it may be correct to make the point that the above-mentioned criteria, alleged to be distinctive of adults, cannot be regarded as such, this does not preclude substantive differences in the form in which such similarities are expressed or manifested. In addition, the very concept of life-span development (Baltes et al., 1980), which is prevalent within developmental psychology, contradicts the notion of a clear-cut division between childhood and adulthood, the research findings of which generally reflect a highly complex pattern of continuities and discontinuities between earlier and later periods of the life span (e.g. Brim and Kagan, 1980).

It is not being suggested that there are no differences between adults and children. On the contrary, there are probably many, but, whatever the nature and extent of such differences, it is very doubtful whether they can be accurately described and encapsulated within gross and simplistic dichotomies such as those suggested by Knowles. As a theoretical basis for a distinctive adult education, such dichotomies, it is suggested, are weak and display a lack of conceptual understanding and sophistication. The possible utility of andragogy as one approach (i.e. within humanistic psychology) to applied adult learning is not being denied, but the status of its theoretical distinction between adults and children is questionable. Paradoxically, the epistemological status of andragogy's theoretical basis within psychology is good but would not appear to be adequately recognized or acknowledged.

The problem of the theory/practice relationship

Because the epistemological issues raised in the present chapter are rarely discussed within the adult education literature, pragmatism as a justification for the above problems is usually implicit rather than explicit. However, the latter is apparent in discussions concerning the nature of adult education (e.g. Brookfield, 1985; Usher, 1986) although the full epistemological implications are not investigated. Also, the inescapable practical ethos and orientation of education have been the subject of debate within the philosophy of education (Hirst, 1974, Phenix, 1964; O'Connor, 1973). Thus the justification for 'bad eclecticism' and weak theoretical bases for specialized orientations within adult education is the view that, because of the latter's practical nature, theoretical and epistemological niceties and imperatives can be ignored, the overriding rational being the practical utility of theoretical prin-ciples.

Although the pure/applied distinction is entailed by conventional epistemology's 'form' and 'field' categories and relations, the latter can correspond to theoretical or practical activities (Bright, 1985), i.e. fields can be theoretical or practical in orientation. Also, it is suggested, where a 'field' defines itself as a practical activity, this does not justify either ignoring or mimicking knowledge content

from source disciplines. Indeed, the conventional epistemological structure would suggest that good practice is based
upon authentic incorporation of source discipline knowledge
and its elaboration within the practical domain of a given
field. In this sense, and in the manner of the logical
relationship between content and method, adult education
has the problem of reflecting the content-method relationship involved in the generation of knowledge by its source
disciplines. It also has the problem of simultaneously doing
this in such a way that it retains the authenticity of that
knowledge but also expresses a valid content-method
relationship in terms of its own activity as a transmitter
and/or applier of that knowledge. In its current solution to
this double problem, adult education displays obvious and
understandable tensions and conflicts. The practical and
applied nature of education generally would appear to
conflict with the academic and theoretical ethos of
university institutions within which adult education departments are found.

It also conflicts with the theoretical 'topping up'
perspective adopted in the provision of many postgraduate
degrees in adult education. In addition, whilst 'hard'-
knowledge, practical fields such as engineering and medicine
have a much clearer remit in terms of the source discipline
content they have to include, and a much reduced remit in
terms of the elaboration of this content, 'soft' interpretive,
theoretical, and practical areas, such as adult education,
face a much more difficult task. The criteria for inclusion
and exclusion of source discipline content, and, indeed, the
criteria for remaining in touch with theoretical advances
and developments in source disciplines, are more ambiguous
and value-laden. It is suggested that, in its attempt to
resolve these problems, adult education has effectively
decontextualized its knowledge sources and has decoupled
itself from them in the mistaken, and contradictory,
expression of itself as a practical activity which legitimizes
its current use and treatment of its source knowledge.

A further problem is that, whilst, for example, Squires's
contingency model (1982) and andragogy eschew conventional theory in the name of pragmatism, they also
represent theory. This, obviously, refers to the inextricable
relationship between content and method and raises the
question of the status and defining criteria of such
pragmatically oriented theory. It must be noted that
Squires, and presumably andragogy, may not accept this

explicit distinction between theoretical theory and prag-matic theory. Squires, for example, regards his model as fully consistent with the demise of grand theory within psychology and the movement towards contingent and less deterministic theories (e.g. Fiedler, 1967). Similarly, andragogy could claim accurate representation of a psychological theory and a distinctive adult educational elaboration and application of it. Indeed, Usher (1986) suggests that only psychological theories with a therapeutic and, therefore, applied nature should or can be used by adult education. Andragogy can be regarded as an example of this.

However, it can be argued that the 'theoretical' basis of such approaches amounts to a self-fulfilling prophecy - that, in eschewing conventional theory, they substitute even grander and weaker (i.e. unfalsifiable) theories which involve intradisciplinary and interdisciplinary eclecticism (Squires's model), or which emphasize one particular theory within psychology (humanistic psychology within andragogy). Both regard their views as the definition of adult learning/teaching which can be applied in all adult learning situations. Rather than representing a commitment to actual practice, they represent theoretical assumptions within which practice may be interpreted. In other words, they do not represent a primary emphasis upon practice, and are further examples of the 'theory-driven' nature of the academic, theoretical model of conventional adult education. Castell and Freeman (1978) offer an inter-pretation of a 'practice-driven' approach to education which clearly and honestly surrenders the pre-eminence of theory in the name of utility in resolving practical problems. Whilst this strongly implies eclecticism, it also suggests the need for detailed and extensive knowledge in source discipline theory in addition to an equally extensive knowledge of practical situations. It also represents an explicit and articulate justification for the pragmatism and eclecticism it entails.

The problem of interdisciplinary relations

Consistent with conventional epistemology and adult education's imitation of the theoretical, academic model, the independence between different source disciplines is reflected in publications (e.g. Jones, 1984: sociology; Bright, 1986a: psychology; Paterson, 1979: philosophy), teaching (sociology/psychology/philosophy of adult education), and in the professional emphasis placed upon subject specialists (Bright, 1985). The interdisciplinary nature of adult education is potentially a positive feature for both its subject specialist teachers and students, yet this is rarely exploited or developed, even within the vertical framework of conventional epistemology. Also, it must be noted that many students (especially overseas students) do not possess a first degree in the social sciences and are relatively unfamiliar with their isolated nature and the lack of integration between them, a feature which is exacerbated by the abbreviated form and introductory nature of most teaching and research in these subjects within adult education. Despite the impossibility, from conventional epistemology's perspective, of integrating these subjects, it is suggested that an approach towards this could be made in terms of addressing higher-level epistemological theories and categories which may facilitate identifying common orientations within different disciplines. In the absence of this, lower-level approaches could be made in generating discussion between subject specialists and reflecting this within teaching and research.

The problem of subject specialists

From all the above, it is suggested that the subject specialist is in an epistemologically contradictory position. Adult education simultaneously emphasizes its composite source disciplines in terms of its teaching, research and personnel whilst claiming its independence from them. Because of the introductory level of teaching and research in its source subjects, adult education converts its 'specialists' into outdated generalists within their first discipline whilst maintaining their specialist status; obstructs inter-collegiate relations with other subject specialists because of the emphasis upon, and epistemological independence between, such other subject specialists; and systematically fails to provide a comprehensible and epistemologically distinct definition of adult education content, a failure it denies. In the manner of the 'double bind' hypothesis (Bateson et al., 1956), adult education simultaneously emphasises and denies the importance and role of subject specialists and then denies its denial.

FUTURE APPROACHES

It is suggested that the study of adult education needs to address the following major areas of its activity in order to ameliorate the above-mentioned epistemological and professional problems. These may be summarized by the simultaneous need to adopt a more general, meta-model epistemological orientation and a more knowledgeable awareness of detail at the theoretical and practical levels.

Epistemological contextualism

Apart from reference to conventional epistemology sources, adult education appears to be marked by the lack of epistemological awareness concerning the nature, type, and categories of knowledge. This is all the more noticeable because of its interdisciplinary character and its heavy dependence upon source discipline material, both of which would suggest the need for an awareness of epistemological theories and categorical characterizations of different types of knowledge. There is a suggestion (Usher, 1987), which is confirmed by the current author's own experience, that subject specialists within adult education are drifting, as it were, towards higher-level philosophical and epistemological approaches in their teaching. Bright (1986a) explicitly reflects this tendency within research literature; however, most research does not seem to adopt this orientation. Squires (1984), for example, suggests a thoroughly contextualist model, yet no reference is made to the epistemological model of contextualism (Pepper, 1942). Similarly, andragogy can be regarded as a contextualist model in a subjective sense, but, again, no reference is made to this idea or the epistemological genre of organicism within which humanistic psychology falls. Indeed. most of adult education's epistemological function, it can be argued, may be categorized as contextualization (e.g. Cross's model, 1981; Boyd and Apps's model, 1984). If this is the case, and because adult education is dealing with knowledge, it can be argued that it should be attempting to place this knowledge in its context, which a meta-theoretical epistemological orientation would facilitate. The notion of epistemological contextualism applies not only at an interdisciplinary theoretical level but also at both intradisciplinary theoretical and intrafield, practical levels.

Closer involvement with intradisciplinary theories

As indicated, it is suggested that subject specialists within adult education operate as generalists within the terms of their first discipline. This occurs as a result of the combination of the subtle processes of abbreviated teaching to non-specialist students, lack of time for specialists to keep in touch with their discipline and the lack of relevance of doing so within the current epistemological approach of adult education. As a contrary measure, it is suggested that it is imperative for subject specialists to remain knowledgable in their first discipline at a relatively detailed level. Academic status and the need to articulate a representative and useful curriculum for adult education compel this. Similarly, if adult education is defined as a practical rather than theoretical activity, the need for good theory at a detailed level is also suggested. The demands of 'good eclecticism' in both its theoretical and its practical senses also entails this. Quite simply, if the epistemological origins of adult education are to be recognized and this knowledge content is to be used, either theoretically or practically, the status and level of such knowledge needs to be taken seriously.

Closer involvement with practical adult education

Neither the need for meta-model epistemological contextualization nor the need for closer involvement with detailed intradisciplinary theories and interpretations necessarily excludes a complementary orientation towards practical problems in adult education. To believe otherwise is to accept the formal, theoretical model and its concomitant formal lecture method and the objective truth fallacy it represents. The possession of meta-model epistemological contexts and detailed theoretical perspectives within a discipline may be used within a problem- and practice-led educational activity. This would also facilitate further understanding of the relationship between formal theory and the informal theories that practitioners implicitly use in their everyday professional life. Since the vast majority of students in adult education are already experienced practitioners, it may be pertinent to their education and the deeper understanding of adult education itself to utilize this resource as a way of elucidating and applying formal theories to practical problems. Such an approach, which assumes the previous two approaches outlined above, would appear to satisfy the epistemological and academic status problems found within adult education, and provide it with a means of integrating these within a distinctive adult educational form.

REFERENCES

Allman, P. (1983) Toward a Developmental Theory of Andragogy, Nottingham: Department of Adult Education, University of Nottingham.

Anastasi, A. (1958) 'Heredity, environment and the question how?', Psychological Review 65: 197-208.

Baltes, P. B., Reese, H. W., and Lipsitt, L. P. (1980) 'Life span developmental psychology', Annual Review of Psychology 31: 65-110.

Bateson, G., Jackson, D., Haley, J., and Weakland, J. (1956) 'Towards a theory of schizophrenia', Behavioural Science 1: 251-64.

Bell, R. Q. (1968) 'A reinterpretation of the direction of effects in studies of socialisation', Psychological Review 75: 81-95.

Boyd, R. D., Apps, J. W., and associates (1984) Redefining the Discipline of Adult Education, London: Jossey-Bass.

Bright, B. P. (1985) 'The content-method relationship in the study of adult education', Studies In the Education of Adults 17 (2): 168-83.

—— (1986a) Adult Development, Learning and Teaching, Newland Paper No. 12, Hull: School of Adult and Continuing Education, University of Hull.

—— (1986b) 'The study of adult education: epistemology, the subject specialist and research', in M. Zukas (ed.), Standing Conference on University Training and Research in the Education of Adults, papers of sixteenth annual conference, University of Hull.

—— (1986c) The Study of Adult Education in the UK, paper given at the Adult Education Research Conference, Syracuse, N.Y.

Brim, O. G., and Kagan, J. (eds) (1980) Constancy and Change in Human Development, Cambridge, Mass.: Harvard University Press.

Brookfield, S. D. (1985) 'Training educators of adults: a comparative analysis of graduate adult education in the United States and Great Britain', in G. J. Conti and

R.A. Fellenz (eds), Dialogue on Issues of Lifelong Learning in a Democratic Society, working papers from a British and North American faculty exchange, Texas A & M University.

—— (1986) Understanding and Facilitating Adult Learning, London: Jossey-Bass.

Bruner, J. S. (1974) Beyond the Information Given: Studies in Cognitive Growth, London: Allen & Unwin.

de Castell, S., and Freeman, H. (1978) 'Education as a socio-practical field: the theory practice question reformulated', Journal of Philosophy of Education 2: 13-28.

Cattell, R. B. (1963) 'Theory of fluid and crystallised intelligence: critical experiment', Journal of Educational Psychology 54: 1-22.

Child, D. (1981) Psychology and the Teacher, third edition, London: Holt Rinehart & Winston.

Clarke, A. M. and A. D. B. (1977) Early Experience: Myth and Evidence, London: Tavistock Publications.

Cross, K. P. (1981) Adults as Learners: Increasing Participation and Facilitating Learning, San Francisco: Jossey-Bass.

Danziger, R. (1978) Socialisation, London: Penguin Books.

Erikson, E. W. (1974) Identity: Youth and Crisis, London: Faber & Faber.

Fiedler, F. E. (1967) A Theory of Leadership Effectiveness, New York: McGraw-Hill.

Griffin, C. (1986) 'A researchable politics of adult education?', in M. Zukas (ed.), Standing Conference on University Teaching and Research in the Education of Adults, papers of sixteenth annual conference, University of Hull.

Heather, N. (1976) Radical Perspectives in Psychology, London: Methuen.

Hirst, P. (1974) Knowledge and the Curriculum, London: Routledge & Kegan Paul.

Hultsch, D. F., and Hickey, T. (1978) 'External validity in the study of human development: theoretical and methodological issues', Human Development 21: 76-91.

Jones, K. (1984) The Sociology of Adult Education, Aldershot: Gower.

Knowles, M. (1980) The Modern Practice of Adult Education: from Pedagogy to Andragogy, New York: Cambridge Books.

—— (1984a) The Adult Learner: a Neglected Species, Houston, Tex.: Gulf.

—— (1984b) Andragogy in Action: Applying Modern Principles of Adult Learning, San Francisco: Jossey-Bass.

Knox, A. (1977) Adult Development and Learning: a Handbook on Individual Growth and Competence in the Adult Years, San Francisco: Jossey-Bass.

Labouvie-Vief, G. (1980) 'Adaptive dimensions of adult cognition', in N. Datan and N. Lohman (eds), Transitions of Ageing, New York: Academic Press.

Lerner, R. M. (1976) Concepts and Theories of Human Development, Reading, Mass.: Addison-Wesley.

—— (1978) 'Nature, nurture and dynamic interactionism', Human Development 21: 1-20.

—— and Busch-Rossnagel, N. A. (eds) (1981) Individuals as Producers of their own Development, New York: Academic Press.

—— and Spanier, G. B. (eds) (1978) Child Influences on Marital and Family Interaction: a Life-span Perspective, New York: Academic Press.

Mackie, K. (1981) The Application of Learning Theory to Adult Teaching, Nottingham: Department of Adult Education, University of Nottingham.

Maslow, A. (1973) The Further Reaches of Human Nature, Harmondsworth: Penguin Books.

Novack, G. (1978) The Logic of Marxism, London: Pathfinder Press.

O'Connor, D. J. (1973) 'The nature and scope of educational theory', in G. Langford and D. J. O'Connor (eds), New Essays in the Philosophy of Education, London: Routledge & Kegan Paul.

Okum, M., and Dubin, S. (1973) 'Implications of learning theories for adult instruction', Adult Education 24 (1): 3-19.

Osborn, M., Charnley, A., and Withnall, A., (1981) Review of Research in Adult and Continuing Education: the Psychology of Adult Learning and Development, Leicester: National Institute for Adult Continuing Education.

Paterson, R. W. K. (1979) Values, Education and the Adult, London: Routledge & Kegan Paul.

Pepper, S. C. (1942) World Hypotheses, 1961 edition, Berkeley, Cal.: University of California Press.

Phenix, P.H. (1964) Realms of Meaning, London: McGraw-Hill.

Piaget, J. (1972) 'Intellectual evolution from adolescence to

adulthood', Human Development 15: 1-12.
Reese, H. W., and Overton, W. F. (1970) 'Models of development and theories of development', in L. R. Goulet and P. B. Baltes (eds), Life-span Developmental Psychology: Research and Theory, New York: Academic Press.
Riegel, K. F. (1976) 'The dialectics of human development', American Psychologist 31: 689-700.
—— (1979) Foundations of Dialectical Psychology, New York: Academic Press.
Rotter, J. B. (1966) Generalised Expectancies for Internal Versus External Control of Reinforcement, Psychological Monographs, No. 80.
Sameroff, A. J. (1975) 'Early influences: fact or fantasy?', Merrill Palmer Quarterly 21 (4): 267-94.
Schaffer, H. R. (1976) The Growth of Sociability, Harmondsworth: Penguin Books.
Schaie, K. W. (1965) 'A general model for the study of developmental problems', Psychological Bulletin 64: 42-107.
Shotter, J. (1975) Images of Man in Psychological Research, London: Methuen.
Squires, G. (1982) The Analysis of Teaching, Newland Paper No. 8, Hull: Department of Adult and Continuing Education, University of Hull.
—— (1986) 'Discipline-based research: briefing paper', in M. Zukas (ed.), Standing Conference on University Teaching and Research in the Education of Adults, papers of sixteenth annual conference, University of Hull.
Usher, R. (1986) 'The theory-practice problem and psychology as a foundation discipline in adult education', in M. Zukas (ed.), Standing Conference on University Teaching and Research in the Education of Adults, papers of sixteenth annual conference, University of Hull.
—— (1987) Personal communication.
Westland, G. (1978) Current Crises of Psychology, London: Heinemann.
Youngman, F. (1986) Adult Education and Socialist Pedagogy, London: Croom Helm.
Zukas, M. (ed.) (1986) Standing Conference on University Teaching and Research in the Education of Adults, papers of sixteenth annual conference, University of Hull, published by the Department of Adult and Continuing Education, University of Leeds.

Chapter four

LOCATING ADULT EDUCATION IN THE PRACTICAL

Robin S. Usher

Since this chapter is centrally concerned with the notion of 'frameworks of understanding', I must start by making clear, at least in outline, what my own 'framework' is. First, I am assuming that adult education is a branch of education, both in theory and in practice. Accordingly, I have used the term 'education/educational' and would wish 'adult education' to be read also into this usage. Where there is a difference or where I intend an emphasis the latter term is specifically used.

Second, my primary concern is to examine what it means to say that education, including adult education, is a practical activity. The starting point is Bright's (1985) analysis of adult education as a practical a field of knowledge. I want to agree with this partially but at the same time suggest an alternative way of locating adult education in the 'practical'. My focus is adult education as a field of study and its relationship with adult education as a field of practice. I am therefore assuming that those to whom the former is directed are themselves engaged in the latter. Finally, I have used the term 'professional formation' as a kind of shorthand to embrace both education and training through award and non-award-bearing courses.

After outlining the main characteristics of education as a practical activity I discuss the nature of the 'technical-rationality' model which, in my view, has constituted a dominant paradigm both in professional practice and in professional formation. The consequences of this model are considered in terms of, first, the dilemma generated between rigour and relevance, second, the conception of 'theory' contained within it and, third, the implications of the model for education. From this critique I then suggest

65

an alternative to the technical-rationality model and discuss the implications of this alternative for the theory-practice relationship, the conceptualization of theory, and the design and implementation of curricula for professional formation.

EDUCATION AS A PRACTICAL ACTIVITY

Hirst (1974) in his epistemological analysis distinguished between 'forms' of knowledge which occur naturally and 'fields' of knowledge which are composites derived from the 'forms'. Thus, for example, the natural sciences are 'forms' of knowledge whilst engineering is a 'field', a composite with elements drawn from the 'forms' in an integrated way. The principle of integration depends on the forms and purpose of the 'field' and, according to Hirst, it is possible to distinguish between theoretical and practical 'fields'. Broadly speaking, a theoretical field is concerned with 'finding out' about the world, discovering 'truths', whereas a practical field is concerned with acting on the world and changing it in certain ways.

This analysis of 'forms' and 'fields' has been used by Bright in considering whether adult education can be characterized as a field of knowledge. In general, he seems to think it can be, although he deploys powerful arguments to demonstrate that it cannot be seen as a <u>theoretical</u> field of knowledge. He argues rightly that adult education has, in fact, tended to see itself this way but that it is a mistaken view which is based on an 'illogical adoption of the independent, theoretical academic disciplines model' (Bright, 1985: 179).

If adult education cannot be a theoretical field of knowledge cannot it, therefore, be characterized as a <u>practical</u> field of knowledge, as in, let us say, engineering and medicine? Bright's answer is not entirely clear. On the one hand, he maintains that, since in adopting the 'disciplines model' adult education cannot legitimately be a theoretical field, it is for the same reason debarred from being a practical field, although it could be if it abandoned the disciplines model. On the other hand, he seems to be supporting the case put forward by Castell and Freeman (1978) that education is a 'socio-practical' field of inquiry and that adult education can be similarly characterized.

The problem here (and the reason why I earlier signalled my partial disagreement with Bright's analysis) is that the notion of education as a 'socio-practical' field is not the same as education as a practical 'field' of knowledge. The latter is still based on disciplines, albeit not independent but composite, interdisciplinary and with an integrating theory and concepts, but disciplines all the same. The 'socio-practical', on the other hand, is not based on disciplines; there is a place for disciplines but that place is pragmatic, not foundational. Knowledge in the 'socio-practical' is practical knowledge and therefore not the same as the knowledge accumulated and organized in disciplines.

The notion of practical knowledge and its correlate practical reasoning forms a central theme in my analysis, which seeks to locate adult education in the 'practical' but not as a 'field' of knowledge. I will start, therefore, by considering briefly what Castell and Freeman have to say about education as a 'socio-practical' field of inquiry.

The existence of a context which includes values relating to human welfare are crucial components in this notion. The 'socio-practical' is characterized as a field of inquiry where considerations of welfare and contextual constraints are paramount and where knowledge and understanding (theory) are practical and 'instrumental to taking effective action to solve acknowledged practical problems' (p. 17).

A distinction is drawn between the 'socio-practical' and the 'theoretico-practical'. The latter as a field of inquiry assumes context to be irrelevant to its concerns or at least invariant. The problems towards which inquiry is directed are intrinsic to itself and are identified by the theory within the field. The socio-practical, on the other hand, assumes variable social contexts, and the problems towards which inquiry is directed are intrinsic to these contexts and are identified by the need for continually effective action 'as a matter of urgent concern' (p. 15).

Socio-practical fields can be specifically demarcated from theoretico-practical fields in terms of their content, method, and goals. First, there is no restriction on substantive content - the only consideration is the 'necessary concern' with purposeful action, a premium on the urgent solution of problems, and the practical use of knowledge. Second, method is defined in terms of function and purpose; there can be no restrictions on theory, since any theory which facilitates effective action is acceptable - in other words, method is eclectic and the justification for use is pragmatic. Third, in terms of goals, the most important area of demarcation, the reasons for action are always the need to solve urgent problems where the resolution of the problem and the means used 'affect directly the lives of other human beings' (p.17). The generation and use of knowledge are therefore always in relation to a context and never an end in themselves.

Given the orientation of socio-practical fields it is clear that, in emphasizing socially defined problems and their resolution in contextually acceptable ways, the role of educational practitioners is crucial. It is they who are in the best position both to define and to help resolve such problems and to incorporate within them their knowledge and understanding of the specificities of contexts, particularly the constraints to be found therein.

At this point a comment on Castell and Freeman's notion of 'praxis' is in order, although I shall take up this point and the related one of the relationship between theory and practice in greater detail later. Given the necessary need for practitioner involvement in socio-practical fields, within these, the practitioner is not merely a 'technician'. In this sense the position is entirely different to the more common 'applied science' view of the practitioner. Castell and Freeman refer to the practitioner being involved in 'internally instrumental action' which they characterize as 'similar to the concept of praxis' (p. 19), and which brings together theory and practice in a process of dialectical engagement. The prescriptions which are generated by 'internally instrumental action' cannot be adopted in the abstract but must be filtered through the contextual constraints within which action is located. Practice is therefore neither a matter of applying abstract theory nor is it action not guided by theory. Theory provides the reasons and motives for purposeful practical action and thus 'guides' practice but within situations where contextual variables have to be taken into account.

Clearly, this analysis is fruitful in relation to adult education. Given the relationship of adult education to education, it seems logical to postulate that if the latter can be considered a 'socio-practical field' then so too can the former - and perhaps, in a real sense, even more so. In conceptualizing adult education as a 'socio-practical' field we underline what is undoubtedly the case, that it is an activity directly and ultimately concerned with human welfare whereby value judgements concerning ends and means are unavoidable. At the same time there are other factors which reinforce this; for example, the nature and status of its clientele, its strong and long-standing humanistic orientation, and the fact that much adult education practice takes place outside the institutional contexts of mass schooling.

Although adult education does not currently, see itself this way there is no reason why, in principle, it cannot do so. At the moment adult education 'theory' in both teaching and research barely merits the epithet, consisting, as Bright rightly points out, of a rag-bag collection of bits of theoretical knowledge from so-called foundation disciplines, lacking in focus and integration. This has its unfortunate effects on curriculum design and implementation and on the content and methodology of research. The gap between theory and practice constitutes a veritable chasm, and no way has been found of properly assimilating the knowledge and understandings of practitioners. My point is that there is no way this can be done until there is greater clarity about the nature of the 'practical' and of practical knowledge. Unfortunately, this is easier said than done, since there is a fundamental problem which cannot be easily overcome.

THE DILEMMA OF RIGOUR AND RELEVANCE

One way in which the problem manifests itself is in terms of this dilemma. If we examine the professional formation of adult educators, the issue of 'relevant' content appears as a constant theme. On the face of it, relevance means making content relate to the world of practice where the concern is with the instrumental aims of helping the practitioner through developing skills and capabilities and generally enhancing effectiveness in coping with practice. Within adult education studies, relevance is always given a prominent, if not an exclusive, place.

At the same time, the bulk of the content in such courses consists of what I will call 'formal' theory: normally the theoretical knowledge contained in disciplines such as psychology and sociology or fields of knowledge such as management and organization studies and sub-divisions of the disciplines and fields, e.g. psychology of education, management in adult education. This strong emphasis within content on theoretical knowledge is clearly an attempt to impose rigour which can be characterized as making content relate to the world of formal theory.

An examination of the kinds of curricula found in professional courses for adult educators reveals that, ostensibly at least, the design of such curricula attempts to incorporate both relevance and rigour. However, in most cases the incorporation does not work, the reconciliation fails, with rigour or formal theory inevitably privileged. There is an inherent dilemma, therefore, whether to emphasize relevance or rigour, a dilemma which is made even more acute by the question of how teaching methods can be made congruent to both.

Given this dilemma and the problems it poses for the design and implementation of curricula in professional formation, it is interesting to speculate whence it arises. Schon (1983) has pointed out that it also exists within professional practice and he attributes this to the power of an underlying 'technical-rationality' model where theoretical knowledge (or formal theory) is deemed fundamental and can be applied to the instrumental problems of practice. Theory is therefore privileged as 'real' knowledge whilst practice is merely the application of this knowledge to the solving of problems. The implication is that there is no knowledge contained in practice.

The power of the model lies in its assumption that the application of theory is the only certainty of rigour in practice and produces the dilemma of rigour and relevance as we find it in both practice and formation. The achievement of rigour is normally at the expense of relevance, although, as Schon demonstrates, the notion of 'applying' theory to practice is problematic. If practitioners followed the technical-rationality model as a guide for rigorous practice they could end up failing to be relevant, failing to address practice as it really is.

The parallel in professional formation is the privileging of theory in order to give rigour to content. Rigour is seen as the main priority, with relevance a matter of students somehow relating the theory to their practice. This results in a pedagogy which stresses transmission of theory by methods which make it difficult for students to relate it to their practice either during or after their studies.

Essentially, what the technical-rationality model does is create a 'gap' between theory and practice which is at the heart of the dilemma. The existence of the gap creates a problem of how it can be bridged. For teachers and trainers this normally takes the form of attempting to find more effective ways of communicating theory to practitioners and of practitioners attempting to implement theory in practice situations (Carr, 1980). In the main, however, practitioners are more than likely to quietly abandon formal theory when its prescriptions do not actually work.

The bridging of the gap between theory and practice is not really about making theory 'simpler' so that practitioners can more readily understand it, since no amount of simplification will make it more readily relatable or applicable to practice. The same too is the case with attempts to make the content of teaching more <u>directly</u> relevant to practice. The difficulty of bridging the gap lies in the perceived existence of the gap itself, which is really a problem about the way that both theory and practice have been conceptualized.

THE CONCEPTUALIZATION OF THEORY IN THE TECHNICAL-RATIONALITY MODEL

Within this model, theory is conceptualized as revealing the nature of the world through scientific inquiry, thus enabling a body of knowledge to be constructed which explains the world and allows for prediction and control. In professions such as medicine and engineering theoretical knowledge both guides and justifies practice. It is the base upon which practice is founded, and is also the means of assessing practices and providing their scientific warrant.

The role of theory, therefore, is to tell the practitioner what is the case and what will happen if certain things are done. In medicine and engineering ends are considered unproblematic - restoring a patient to health or building a bridge. Theory provides the empirically validated knowledge about the physiology of patients, the physical properties of structures and an integrated system of concepts and principles. The task of the practitioner is then to use the know-ledge appropriately and apply it to the achievement of the unproblematic ends in the most efficient and effective manner.

The technical-rationality model takes for granted that those who generate the knowledge will be different from those who use it. The generation of knowledge is, in the main, the prerogative of the 'academy' which can engage in scientific research detached from the pressing everyday concerns of practice. Essentially the practitioner is a <u>knowledge-user</u>, a skilled craftsman implementing the 'design' of the theorist.

There is now a well established critique of the technical-rationality model and its conceptualization of theory which I will briefly summarize. First, theory cannot simply be 'mapped' on to practice as the model suggests. Within practice, certain kinds of judgement have to be made which do not follow or are implied by theory, or, to put it another way, 'facts' do not unequivocally point to action. The facts are often incomplete and practice situations are never fully understood. Practical judgements are always made in conditions of 'bounded rationality' (Hartnett and Naish, 1976); practice is therefore always underdetermined by theory.

Second, although practical judgements are often justified by appeal to the 'facts', this justification requires the exercise of judgement as to which 'facts' are relevant and what criteria for assessing relevance are appropriate. The facts will not themselves provide the answers; within practice, therefore, there is always an <u>interpretive</u> process at work.

Third, there is the rather complex point that theory cannot tell us how to practise. The twin phenomena - of knowing something in 'theory' yet being unable to practise it and its obverse, being able to practise but unable to specify what one does in 'theory' - are well known. What the former situation illustrates is that practice is not simply the application of theory or precepts derived from theory. Most skilled activity does not involve the conscious prior application of principles as such - in a sense, that is the essence of the skill. Even with activities that are not entirely routinizable, such as teaching, the skill consists not in the ability to apply theory to particular situations but in such things as attending and being sensitive to the situation, anticipating, making <u>ad hoc</u> decisions, none of which would be possible if we had to stop and find the appropriate theory before we acted.

In general, the view seems to be that the technical-rationality model, rather than being a reflection of reality, is actually part of a paradigm which is both oppressive and limited in its usefulness. For many practitioners it does not seem to provide much help as a working model. The privileging of a particular kind of theory appears to have a number of unfortunate effects. Rather than being 'relevant' the theory becomes a kind of ritualistic language with little resonance in practice. By equating practice merely with craftsmanship and technique, practice is thereby relegated to an instrumental and hence subordinate position in relation to theory. Practice is conceived solely as 'activity' and practice-derived knowledge is seen, where it exists, as specific, intuitive, and unsystematic, thus failing the test of 'true' knowledge.

THE TECHNICAL-RATIONALITY MODEL
AND EDUCATION

Whatever the merits of the technical-rationality model as a paradigm guiding professions such as medicine and engineering, it has been seen to have insuperable problems as a paradigm for education, particularly in the conceptualization of theory and its relationship to practice. The technical-rationality model in education sees educational theory as consisting of the so-called foundation disciplines such as psychology and sociology. This, however, is an extremely problematic assumption.

First, as Carr (1982) points out, these disciplines reject each other's theoretical frameworks and underlying assumptions. Within each discipline there are conflicting frameworks - in psychology, for example, between behaviourists and humanists, in sociology between functionalists and Marxists. It is difficult to see, therefore, how educational practice in 'applying' theory is to choose among this plethora.

Second, in medicine and engineering, the theory that is applied is relatively secure and commands general agreement, certainly in terms of its fundamentals. This is hardly the case, however, with the social sciences. Psychology, for example, as a body of knowledge which purports to describe and explain the world is highly problematic in terms of both its security and the assent it commands. Psychology, in general, still tends to see itself as a science modelled on the natural sciences. Whilst opinions differ as to the appropriateness of this aspiration and the extent of its realization, the search for scientific status has undoubtedly resulted in the well known problem of 'ecological validity'. By opting for experimental control and the rigour of 'objectivity' theory has little validity in accounting for 'normal' life. Unfortunately, it is precisely this kind of theory which education requires.

All this leaves practice with a number of unanswerable questions. One of them is <u>what</u> theory? Another is, does any theory purporting to be about human beings in a social world have the same kind of relationship to education as theories of the physical world have to activities such as medicine and engineering? Not only is one hard pressed to decide which theory is appropriate but to find theory which is both scientifically 'respectable', ecologically valid, and commands agreement beyond its own proponents is even more difficult.

At the same time, however, it is important to stress that this is not just a provisional matter which can be put right in time. Whilst it is undoubtedly the case that the search for theory of this kind seems immune to success we have to recognize that since education is a 'contested concept' (Hartnett and Naish, 1975) the search is <u>always bound to fail</u>.

The notion of a 'contested concept' is a useful one in looking at education, again in contrast to activities such as engineering and medicine. Within education, ends are not unproblematic, since they are bound up with value conflicts about the nature of education; conflicts about goals and purposes are endemic and intrinsic to the very nature of education. Any set of educational principles which purported to guide practice would only be 'educational' within a particular set of values which constituted educational ends and thus these principles could not be derived solely from theory. In effect one could say that since there is a <u>contest</u> of values it is not theory which influences the relevance of choices but the choices in the contest which influence the relevance of theory.

However, the matter goes further than this, for in education it is not only ends but means also which must be seen within a framework of values. Education is about changing people in desired directions, using desirable means, and it is impossible therefore to say, as the technical-rationality model does, that whilst ends may involve values, means are always a technical matter involving criteria of efficiency and effectiveness.

Within education, therefore, ends and means cannot be separated. Ends are the values which constitute means as properly educational. Means cannot, thus, be derived from theory; they are not mere instrumentality. Ends and means are intrinsically related within value frameworks, and the 'contest' in education encompasses both.

PRACTICAL KNOWLEDGE AND PRACTICAL REASONING

The critique of the technical-rationality model and the notion of the 'socio-practical' set the scene for an examination of practical knowledge and reasoning. In undertaking this task I will draw upon contemporary analysis of the nature of hermeneutic understanding which takes as its starting point the Aristotelian conception of different kinds of knowledge and reasoning.

Briefly, the argument is that there are three kinds of knowledge, each with its own mode of reasoning and which can be differentiated in terms of purpose. The first is theoretical knowledge, whose purpose is to discover the nature of the world, what 'necessarily' exists; the mode of reasoning is 'scientific', contemplative, and geared to uncovering universal laws. The second is technical knowledge or technical 'know-how' whose purpose is to make things; the mode of reasoning here is an instrumental or a 'means-end' type of reasoning. The end, the finished product, as it were, is known in advance; the question is how to use the proper means to achieve that end most effectively.

The third kind of knowledge is practical knowledge whose purpose is to act appropriately in the world. The mode of reasoning is praxis, which, broadly speaking, is informed and committed action. The important point to note is that practical knowledge is different from both theoretical and scientific knowledge. Practical knowledge is knowledge not of the world, but of how to act in the world. Equally, although, like technical knowledge, it is a form of 'know-how', it differs in three important respects (Bernstein, 1986).

First, because we are always situated we cannot help but act in the situations we find ourselves in and thus we cannot help but use our practical knowledge to cope with the circumstances of those situations. The use of technical knowledge, on the other hand, is not situationally dependent; we can know how to make something when required to do so but if not we can forget; but since we are always in situations we cannot 'forget' how to act within them, although we can act more or less appropriately.

Second, as we have seen, the purpose of practical knowledge is informed and committed action. The implication of this is that with practical knowledge the end is not predetermined. We need technical knowledge (technique), for example, in order to sculpt, and we can know in advance what we are going to produce - e.g. a pot. Furthermore, even though we might make different pots on different occasions, the techniques (means) by which we make them will remain the same on each occasion. But this is not the case with practical knowledge, since we cannot know in advance what the right means will be to achieve a particular end. 'For the end itself is only concretely specified in deliberating about the means appropriate to this particular situation' (Bernstein, 1986: 100). Ends and means are co-implicated, co-determined and shaped by the nature of the situation.

Third, practical knowledge has an important and necessary ethical dimension. Technical knowledge orients the self towards the end-state. It is essentially instrumental, so, for example, in making a pot ethical questions do not have to be taken into account. Practical knowledge, since it is concerned with appropriate action, in the world, must consider 'right' action. It is a kind of knowledge which must inevitably take account of others, since those others are part of the situation. Instrumentality is replaced by the need to make choices about means, and value decisions are unavoidable.

It would be possible to say, therefore, that both technical knowledge and practical knowledge are developed in and through practice. But the relationship of each to situatedness is very different. Let us consider this a little more closely. Earlier I said that practical knowledge was about praxis-informed and committed action; but what is it that 'informs' and to what is the action 'committed'? In so far as the former is concerned, one could say that action is informed by some 'universal', which could be a universal law discovered by theoretical knowledge or perhaps some universal ethical principle. Whichever it is, the point is that the 'universal' is never simply applied as it is but must always be 'mediated' in the light of a particular situation. As Warnke (1987) points out, practical knowledge involves understanding how a universal is given 'concrete content - or what its meaning is ... with regard to a particular situation' (p. 93). With technical knowledge, however, the task is to find the most effective and efficient means to fulfil an end in the light of what the universal tells us about the nature of the world.

The implication of this is that practical knowledge is reflexive; knowledge of the universal itself is changed as a result of its application to particular situations. Whilst the universal may allow us to understand our situation better and thus act appropriately the application of that knowledge requires not only that the universal be modified but that the understanding generated through the application may itself lead to further modification of the universal. There is, in other words, a constant interplay between the universal and the particular. The universal helps us to understand the particular and the particular helps us to understand the universal, and in this interplay both understandings may undergo change.

This reinforces the point made earlier about the co-implication of ends and means. In both cases we are talking about a relationship that is essentially reciprocal. The implication is that the mode of reasoning associated with practical knowledge is reflective. Reflection involves choosing how to act in the light of a particular situation where we 'cannot be spared the task of deliberation and decision by any learned or mastered technique' (Gadamer, 1981: 92). It now also becomes clear that the 'commitment', mentioned earlier, has two related aspects; first, it is to an understanding of 'universals' or general principles and, second, to being attuned to the circumstances of particular situations or to situatedness.

Practical knowledge is hermeneutic understanding, and the latter is always situated, so that when I understand X I do so within the circumstances of my particular situation. Hermeneutic understanding involves the application of universals to particular situations where the relationship is mediated. In practical reasoning, we apply as part of the moment of understanding but the nature of the application is such that the universal and particular are co-implicated and co-determined.

The implication of this - rather a startling one - is that all understanding is hermeneutical; it is not 'totally different from everyday human understanding [but] just one example of an everyday process through which persons make sense of their world' (Rowan and Reason, 1981: 132). Following this a little further, Rowan and Reason elaborate by pointing out that we and our understanding are finitely situated in time, history, and culture. Every act of understanding is also an act of interpretation (giving 'meaning', thus hermeneutic). We interpret, we place things within a context, we connect them to other things; we therefore never understand outside a context. The boundaries of interpretation, our frameworks or paradigms, as it were, 'derive from our circumstances and experience and these circumstances and experiences are always already informed by the history of the society and the culture to which we belong' (Warnke, 1987: 168-9). If this is the case, then theoretical knowledge and technical knowledge are themselves implicated within history and culture; they too are located within frameworks and paradigms.

Understanding therefore involves interpretation, and the latter in turn involves 'prejudices' or prejudgements which constitute us as historically situated beings. We cannot abolish our prejudices by an act of will - stand outside them, as it were - since this in itself would be a 'prejudice'. At the same time 'prejudices' are always co-implicated with 'tradition' and our interpretations are, therefore, not subjective in an arbitrary or egotistic·sense but are influenced both by our circumstantial concerns and by our 'effective history'; interpretive traditions which transcend us and are given by history and culture. 'Prejudice' and 'tradition', therefore, far from being arbitrary expressions of personal preference, are actually influences which shape interpretation in a way which brings together the 'subjective' and the 'objective'.

As well as interpretation, application is also always involved in the moment of understanding. We have touched upon this already where I made the point that understanding is always situated. The meaning of X is a meaning <u>for me in my particular situation</u>. When I try to understand X I assume that there is truth in X, i.e. that it is trying to 'tell' me something; but it can do this only in terms of my particular situation and the questions and concerns located in that situation. Rowan and Reason give the following example, which I think nicely illustrates the point I am trying to make. 'Feminists ... are reinterpreting the position of women in history and in culture in the light of their present understanding of the position of women; in reinterpreting history they give themselves new possibilities as women in the future' (p. 133). Thus through our prejudices and traditions, which define our questions and concerns, we understand the past in terms of the present, but by so doing we also deepen our understanding of the present and at the same time orient ourselves to the future.

At this point we are now in a position to relate the analysis to our specific concerns. The analysis presented so far of the nature of practical knowledge and hermeneutic understanding indicates a close identity with certain points made earlier about education. In particular, one could highlight the situatedness of the 'socio-practical' with the emphasis on solving problems (acting appropriately) and concern for human welfare (acting rightly); the concept of praxis, involving the dialectical engagement of theory and practice; the mutual determination of means and ends and Schon's notion of knowledge contained in practice (practical knowledge).

The case I am seeking to make is that practitioners are always in the process of 'making sense' of their world of practice. They are thus always acting hermeneutically. This involves acting rightly and appropriately within the particular situations of practice. They do this by using a certain kind of knowledge and reasoning which is neither theoretical nor technical. It may involve theoretical knowledge and it is a kind of 'know-how' but it is always mediated in the light of the circumstances of the situation, and is, therefore, situational and ethical.

Understanding or 'making sense' is not a special kind of activity but is always present and always involves interpretation and application. But this application is not that of the technical-rationality model but rather an appropriation to oneself - one can only 'make sense' in terms of one's own perspective, framework or paradigm. At the same time, however, the latter is not purely subjective but is influenced by culture and history, by a 'tradition' which can be societal, professional, institutional, informal, or more likely a combination of all. There are, as it were, frameworks and paradigms <u>within situations</u>, and <u>within practice</u>. One 'makes sense' from within one's own framework or paradigm, but this is always part of these larger frameworks or paradigms.

If we conceive of the 'practical' in this way we end up with a very different picture from that projected by the technical-rationality model. The 'practical' is not merely routinized, habitual activity but a realm of knowledge in its own right. It is concerned with action of a particular kind and has its own appropriate modes of reasoning and understanding. Indeed, a case could be made that practical reasoning and hermeneutic understanding are involved in the theoretical, the technical, and the practical. This has been denied within the 'tradition' of our scientific-technological culture, with the consequence that the practical has been subordinated to the theoretical and the technical. What I want to suggest is that we see theoretical and technical knowledge and instrumental reasoning as <u>special</u> cases of practical knowledge, reasoning, and hermeneutic understanding.

AN ALTERNATIVE APPROACH TO THE THEORY-PRACTICE RELATIONSHIP

Enough has been said to indicate that the technical-rationality model does not serve education well. An alternative, which we have already started considering, is more likely to emerge by relating education to the 'practical'.

Given that the practical is concerned with action, and that all actions are embedded within a framework, then within practice there is always an implicit or informal 'theory'. Indeed, as Pring (1977) points out, one cannot practise without this informal theory, since it renders practice intelligible; theory and practice are thus <u>conceptually</u> not contingently linked - a point supported by Castell and Freeman when they talk of practice as 'internally instrumental action'. Carr (1980, 1986) also points out that practice consists of intentional activity implicated in conceptual frameworks through which practitioners make sense of what they are doing. The frameworks enable one's own and others' practice to be both characterized and assessed. This notion of 'theoretical' practice is an interesting one, since it contradicts the conventional view of practice as 'thoughtless behaviour which exists separately from "theory" and to which theory can be applied' (Carr and Kemmis, 1986: 113). Since theory is always present in practice, it structures the experience of practice.

At this point, it is perhaps worth pausing to unpack the notion of 'theory' further, particularly as there is a danger that my examination of 'practitioner theory' may cause some confusion in terms of the relationship between this kind of theory and what would conventionally be termed 'theory', which I have earlier called 'formal' theory.

I want to suggest that we can conceptualize 'theory' in terms of two dimensions. One is the <u>formal-informal</u> dimension, the other a <u>framework-products dimension</u>. The first dimension points to a distinction between theory as organized, codified bodies of knowledge most commonly embodied in disciplines and normally expressed in academic discourse and theory in the practice sense which is not organized and codified, is closely bound up with action, and finds expression in practical discourse. The framework-products dimension, on the other hand, points to a distinction between 'theory' in the sense of a framework of understandings, concepts, beliefs, and values which characterize and underlie any activity, be it theoretical or practical and the particular theories which in a sense are rooted in these frameworks and are their product.

In principle, the two dimensions yield four permut-ations, each of which is a different form of 'theory': (1) formal theory as framework, (2) informal theory as framework, (3) formal theory as product,(4) informal theory as product. I will say more about formal theory later but an example of theory as framework would be behaviourism and, as product, operant conditioning.

Mee and Wiltshire (1978) provided examples of informal, practitioner theory when they referred to 'concepts' held by practising adult educators. These could be seen as part of a framework of principles, assumptions, values, and beliefs which structured the general approach to practice and influenced the kind of action taken in particular practice situations. An adult educator with a 'learning' framework might organize very different programmes from one with a 'community' framework and would tackle problem-solving and decision-making in a very different way.

The relationship between the various kinds of theory is a complex one. However, we can see 'theory as framework' as similar to the Kuhnian notion of a paradigm which defines a particular way of seeing the world and thus working within it. 'Theory as product' is therefore perspective - or paradigm-dependent and generating it is an activity carried out by a community who share the beliefs, values, and assumptions of the paradigm. This is the case whether we are talking of formal or informal theory. 'Informal theory as product', or working theory, situationally-dependent and action-oriented, will be influenced by and draw upon frameworks, located in the practice.

An important point which emerges from this analysis is that in both formal and informal theory, framework and product are related in and through practice. Theory is produced through practioners engaging in certain kinds of practice guided by a framework. This clearly suggests, therefore, that theorizing is itself a practice. Furthermore, the relationship is not unidirectional, since theory as 'product' can 'loop-back' to affect practice and practice can itself affect frameworks. Indeed, this is an important way in which frameworks change over time and is akin to the process of Kuhnian paradigm shifts. Practice throws up so many problems or 'anomalies' that frameworks have to change to accommodate them - a process which involves change in beliefs, assumptions, and values, and consequently different ways of interpreting 'reality' and different kinds of theory as 'product'.

Whether we are referring to theory in a formal or informal sense the position of practice is crucial. Both kinds of theory emerge from certain kinds of practice and practice is itself guided by theory. As Carr and Kemmis (1986: 113) point out, 'the twin assumptions that all "theory" is non-practical and all "practice" is non-theoretical are, therefore, entirely misguided'. Theorizing and practising are both practical activities which although carried out by different practitioners share the common aspect of having a theory which guides and structures the activity. Since all theory is a construct, it emerges through practice and, since all practice is framework-dependent, practice always involves theory.

Having said this, however, I would emphasize that it does not mean that any distinction between theory and practice thereby melts away or is unnecessary, nor does it mean that when referring to 'theory' informal theory is being privileged. This would be to treat informal theory as unproblematically as the technical-rationality model treats formal theory.

THE LIMITATIONS OF INFORMAL THEORY

It could be argued that informal theory in the sense in which I have described it appears to be virtually indistinguishable from commonsense knowledge. Furthermore, it would appear to have conservative implications, since if educational practitioners already have a theory which guides and structures their practice and which they seem to get along well with, then there is no need for change and thus no need for any kind of professional formation.

It is undoubtedly the case that educational practitioners do work with commonsense knowledge to a very large degree and it is the essence of this kind of knowledge that it has a taken-for-granted quality which does not encourage critical reflection. Equally, not all the knowledge contained in informal theory is of this kind. Whilst it must be the case that informal theory implies awareness, it cannot be assumed that this is found to the same degree in all practitioners. A variety of factors, some relating to the individual, others contextual, will operate as constraints in limiting awareness and thus the extent to which informal theory is more than just commonsense knowledge. This has important teaching implications which I shall examine later.

Squires (1982) isolates three problematic areas. Informal theory tends to be private and does not facilitate dialogue; its concern is with coping with immediate problems and it tends to 'tap only the most immediate and obvious causes and explanations ' (p. 48). He concludes that it can be limited in scope and depth. Essentially the problem is that the strength of informal theory is also its weakness. As we have seen, practice can be informed and committed action (praxis); unfortunately it may also be routine and habitual practice. Informal theory may well guide and structure practice but it does not follow that this is being done in the most aware and productive way. This links with the point about the possibly conservative effects of informal theory. If theory is not always optimal in terms of the outcomes of practice, then there is a need for improving and refining it and hence the possibility of educational intervention as a means of facilitating this.

As Carr and Kemmis (1986) point out within educational practice, problems arise through a failure of informal theory. The latter by its very nature generates expectations about practice of the kind 'If I do X, then Y should result'. Action is both directed and justified: 'I did X because I expected Y to happen.' Now if these expectations are not realized, if the outcomes of practice are different from those expected, so that what was supposed to happen does not actually happen, then practice no longer works and a problem exists. It is clear, however, that it is not only practice which is not working but also, and perhaps more significantly, informal theory, since it is the latter which generated the expectations. This means, therefore, that an educational problem denotes not merely a failure of practice but also a failure in informal theory.

Furthermore, the resolution of the problem does not lie in merely adjusting practice, as a change in informal theory is a prerequisite. Such changes may be marginal or they may be more in the nature of fundamental changes in 'informal theory as framework' - an entirely new way of understanding practice and a consequent fundamental change in practice itself.

DEFINING EDUCATIONAL THEORY

At this point it is worth considering the implications of what has been said so far for understanding the nature of educational theory. The technical-rationality model sees educational theory as a kind of applied science. However, the emphasis on the 'practical' leads to a recognition of the centrality of context and thus a need to focus on educational practice and practitioners' informal theory. The practitioner is now seen not as a technician but as someone who can possess wisdom, judgement, and a certain kind of knowledge.

This conception of the practitioner is very much in line with the hermeneutic, interpretive conception that was discussed earlier. The emphasis is on practitioners and their actions, and the way educational practice and problems relate to contexts and frameworks. Practice is to be understood from practitioners' viewpoints, and the way they understand, interpret, and appropriate their contexts. The framework of educational theory is defined in practitioners and their activity within situated contexts. The content of educational theory is the contextual problems which enable situated understandings to be explored and systematized. The purpose of educational theory is essentially pragmatic in helping practitioners to enhance and refine their understanding and hence their praxis.

If practitioners already possess a 'theory' which is to a very large extent common to a community of practitioners, then educational theory refers to this 'theory' rather than the 'theory' in scientific disciplines. Carr and Kemmis, who have argued this standpoint cogently, maintain that educational theory is the theory which guides the work of practitioners. It is a mistake to suppose that a theory which is located <u>outside</u> the context of educational practice could properly be <u>educational</u> theory and the result of this mistake has been the creation of the so-called 'gap' between educational theory and practice. They point out furthermore that it is hardly surprising that efforts to eliminate the gap by attempting to persuade educational practitioners to 'apply' the theory of scientific disciplines have met with limited success. In other words, the problem is not one of inadequate 'communication', or poor teaching, even less that practitioners are incapable of understanding; rather it is a problem that is <u>of necessity insoluble</u> so long as a particular conception of educational theory is held.

At the same time, however, they recognize that characterizing educational theory <u>simply</u> as the theory already possessed by educational practitioners is not enough. I have already indicated some of the limitations of informal theory, and these are conceptually rooted in the weaknesses of the hermeneutic approach.

It will be recalled that when I discussed the situatedness of practical knowledge and understanding I emphasized the influence of our 'prejudices' and our location in a 'tradition'. Part of the difficulty lies in distinguishing between 'blind' and 'productive' prejudices and tradition which can either inhibit or expand one's horizons of understanding. The most problematic feature is the part played by power and ideology in shaping knowledge and understanding, and this raises questions as to the extent to which, first, practitioners' frameworks and informal theory are genuinely their own and second, their efficacy in dealing with problems which are to do with the structural features of social contexts. The weakness of the hermeneutic approach is that it is not self-referential. Its critique of the technical-rationality model is that it fails to take account of situatedness, seeing theory as a universal which stands outside contexts. Yet it too has to recognize, but often fails to do so, that the very notion of practical knowledge both in general terms and in terms of specific instances is itself situated in a context where praxis can be distorted.

Informal theory, therefore, may be the <u>starting point</u> of educational theory but cannot constitute its exclusive content. Educational theory must also include a critical evaluation of the nature and adequacy of informal theory. One thing, however, is clear from the analysis so far; education is not a field of knowledge and educational theory is not the integrating, interdisciplinary theory of a field. Education as a study and education as a practice are both 'practical' and therefore cannot be founded or based on disciplines. Equally, however, any educational theory located in the 'practical' must take account of its limitations.

IMPLICATIONS FOR CURRICULUM DESIGN
AND TEACHING

It is clear, therefore, that an appropriate curriculum for professional formation would not be <u>founded</u> on the disciplines. In the argument I have presented adult education, like education, is neither a theoretical nor a practical field of knowledge in the Hirstian sense but is properly located in the 'practical'. Hence its curriculum must appropriately reflect this.

Specifically, I would want to emphasize that adult education as a field of study has to recognize that adult education as a field of practice is a practical activity. As such the latter, as we have seen, has its own realm of knowledge and its own mode of understanding which I have described as hermeneutic. It follows, therefore, that adult education as a field of study must incorporate this realm of knowledge and mode of understanding in its own practice, and thus it too must be hermeneutic. There is, in other words, a 'double hermeneutic', since both the study and the object of study are located within paradigms, 'theoretical' frameworks, or hermeneutic situations from which they cannot be detached.

The elucidation of these hermeneutic situations can come about only through <u>dialogue</u>, and it is this which must form the guiding principle of curriculum design. Equally, the mode of teaching must be such as to facilitate dialogue. At the same time, however, it is important that dialogue must be <u>critical</u>, otherwise the constraining factors mentioned earlier which distort dialogue and hence understanding will never be acknowledged and assessed.

This would suggest, therefore, that the starting point is practice <u>problems</u> rather than practice <u>per se</u>. These need to be articulated so that frameworks of practice can be surfaced and analysed and the effects of discursive and material constraints assessed. In effect the process is one of examining the way in which practice is <u>framed</u> and <u>constrained</u>. It can be characterized as 'denormalizing' practice, since its effect is that practice is no longer seen as 'normal' or routinized (Usher, 1987). Practice, as we have seen, can be routine, habitual, and unproductive, and perceived as 'immutable'. The 'denormalizing' of practice is, therefore, the beginning of a critical self-questioning approach to practice; the beginnings of a dialogue with and about practice which can lead to an appreciation of alternative possibilities.

This, by itself, is not enough. A great deal of professional formation which uses experiential approaches does this but takes things no further. To surface and question the frameworks of informal theory is an essential first step but the frameworks may themselves be so constraining that they do not suggest the possibility of better options. It is at this point that formal theory can play a useful part.

Formal theory, as we have seen, takes the form of a 'universal' which aims to describe and explain the world, whereas informal theory is situated and concerned with action and change. We have seen that we cannot 'apply' formal theory to informal theory; it cannot be directly 'mapped' on to informal theory, but may none the less help in perceiving the 'terrain' of the latter more clearly.

To clarify what I mean here I need to backtrack a little to a point made earlier, that 'formal theory as product' is generated out of a practice informed by 'formal theory as framework'. The end to which the practice is directed in the case of formal theory is the generation of conceptual representations of an abstract kind designed to reflect and model the world. In this sense, the formal theorist is o̲f̲ the world but not i̲n̲ it and; thus the resulting theory i̲s̲ not ostensibly situated. This is similar to the 'theoretico-practical' described by Castell and Freeman (1978: 20) as a mode of theorizing carried out 'as an end in itself' and which treats contextual factors as invariant.

The practice of generating 'formal theory as product' is not the practice of practitioners; thus the kinds of choices and judgements that have to be made are, as it were, one step removed from the action. Informal theory, however, is concerned not with representation and explanation but with understanding, interpretation, and appropriation. The question is, therefore, how can representation and explanation help the latter? Formal theory in the sense that it is 'outside' the immediate world of everyday practice can help through facilitating the 're-presentation' of practice problems, not through direct application to those problems but 'as a source of metaphor and sensitising concepts with which to view in a different way and to reformulate the problem' (Usher and Bryant, 1987: 209).

The term 'review' seems an appropriate one for characterizing this process, given its connotation of 'looking back' and 'reconsidering'. We can see formal theory, therefore, as a kind of resource and 'sounding board' for the development and refinement of informal theory - a way of bringing critical analysis to bear on the latter. Instead of formal theory being applied to practice we have the notion of informal theory (and practice) 'reviewed' through formal theory. Here, therefore, we see formal theory not as foundational but more as an ingredient in a developing and edifying discourse (Rorty, 1980) which helps us both to cope with the world and continually to 'create' ourselves in the world. As Macdonald (1982) puts it, formal theory is not so much a body of knowledge as a 'bundle of illuminations'.

The biggest problem is that, in reality, formal and informal theory are always found together anyway. Moore (1981) makes the point that formal theory is always already present because the commonsense knowledge of educational practitioners inevitably contains elements of formal theory. Formal theory as 'product' clearly influences informal theory as 'framework'. It is important to surface the extent of this influence and examine the degree to which it may be contributing to problems in educational practice.

From a pedagogical viewpoint, dealing with formal theory as 'product' presents its own difficulties, since it is part of the 'taken for granted' - it is part of the 'tradition'. Educational practitioners when they become students tend to be overawed; they find it difficult to question, given the status of formal theory as codified knowledge and the attached aura of 'academic' legitimacy. At the same time, they do often feel that its concerns are not directly theirs even though they invariably cannot articulate the reasons.

There are, however, good reasons for this uneasiness on the part of practitioners, given that education is a practical and not a theoretical activity in the way that, for example, psychology is. Whilst the production of psychological theory is located in a framework, the content of that framework will be very different from the framework of educational practice. The difference is not immediately apparent, since there are concepts common to both which have the same verbal labels.

A good example is the concept of 'learning', which means different things to the psychologist and the educational practitioner, as anyone who has taught psychology of learning will have experienced at first hand. Psychological theories of learning are inevitably impersonal and generalized and exclude matters such as individual biography, relationships, or the social location of learning which practitioners recognize to be important (Salmon, 1980). For educational practitioners, therefore, psychological theories do not appear to be about 'real' learning, they do not seem to engage with learning as they have come to understand it through their own practice. In other words, their informal theory is telling them a different story, and although this story is no more 'right' than the psychologist's story, it cannot, from a pedagogical viewpoint, be dismissed as 'unscientific', 'imprecise', and 'lacking in rigour'. The root of the problem is that psychological theory and practitioners' informal theory have <u>different</u> sites of origination but the <u>same</u> site of application, i.e. educational practice, and it is this which causes the difficulty both in practice and in pedagogy.

Formal theory as 'product' is therefore very difficult to deal with in the classroom. On the other hand, given that it is the product of practices guided by formal theory as 'framework', it can be more productive to start with the latter. When students examine the underlying theoretical framework they can see how, for example, theories of learning take the particular form they do and how they are as much a construct and therefore as much capable of problematization as their own informal theory.

In a sense, one can see this as a process of putting formal theory as 'product' into a <u>context</u> by explaining the assumptions, concepts, values, and language of formal theory as 'framework'. Thus contextualized it can then be seen as explaining the world in a particular way and from a particular standpoint, rather than discovering 'truths' about the world, and being more or less helpful in so doing - ultimately, therefore, a pragmatic test. At the same time, formal theories can be differentiated in terms of their affinity and edifying force for informal theory.

'Review' is essentially a dialogical process which mediates formal and informal theory, enabling counterposing and mutual questioning; it is a 'fusion of horizons' between formal and informal theory which deepens understanding and opens up the possibility of new experience and changes in practice. Informal theory goes beyond 'commonsense', practice beyond routine, and formal theory is seen as pragmatic and edifying.

CONCLUSIONS

If we accept that adult education both as a field of study and as a field of practice is a practical activity it must follow that the primary aim of a curriculum for professional formation should be the enhancement and improvement of practice. Such a curriculum would enable practitioners to develop a reflexive awareness of practice and to engage truly in praxis.

Earlier I discussed the dilemma of rigour and relevance arising from the technical-rationality model and suggested the alternative of practical knowledge and hermeneutic understanding as a more adequate conceptualization of practice and of the theory-practice relationship. However, we cannot merely through an act of will 'wish away' the technical-rationality model. As Habermas, Foucault, and other contemporary scholars have pointed out, all forms of knowledge are always co-implicated with power and ideology. This points to the need for a critical approach both in curriculum design and in teaching.

The dilemma of rigour and relevance can be reconciled, in formation at least, by the approach described. By focusing on practice and by recognizing the existence of informal theory the curriculum can be made 'relevant'. At the same time, narrowness, triviality, and anecdotage can be avoided. 'Rigour' is preserved through starting with informal theory but recognizing that formal theory has its pragmatic place.

There is a further point that needs to be stressed. The use of techniques such as 'denormalizing' and 'reviewing' ensure that teaching is congruent with both rigour and relevance. If the aim is to improve practice through enabling the development of reflexive awareness, then the classroom must provide the means for this to happen, with teachers/trainers themselves engaging in praxis.

There are, however, a number of wider implications. The first is that the distinction between 'theorists' and practitioners needs to be softened. Theorists' and teachers (who in adult education tend to be one and the same) need to be both more aware and more knowledgeable about practice 'in the field'. Certainly in school education it now seems to be accepted that teachers/trainers should periodically spend some of their time teaching in schools. Equally, however, practitioners need to become more aware of the place of 'theory' and theorizing in their work. Project work and placements may have a part to play here. As Squires (1987) points out, these are an essential part of adult education curricula in the rest of Europe and are seen as a means of furthering praxis through a critical engagement with the 'real' world. Practitioner-based inquiry and research are also another means of heightening an awareness of 'theory' and facilitating praxis. The teacher-as-researcher movement provides a useful and successful example from school education.

The second point to stress is that adult education in adopting the 'practical' needs to reconceptualize its notion of 'theory' and thus its epistemology generally. Theory is not confined solely to the theoretical knowledge contained in disciplines. The existence of an epistemology of practice has to be acknowledged. Practitioners have to be seen not merely as actors but as informed and committed actors. The importance of the contexts of practice has to be recognized and 'theory' has to take on board the consequent social and moral dimensions of practice.

A pragmatic orientation to theory and method is justified in terms of a commitment to practical issues and problems. But this justification is itself conditional on a commitment to the critical. Without such a commitment, theory could become mere anecdotage and teaching could become inspirational 'ego-boosting'. This commitment to the critical must operate in terms of the content both of theory and of teaching. In abandoning the traditional 'academic disciplines' model adult education must endeavour to develop a critical theory appropriate to its nature as a practical activity. The disciplines have a part to play but the role is to help ensure that horizons of understanding are as 'open' as possible. Locating adult education in practice and practice problems ensures its coherence as theory. At the same time, 'open' horizons of understanding ensure, by providing a context of relevance, that theorists do not get 'lost' in disciplines (Vandenberg, 1974).

If the aim of adult education as a field of study is to develop the praxis which is always present, albeit in a distorted and incomplete form, in adult education as a field of practice, then practitioners as students need a mode of professional formation which brings that about. The emphasis has generally been either to transmit formal theory or to work with 'experience' or an uneasy attempt to integrate the two through 'application'. But we now recognize that these approaches have not worked too well and so it is important to switch our gaze and see that adult education both as a field of study and as a field of practice are located in the 'practical'. It follows that the knowledge, 'theory', and understanding distinctive of the 'practical' must inform the content of and the approach to teaching. But since praxis is about acting appropriately in concrete situations, and since, within the latter, power and ideology are always present, then the 'practical' and the critical are conjoined. Understanding and dialogue, the basis of praxis, can function both in the world of practice and in the world of the classroom only through a recognition of the possibilities and the limits of situatedness.

REFERENCES

Bernstein, R. (1986) Philosophical Profiles: Essays in a Pragmatic Mode, Oxford: Polity Press.

Bright, B. P. (1985) 'The content-method relationship in the study of adult education', Studies in the Education of Adults 17 (2): 168-83.

Carr, W. (1980) 'The gap between theory and practice', Journal of Further and Higher Education 4 (1): 60-9.

—— (1982) 'Treating the symptoms, neglecting the cause; diagnosing the problem of theory and practice', Journal of Further and Higher Education 6 (2): 19-29.

—— (1986) 'Theories of theory and practice', Journal of Philosophy of Education 20 (2): 177-86.

—— and Kemmis, S. (1986) Becoming Critical, Lewes: Falmer Press.

de Castell, S., and Freeman, H. (1978) 'Education as a socio-practical field: the theory-practice question reformulated', Journal of Philosophy of Education 12: 12-28.

Gadamer, H. G. (1981) 'Hermeneutics as practical philosophy', in Reason in Age of Science, trans. F. Lawrence, Cambridge, Mass.: M I T Press.

Hartnett, M., and Naish, A. (1975) 'What theory cannot do for teachers', Education for Teaching 96 (1): 12-19.

—— (1976) Theory and the Practice of Education, London: Heinemann.

Hirst, P. (1974) Knowledge and the Curriculum, London: Routledge & Kegan Paul.

Macdonald, J. B. (1982) 'How literal is curriculum theory?' Theory into Practice 21 (1): 55-61.

Mee, G., and Wiltshire, H. (1978) Structure and Performance in Adult Education, London: Longman.

Moore, P. (1981) 'Relations between theory and practice: a critique of Wilfred Carr's views', Journal of Further and Higher Education 5 (2): 44-56.

Pring, R. (1977) 'Commonsense and education', Proceedings of the Philosophy of Education Society 11: 57-77.

Rorty, R. (1980) Philosophy and the Mirror of Nature, Oxford: Blackwell.

Rowan, J., and Reason, P. (1981) 'On making sense', in P. Reason and J. Rowan (eds), Human Inquiry: a Sourcebook on New Paradigm Research, Chichester: Wiley.

Salmon, P. (1980) Coming to Know, London: Routledge & Kegan Paul.

Schon, D. A. (1983) The Reflective Practitioner: how Professionals Think in Action, London: Temple Smith.

Squires, G. (1982) The Analysis of Teaching, Hull: Department of Adult Education, University of Hull.

—— (1987) The Curriculum beyond School, London: Hodder & Stoughton.

Usher, R. S. (1987) 'The place of theory in designing curricula for the continuing education of adult educators', Studies in the Education of Adults 19 (1): 26-36.

—— and Bryant, I. (1987) 'Re-examining the theory-practice relationship in continuing professional education', Studies in Higher Education 12 (2): 201-12.

Vandenberg, D. (1974) 'Phenomenology and educational research', in D. Denton (ed.), Existentialism and Phenomenology in Education, New York: Teachers College Press.

Warnke, G. (1987) Gadamer: Hermeneutics, Tradition and Reason, Oxford: Polity Press.

Chapter five

RIGHT FOR THE WRONG REASONS: A CRITIQUE OF SOCIOLOGY IN PROFESSIONAL ADULT EDUCATION

Paul F. Armstrong

In recent years there has been growing acceptance of the place of sociology in the curriculum of adult education training courses. This is part of a general trend in professional and vocational training after many years of suspicion of what is a relatively young discipline, whose content and epistemological status is still uncertain. Nevertheless, Heraud (1979) was able to report in 1979 that sociology is now required to provide part of the basic training curriculum of many professional courses, even those of the long-established, powerful, and prestigious professions, such as law and medicine. In areas such as health visiting, social work, and education - 'people-processing' professions - sociology has come to command a place in the standard training curriculum, though not without much debate. In health visitors' training, for example, the Central Council for the Training of Health Visitors first introduced sociology as a core subject into its curriculum in 1965. At the time many health visitors, students and tutors 'were dubious about the wisdom of introducing an academic discipline of such a complex nature into an applied professional course' (Owen, 1977: 95). The relevance of sociology to health visitors has been an on-going concern ever since. A number of authors have written to defend the place of sociology on the curriculum of such a training course:

> ... it is likely that sociology will have a considerable contribution to make in providing a short cut to the formation of attitudes in health visitors which previously were gained only through several slow years of actual casework experience. [Barber, 1968: 185]

Although sociology leads to an understanding rather than practice, it is an understanding that can be recommended to people like social workers and nurses (and naturally to health visitors). In fact it can be 'recommended to anyone whose goals involve the manipulation of men'. This kind of understanding can influence our attitudes and increase our effectiveness in helping people with whom we are concerned ...

... as a means of communication ... it offers an understanding of groups and different cultures and therefore helps in establishing social contact. It may well also help to overcome any rigidity or authoritarianism ... and could be very important in helping to establish suitable attitudes and developing a sense of maturity and a readiness to question their own value systems where necessary. [Owen, 1977: 98, 100]

One suspects from the plethora of articles written supporting the inclusion of sociology into the health visiting training course that the tutors themselves were not entirely convinced and were trying to produce justifications. As North admits:

What's the use of sociology to the health visitor? One possible answer is: no use. At least, no more use than history, philosophy or comparative religion. [North, 1975: 113]

And as one critic has posed:

For much too long there has been a lack of public discussion on the philosophical differences which so often separate the health visiting professionals and sociologists. The divisions are deep and cannot be resolved easily, if at all. It is not simply a matter of amending or abolishing a central syllabus underlying philosophy which we use to justify sociology's inclusion in health visitor education, how it got there in the first place, how it should develop in the future. We must, in short, return to first principles and ask the question 'why sociology?' of ourselves. [Anderson, 1979: 187]

It is the intention of this chapter to take up this question and relate it to professional training in education. Although mainly concerned with the education of adults, the discussion will focus on more general issues, and then seek to relate this to professional training in adult education where appropriate. It will be suggested that the inclusion of sociology on all education training programmes is problematic, but that those who have presented arguments for its removal from the curriculum of education training courses have done so largely on misguided grounds. Many recent arguments against the teaching of sociology to training teachers (and on other professional and/or vocational training courses) emanate from right-wing views, whose exponents believe that the discipline of sociology is in itself subversive, especially in the way that it supposedly undermines professionals' participation in modern and developing capitalist economies. My argument is that this is rather 'optimistic', and, far from being subversive of the dominant ideology, the discipline of sociology is either reduced to abstract theorizing, without practical intent, or is a form of technicism that can actually serve to make professional educators more effective in their maintenance of the status quo, and reproduction of unequal capitalist relations. This has been recognized in the training of health visitors:

> ... it is not true that most sociology is overcritical of the family, religion and the dominant morality. Most sociology affirms and applauds the alleged crucial role of the family in preserving the status quo for the benefit of all. This is another point about sociology which is continuously misunderstood by students. Far from being a radical left-wing discipline or subject, sociology is a conservative one ... Radical sociology is a minority occupation. [Kornreich, 1977: 264]

Thus the question to be addressed is not only 'why sociology?' but what sociology those on professional teacher training and adult education training courses should be exposed to.

WHY SOCIOLOGY?

Like sociology in social work training (Armstrong, 1980), the relationship between sociology and teacher education has been far from straightforward. By the turn of this century there was a possibility that sociology would begin to inform the training of teachers, particularly when one of sociology's founding fathers, Emile Durkheim, was appointed to the Chair of the Science of Education (later renamed Sociology and Education) at the Sorbonne in 1906. Education was one of Durkheim's main sociological interests. He wrote, 'the first postulate of all pedagogical speculation: that education is an eminently social thing in its origins as is its functions, and that therefore pedagogy depends on sociology more closely than any other science' (Durkheim, 1956). But his view of education was not widely shared outside his own institution, and it was not until after the Second World War that interest in the sociological basis of teacher education was awoken. There were many reasons for this, and none can be considered more important than any of the others, but it was the favourable historical conjunction of these factors that stimulated the rapid establishment of sociology as one of the basic curricular subjects of teacher education in Britain.

After Karl Mannheim's appointment to the Chair at the University of London's Institute of Education, there was increasing recognition of the epistemological significance of sociology as a discipline, as well as stimulation of empirical research within the area of the sociology of education. Such research was not purely academic, but was beginning to inform educational policy. Indeed, many of the government committees reporting from the end of the 1950s through the 1960s took account of a sociological perspective. The Newsom Report (1963), for instance, suggested that teachers should 'put their job into social perspective and be better prepared to understand the difficulties of pupils in certain types of areas'.

Thus at this time the discipline of sociology itself was growing in stature and in numbers of graduates. After the Robbins Report (1963), not only was there a general expansion of further and higher education, which facilitated the development of the teaching of sociology in universities and colleges, but the expansion of and changes to teacher education paved the way for the introduction of sociology as a contributing discipline. In part this was influenced by developments in the United States, for there education had since the 1920s been informed by sociology, and sociology was taught more widely. According to one American textbook, 'the line of demarcation between "education" and "sociology" seems at times to become almost completely obliterated' (Roucek, 1961). And it was not only the influence of American education and sociology that was significant, for in Britain a sociological perspective in social work training had by this time taken firm root. This not only served to establish the place of sociology in professional and vocational training: there was a feeling at the time that teachers had much in common with social workers. Maurice Craft (1963: 31) refers to teachers as having become 'in many ways skilled social workers' and Jean Floud (Craft, 1963: 32) saw the teacher's role as 'cultural missionary-cum-social worker'. In a climate where social problems were beginning to re-emerge after the post-war illusion of affluence, there was some hope that sociology would be able not only to assist in the identification of the problems but offer guidance on the solutions as well. If social work was recognized as occurring in a social and political context, then so should teaching, which was equally deserving of a sociological approach to the training of its practitioners. And, as McGregor (Halsey, 1965: 27) suggested, 'Educated people must nowadays be <u>sociate</u> as well as numerate and literate.'

In education research had established firmly the significance of the family, parental influence, and social class on educational achievement, and policies in the 1960s, including those deriving from the Plowden Committee, were built around these sociological findings. There was increasingly less suspicion that sociology was a subversive subject. It was a firmly established discipline, a behavioural science with strong epistemological foundations and methods of justification in the pursuit of truth that could assist in the understanding of the nature of education and teaching. This coincided with a 'revolution' in the philosophy of education, which was no longer viewed as a unitary discipline, but a field to which several other disciplines such as history, philosophy, psychology, and now sociology could contribute (Hirst, 1963, 1965). This epistemological change demanded a rethink of the curricula of teacher training courses to take into account a multi-disciplinary approach.

With the structural changes in teacher education and training that were taking place, particularly the extension of the length of training, and the move towards making the profession a graduate one, there was much opportunity for sociology to establish itself firmly alongside the other disciplines. However, it has to be said that there was still some resistance to the discipline of sociology, and there were practical problems of introducing it into teacher training, not least that there were few trained teachers who were qualified in sociology. In terms of the resistance to the introduction of sociology into colleges of education, objections were raised that sociology in itself was not part of the school curriculum, and therefore should not be taught in teacher education. This was to change over the next few years, for as sociology became an integral part of teacher training programmes it also rapidly established itself as a popular subject in the school curriculum, following its increase in popularity in universities and colleges. Now teacher training institutions were able to appoint sociologists both as professional educators and as subject specialists. Similarly, in the field of adult education training, those university adult education departments that had sociology specialists on their teaching staff could add their perspectives to the diploma and higher degree courses in adult education.

This is not to say that the issue of the relevance of a sociological perspective disappeared, for periodically this debate emerges for public discussion. The debate focuses largely around either or both (a) the epistemological nature of sociology, and (b) the problem of bias and objectivity in the subject. The issues relating to (b) will be dealt with in a later section; here we focus on aspects of epistemology.

There are several aspects to the epistemological debate surrounding sociology. Great claims were made for the introduction of sociology into the curricula of teacher education. The claim that sociology, like philosophy, was in pursuit of truth in a scientific and rigorous way was not borne out in practice. The difficulty seemed to be the very nature of sociology. For example, Otley (1966: 56) argued that:

> Sociology is one of those subjects which only seems bona fide when it is taught at the University level in a university setting. It appears to take badly to 'dilution' or 'simplification' ... Hence the erstwhile teacher of sociology in a college of education seems to be faced with an unpalatable choice between a strictly 'academic' university-style sociology course and an eclectic and untheoretical social studies course.

This meant that, if sociology was to be taught outside universities, there had to be some 'middle way' which

99

preserved the unified scientific nature of sociology, and yet could take account of the special conditions and aims of study in a college of education. Such a course needs to be oriented towards topics which are of direct relevance and utility to the student teacher, and should avoid topics of 'undue complexity or abstraction', which include 'property and power structure of modern Britain, the nature of legal and political institutions and religious phenomena, for instance, which are not at all suitable for the ordinary college student' (Otley, 1966: 58).

In a response to this, Chambers (1966) argues that it will lead to 'a very low level of sophistication in our teaching', and makes a plea for the recognition of sociology as a 'serious, scientific discipline'. Part of the disagreement is to do with the lack of consensus as to the purpose of including sociology as part of the teacher training programme. A number of justifications have been put forward. The first follows from what was said above - education does not take place in a social vacuum, and it is therefore important for teachers to take a broader view of their role in society. Second, there is the argument that, as one of the contributing disciplines, sociology as much as any other discipline has as much chance of educating the student teacher (Musgrave, 1965a: 45). Both these stress the education as opposed to the training of teachers. If sociology is to be justified in terms of training, as making a contribution to the technical skills of teaching, then it has to be on the grounds of immediate utility and relevance. It has been suggested that before the development of the sociology of education in the 1950s and 1960s the term 'educational sociology' was used to refer to the use of sociology to illuminate practical and technical aspects of teaching, and that this often took a normative approach, and was characteristic of the way sociology influenced education in America (Taylor, 1966; McNamara, 1972). Educationalists are typically concerned with the practical activity of educating, and sociological evidence is drawn on only if it is useful. Taylor sees this as a potential danger, for when insights are brought to bear on the training of teachers they have usually supported an educational philosophy, or an educationalist's point of view. Thus 'The emphasis has been hortatory rather than empirical, inspirational rather than objective, and synoptic rather than analytic' (McNamara, 1972: 138).

This normative orientation of the technicist educational

sociology is to be avoided, argues McNamara. His argument is that these ideologies need to be made explicit, rather than moving away from a utilitarian view of the sociology of education. A broader approach to this is not acceptable, since it is doubtful that sociology has achieved the status of a 'science', and therefore 'it does not have a necessary claim to be included in the education syllabuses of colleges of education'. These arguments for the removal of sociology as one of the contributing disciplines in the curriculum of initial teacher training courses are expanded further in a later article, in which McNamara (1977) outlines a number of objections to the inclusion of sociology on college courses. To begin with, he says, the sociology of education 'is often badly taught by unqualified persons' and 'it is badly "learned" by uninterested students'. This is a secondary objection, and as McNamara says this argument is 'comparatively unimportant' in so far as the remedies are obvious and not intrinsic to the sociology of education. There are other problems which mean that the discipline does not have strong claims to inclusion in the curriculum of teacher training, but these are not inherent in the discipline of sociology itself, only in its application to teacher education:

> First, sociology is essentially an intellectual enterprise in the sense that it attempts to advance our theoretical understanding of the world in an academic ambience premised upon scepticism and debate.
> Second, the sociologist's models of man whether by methodological implication or theoretical invention often seem deterministic and to question the freedom of the individual to act autonomously.
> Thirdly, because sociology is a theoretical discipline concerned with second order abstractions rather than with the qualities and characters of persons, its attempts at enlightenment can be counterproductive.
> Finally, because sociology is a theoretical and empirical discipline, a rigorous and demanding course of study is a necessary prerequisite to an understanding of the issues and problems within sociology itself, before attempting to apply it in the field of education.
> [McNamara, 1977: 180, 181]

These are McNamara's 'serious grounds' for removing sociology from the curricula of teacher education. In its stead McNamara (1977: 182) suggests that 'In the field of education a body of professional material, skill, and technology is being developed which can more than fill the education syllabus for three years.' Thus McNamara is proposing that sociology with a broader educational aim should be replaced by a more technicist approach that stresses the development of competence and skill acquisition that will make intending teachers more effective in their role.

Not surprisingly, McNamara's views were not received very well by sociologists working in education. Culley and Demaine (1978) responded by stating that McNamara was setting up a false dichotomy between 'theoretical' and 'practical' training. They argue that:

> whilst training teachers to be good technicians is essential, it is also important to prepare them to understand the background to the teaching/learning situation in which they find themselves, and the nature of society, of which education is a central part. [p. 221]

They are thus seeking to reassert the case for the broader view of teacher education, rather than the narrow technicist training that McNamara seems to prefer. Culley and Demaine proceed to go through each of McNamara's criticisms to provide a response. They do, in spite of McNamara's disclaimer, think that his article does constitute an attack on sociology itself. They object to his attack on rationality when questioning the 'mental qualities' that a teacher requires when McNamara (1977: 180) writes, 'To put it crudely: the sociologist thinks and then may think about acting, the teacher acts and then may think about having acted.'

But, in a way, McNamara is right. A sociological perspective may provide teachers with a tool for reflection, but given the working conditions of most teachers in Britain there would be little opportunity to use it, except retrospectively, enabling teachers to think back over what they have been doing, rather than to inform their current and future action. In many ways, a sociological perspective may actually be 'disabling' for teachers. To take an example, once teachers are made aware of the nature of the theory and practice of phenomenology, through which they can think about thinking about teaching, what was previously taken for granted, and even subconscious, now becomes obtrusive and interrupts the normal flow of everyday life. The teacher, thinking about the fleeting classroom micro-decisions that he/she makes from moment to moment in teaching (Eggleston, 1979), is no longer making those decisions. Now this is not to say that this is a bad thing, but the way that education is presently organized does not encourage the teacher to adopt a phenomenological stance in the classroom. The point is that McNamara's critique may hold for the way that things are, but it may not be necessary to continue to accept things as they are, and a sociological perspective may be conducive to challenging and changing the role of teachers and the environment in which they have to work. As Culley and Demaine (1978: 222) say, 'Since teachers are concerned with social entities and since they are to be encouraged to think, it makes good sense that they engage in an intellectual enterprise which attempts to advance theoretical understanding of the world.'

As far as McNamara's second criticism is concerned, that sociology tends towards deterministic accounts of human behaviour, Culley and Demaine point out that he ignores some sociological perspectives that are, in a humanistic way, emphasizing free agency. They are right to pick up McNamara's inconsistency here when he says that 'the essence of the teacher's commitment must be a belief that both he and his pupils are to some degree free agents ...' (1977: 181), for the issue remains as to what degree both teachers and pupils are 'unfree' and why, and this is precisely where some sociological perspectives may provide insight. Again, however, it has to be stressed that McNamara is right, in so far as all sociological perspectives do, at minimum, emphasize some constraints on individuality and freedom, and indeed some of them are overtly deterministic.

Culley and Demaine take McNamara's third and fourth criticisms together. The burden of McNamara's critique is that sociology is a theoretical and, later, a theoretical and empirical discipline, and therefore less relevant, useful, and endearing to teachers, for it would be 'unwise for students to embark upon the study of sociology of education until they have a working knowledge of statistical techniques and research methodologies plus an understanding of the philosophy of the social sciences' (McNamara, 1977: 181). Culley and Demaine think that McNamara is confusing the issue of the best way to introduce sociology to student teachers with the objection to the possibility of teaching sociology on teacher education courses. Furthermore, his:

> sterile epistemological dichotomy drawn between the empiricist and rationalist conceptions of the objects of discourse has met with serious opposition in sociology and elsewhere. It is sufficient here merely to point out that neither theoretical concepts nor empirical identifications can be dispensed with in sociology. Each represents a level of conceptualisation in discourse, but neither represents a privileged level or source of deductions. In this respect the empirical and theoretical status of sociology is not unique. Such is the status of the pursuit of all scientific knowledge, including the pursuit of knowledge in the field of education. [Culley and Demaine, 1978: 223]

Thus it would be possible to argue that the history of education should be studied only by graduate historians, the psychology of education by psychology graduates, and the philosophy of education by graduates of philosophy, if the sociology of education can be studied only by those trained in sociology. On this dilemma Musgrave (1965b: 53-4) comments:

> the student today in many education courses is being asked to apply several distinct disciplines to the field of education. Each has its own criteria and its own ways of thought and judgement. Sociology is only one out of perhaps four disciplines used in the education course alone, the other normally being philosophy, history and psychology. The basic concepts and structure of the subject must therefore be established intellectually during a period when, either simultaneously or consecutively, the student is being asked to carry out the same process in several other disciplines. We are, in fact, trying to socialise the student into the role of the teacher by socialising him into several academic subroles, that of sociologist, philosopher and so on. Each of these has its own mode of thinking ... and this has to be learnt by the student, if he is to order his experience in the way that each particular academic role demands.

In another article Musgrave (1965a: 47) concludes that

'a study of sociology can educate a student in the fullest sense as well as any other discipline'. But he does strengthen the case for sociology by arguing that one of its distinctive features is that it may encourage teachers to develop a sociological frame of reference that might lead them to begin to question concepts and evidence, and, although this may lead to 'considerable doubt and personal conflict', 'This is no condemnation if we want our teachers to be questioning beings. Indeed, courses in any discipline will only be good as much as they have this disturbing effect' (Musgrave, 1965a: 54). But there are two problems with this. To begin with, not all may agree that to have questioning teachers is necessarily desirable. In support of his arguments against the inclusion of sociology in teacher education curricula McNamara arrives at a similar conclusion to the one we arrived at above by citing the work of Philip Jackson (1968), who discovered through interviews with highly respected members of the teaching profession that 'successful' teaching runs counter to the aims and aspirations of sociology courses which seek to develop a critical mode of thought, because the pressures on the teacher's role rarely allow the opportunity for critical reflection, and a sociological frame of reference may be 'disfunctional' for the teacher's role:

> teachers' talk is characterised by conceptual simplicity, four aspects of which are: (1) an uncomplicated view of causality; (2) an intuitive, rather than rational approach to classroom events; (3) an opinionated, as opposed to an open-minded, stance when confronted with alternative teaching practices; and (4) a narrowness in the working definitions assigned to abstract terms. [McNamara, 1972: 146]

Thus it is unlikely that students 'would become better teachers as a consequence' of studying sociology.

The second problem related to the development of critical thinking among teachers is that not all sociology inevitably leads to this; not all sociology seeks to challenge the status quo. From the debate surrounding the inclusion of sociology in the curricula of teacher education courses it should be apparent that the difficulty in taking sides with the McNamara viewpoint or the counter-arguments of Culley and Demaine is that they would both appear to assume that it is possible to talk about the sociological perspective. Indeed, it may be, but the problem is that there is not just one sociological perspective, but a number of often competing frameworks within which to interpret the world.

WHICH SOCIOLOGY?

We have seen that part of the answer to why sociology should be included or not in teacher education courses lies not only in what is taught (that is, what is relevant), and the way it is taught, but also which sociological perspective(s) has or have been introduced, and whether it is carried through explicitly or not. This has not only been recognized by others involved in the debate, but they have gone further, to argue that this is precisely the problem and the strength of sociology in education: 'sociological theory has of necessity centrality of place in the development and practice of syllabuses; indeed, it could be claimed that without it sociology loses any distinctiveness it has' (Reid, 1974: 13). The danger is, of course, that sociology is used to understand other sociologies, not societies: 'Many students today use the sociology they are given to work over other sociologies' (Shipman, 1974: 5).

It is at this point that McNamara begins to worry about sociology being an abstract intellectual exercise, a rigorous and demanding course of study, requiring an understanding of the issues and problems in sociology itself before attempting to apply it to fields in education. Nevertheless the refusal to confront alternative perspectives within sociology is part of the problem of the rejection of sociology. For example, in accusing sociology of being deterministic, McNamara neglects the writings of Alfred Schutz, Max Weber, and Peter Berger (Culley and Demaine, 1978: 222). Writing in the early 1970s, Reid suggested that 'many and serious challenges ... are being made to structural functionalism as the theoretical framework of sociology' and the 'adoption of a strong symbolic interactionist and phenomenological stance has and will be very considerable', for:

> If it is not too cynical to claim that it was the ideology within structural functionalism that sold it to conservative America and which helped it to become such an acceptable framework for the sociology taught in

conservative teacher education establishments, then revised if not new approaches which emphasise the uniqueness of social situations and which carve a place for the individual self, will be quickly assimilated into professional areas where such an understanding is traditional and perhaps utilitarian. [1974: 12]

By this time, Michael Young's Knowledge and Control (1971) had been published and the 'new sociology of education' had emerged and was establishing itself in teacher education courses, given a major impetus in Britain by the Open University, whose education faculty course team had produced School and Society in 1971. By the time they came to rewrite the course in 1977, as Schooling and Society, the 'new sociology of education' had gone beyond interactionism and phenomenology into conflict and critical theories of education, which were increasingly becoming dominant in mainstream sociology. This is important to note for two reasons. First, it firmly established that the sociological perspective was becoming increasingly difficult to maintain, and that there were a number of sociological perspectives. This is reflected in the publication of sociology of education texts. Whilst those used in the 1960s, such as Olive Banks's Sociology of Education (1968), Musgrave's The Sociology of Education (1965), Ottaway's Education and Society (1963), were written in largely atheoretical terms (though the influence of the structural functionalism of Parsons and Merton is there to be seen), by the 1970s a new wave of textbooks were appearing that attempted to come to terms with the growing awareness of a range of sociological perspectives, such as Reid's Sociological Perspectives on School and Education (1978), Demaine's Contemporary Theories in the Sociology of Education (1981), and Robinson's Perspectives on the Sociology of Education (1981). There was also a vast and growing library of education texts written specifically from within the conflict or critical perspective.[1]

So far this chapter has made general comments about education and has not focused specifically on adult education. Most of the preceding discussion is equally applicable to teachers of adults, though their training programmes are not always immediately tied up with a qualifying certificate or graduate certificate in education. In teaching sociology on professional adult education courses, until recently one had to rely on the above range of texts from education, but needed to prefix the word 'adult', change the word 'pupil' into 'student', play down 'parental influence' and discipline, and give emphasis to student roles. In Britain one of the earliest texts on the sociology of adult education was Ruddock's monograph, Sociological Perspectives on Adult Education, published in 1972. In no way could this be construed as a general text on the sociology of adult education, but it did in its own idiosyncratic style expose the student of adult education to a humanistic perspective, but one more akin to social psychology than sociology. Similarly, by the end of the decade, Jane Thompson's (1980) edited collection was one of the first efforts at producing a genuine sociological analysis, but from an inconsistent Marxist or critical perspective. Within that collection, the article by Sallie Westwood focused on the relationship between adult education and the sociology of education, but was primarily intended to introduce the reader to a particular Marxist perspective, based on the ideas of Althusser.

It was not until 1984 that the first general textbook on the sociology of adult education appeared. Jones (1984) recognized the lacuna and set out to produce a text to fill it. However, being written in a developing country (Botswana) gave the book a distinct slant towards (a) social anthropology and (b) development issues. Whilst this is not in itself a criticism, to attempt to encompass so much in a short space (the text itself, not including appendices, is only 132 pages long) was rather ambitious. Inevitably, therefore, the book has shortcomings, especially when dealing with different sociological perspectives. It lacks a framework to assist the student of adult education, with no or little prior knowledge of sociology, in making sense of both a sociological perspective and the range of sociological perspectives which the book covers almost inadvertently and in an eclectic way. There remained a gap to be filled.

The following year Peter Jarvis published The Sociology of Adult and Continuing Education (1985). At least his book does provide a framework which, as well as carefully drawing on relevant examples from British adult education, sets out the nature of sociology, and even introduces the reader to the 'two sociologies', that is, one based on consensus and the other on conflict models of society. The major problem with this text is that it does not adequately reflect the current theoretical development of sociology, sociology of education, nor even the sociology of adult education. It was at least ten years too late. The bulk of the book was rooted in functionalist ideas, even though lip service was paid to other theoretical perspectives, in a simplistic way. The point is that for a student of the sociology of adult education the book gave neither a fair nor an accurate reflection of the current state of sociology.

The next year saw a publication by Barry Elsey (1986) that offered a much more promising title, <u>Social Theory Perspectives on Adult Education</u>. However, upon close scrutiny only the final part of the first section of the book (chapters seven and eight) is devoted to examining adult education from a sociological perspective. The early parts of the book are a mixture of political and philosophical perspectives, with an emphasis on social welfare models, which are not helpfully related to adult education, unless one is specifically interested in the issue of participation. Nor is any explicatory framework offered to assist the reader in making sense of these different ways of analysing adult education. When the author does come to introduce the writings of Durkheim, Parsons, Marx, and Weber the analysis is imprecise and patchy; nor does he relate their writings on education in any systematic way to adult education. Furthermore, in the third section of the book, the attention shifts to 'the sociology of the adult student', and with it comes a focus on the interactionist/phenomeno-logical perspectives, and there is some comparison with Parsonian systems theory. But these ideas are dealt with in a cursory way, and with no justification of the shift between taking a 'macro' and a 'micro' perspective. This is how one reviewer summarizes the book:

> The author of the book was faced with a dilemma: in writing an introductory text he was unsure of how much about either adult education or the social sciences his readers would know. Consequently, he tried to give brief introductions to both and in the process the descriptions interfered with his arguments ... Having tried to produce brief introductions to both elements of adult education and of the social sciences, the author seeks to relate them. Had this been successful this would have been a very important contribution to the development of the study of adult education. Unfor-tunately, this relationship is often insufficiently worked out. [Jarvis, 1987: 263]

In short, the book has leanings towards a liberal and eclectic pragmatism, as the author implies in his introduction:

> It is worth stressing at this point that this book is not designed to tender any personally favoured school of thought. It is best to declare bias although by no means do I believe everything I once thought. Nor am I against pragmatism. I favour the view that it is intelligent to try different ideas in a practical way to see if they work rather than operate exclusively from a fixed theoretical perspective. My personal experience is that people who insist, for example, on a radical perspective on adult education sometimes allow their prejudices, dogma and intolerance to get the better of the need to work with all kinds of people and points of view [Elsey, 1986: 2]

Such a view is what Frank Youngman (1986: 140-5) refers to as 'naive eclecticism'. Whereas 'sophisticated eclecticism' in adult education consciously attempts to synthesize different theories in a coherent way, the 'naive' version 'does not exhibit this self-consciously theoretical stance' but rather, using Hilgard and Bower's analogy:

> stocks a kind of medicine cabinet with aids to solve the problems of the teacher. When a problem arises, the teacher can take a psychological principle from the cabinet and apply it like a bandage or an ointment to solve the educational problem. [Youngman, 1986: 142]

There is no concern for theoretical consistency or philosophical acceptability, but merely with effectiveness in practice. The underlying assumptions behind the principles and methods, provided they are ideologically sound, are conveniently ignored. The problematic feature of this is that it unknowingly brings together what are fundamentally incompatible theories, and leads to a 'patchwork' of principles and practice. As Youngman (1986: 144) argues, 'This in my view is the most typical approach of conventional adult education and it reflects a tendency to atheoretical pragmatism which, in turn, conceals an ideology of liberalism.'

There is little doubt that Elsey's textbook reflects the dominant liberal ideology, and although he states that he is not taking sides with any one perspective, he is clearly against the 'radical' perspective in so far as it is prejudiced, dogmatic, and intolerant. The critical perspective, which we have previously suggested is but one version of sociology, is accused of bias, whereas liberal, eclectic pragmatism is supposedly atheoretical, unbiased, and without ideology. These arguments begin to get complex and abstract, and as textbooks get closer to something approximating an adequate reflection of the nature of sociology and a range of sociological perspectives they inevitably should also become more complex and abstract, even though the authors in each case try hard to make their examples relevant to the adult educator. But the almost insurmountable problems they are faced with would reinforce arguments against the inclusion of sociology into teacher education curricula because it is difficult to convey in a rigorous and systematic way the essence of each of these perspectives in the brief time allotted to the discipline of sociology to students who have yet to develop their sociological imagination. The perceived complexity and abstractness of the 1960s had given way to perplexity by the end of the 1970s. It is not surprising, therefore, to find a renewed demand for a more vocationally relevant input which would focus on the technical skills of performing the teacher's role and classroom competence, focusing on pragmatic issues such as classroom management and discipline without theory or ideology.

This renewed demand, however, was now more insistent. Early fears of sociology being a subversive subject resurfaced, as the critical thinking being developed by student and practising teachers was emerging from sociological perspectives with overt ideologies and distinct biases.

THE RED HERRING: MARXIST BIAS IN THE SOCIOLOGY OF EDUCATION

Having discussed the epistemological objections to the inclusion of sociology in the curricula of teacher education, which is equally applicable to professional adult education training programmes, we now come to the second set of major objections, which are to do with the issue of bias in the sociology of education. As we have already indicated, not all sociological perspectives leave themselves open to the accusation of bias, but those that have become dominant in mainstream sociology during the 1970s are precisely those which are characterized as 'subversive'. We have already mentioned the shift in perspective of the Open University education courses from interactionism to Marxism, which reflects the shift in dominant paradigms within sociology itself. But this led to a wide-scale debate not only about this particular Open University course but about the Open University itself as a 'subversive' institution. The debate took off in 1977 when a professor of sociology, Julius Gould, was asked to review a book of readings which had been produced for use with the course 'Schooling and Society'. At this stage there had already been accusations, from both within and without, that the Open University courses contained 'ideological distortion ... propaganda masquerading as scholarship' (Noble, 1976) and consisted 'merely of dogmatic political statements on the assumption that everyone accepts Marxism as desirable and true' (Freeman, 1976). To begin with, this critique of the Open University stemmed from the liberal tradition, and Gould's attack was very much constructed around the defence of that tradition. There is an implication in the way that throughout his article he places 'liberal' and 'liberal ideology' in inverted commas that he doubts whether that liberalism has an ideology. Indeed, this has always been a fundamental weakness of proponents of liberalism - they see that all other perspectives are ideological, whereas they, almost by definition, are non-ideological. A similar reaction was provoked when Roy Shaw (1980) reviewed Jane Thompson's Adult Education for a Change. It is in such anti-Marxist reactions that their own political biases are made explicit, and their own ideology is held up for examination. We have made the point that this is precisely the stance taken by Elsey in his textbook, supposedly neutral but clearly against 'radical dogmatism'. Why is liberal dogmatism more acceptable than left-wing dogmatism? In a reaction to Gould's review three members of the Open University course team made the following point:

> Even were the course to be as 'Marxist' as he alleges it is, he still has to demonstrate the inappropriateness of Marxist theory, not only as a tool for analysing the social world but also as a guide to understanding the nature of other social theories. His conception of sociology teaching appears to be one from which criticism of the practices and structures of our own

society is absent. Theories of society are presumably acceptable if they are set in the context of the 'history of ideas', and do not relate to the everyday politics of control in contemporary society. How else does one explain his acknowledgement that there may be some validity in a critique of liberalism in the reminder that schools reproduce economic inequality, yet all that he offers in response is a complacent statement that conditions are worse elsewhere? Further his assumption that other - i.e. liberal - types of social theory are somehow non-political, and lacking in policy implications is plainly facile. [Dale et al., 1977]

As the debate continued to rage over ensuing weeks, other eminent academics were drawn in, including other sociologists, such as Professor Macrae (1977) of the London School of Economics, who made four major points in support of the critique against Marxist bias. First, he said, there was a 'curious assumption that to be in some sense Marxist is to be unpolitical, while to be critical of Marxism is to be wickedly political'. This mischievously reverted the point that we have just made, that Marxism is condemned for taking an overtly political stance, but in the process recognizes that all other stances are equally political. Second, Macrae argued that Marx himself was not a sociologist, and therefore until the mid-1950s most Marxists did not think of themselves as sociologists. Indeed, he was right, for there are still some Marxists today who would argue that sociology is a 'bourgeois' activity.[2] The point that Macrae is making is that Marxism is 'an assertion of knowledge prior to investigation' whereas sociology is a 'form of inquiry', presumably carried out by uncritical, unreflexive beings with no preconceived ideas that will affect their detached and objective inquiries. His third point is that:

> Marxist sociology of education has, alas, been misled because it overestimates the role of education in the maintenance and the changing of social structure ... The task of education, tautologous though it sounds, is education. The sociology of education should primarily study the content, socially constructed, of education. It is part of the neglected sociology of culture.

This sounds like a yearning for the LSE tradition in the

1950s of sending out researchers to make social anthro-pological observations of East End families and communities and to regret the 'loss of community' among these groups, as did anthropologists studying the cultural change in other societies. It is almost as if this was apolitical, and could neglect the particular socio-economic formation in which this cultural change took place.

Macrae's final point is that 'the sociology of education is, as practised, too often the work of the mediocre on the trival', with a number of exceptions. This configuration of the adoption of a critical perspective with low intellectual and academic standards has found its way into broader criticisms of the place of sociology in teacher education. We are back to McNamara's secondary reason for not including sociology in the curricula of teacher education.

The point of dwelling so long on Gould's and Macrae's critique of the supposed biases in the sociology of education is to stress that, given that they are distinguished sociologists, their views demonstrate that not all sociology is 'radical' or 'left-wing', which is the point that Kornreich made in a quotation cited at the beginning of this chapter. As he said, 'far from being a radical left-wing discipline, sociology is a conservative one'. It is perhaps no coincidence that Gould and Macrae are known academic supporters of the Centre for Policy Studies, a right-wing 'think tank' that produces research to support the Thatcher government. Behind their position of being non-ideological they are lending their weight and experience to the right-wing attack on the welfare state, health services, and education, including the place of sociology in education.

The 'radical right' view of sociology contains a paradox. Cox and Marks (1982) argue that sociology, 'if appropriately taught', can make a valuable contribution to the education of students on courses in education (as well as other professional training courses). But the key question is, what do they mean by 'appropriately taught'? They warn against the dangers of 'politicized sociology' being taught as 'religious dogma', which is a 'wolf in sheep's clothing - offering Marxism or ideologically bigoted socialism in academic dress'. They view sociology as:

> a dispassionate search for truth and a respect for a plurality of views reflected in genuine open debate. This means that the dogmatism, the arrogance and the intellectual dishonesty which characterises so much

that is written and taught in the name of sociology ...
[Cox and Marks, 1982: 68]

The paradox is reflected in this passage, for, having argued for respect for a plurality of views, they proceed to discredit Marxism by associating the perspective with phrases such as 'academically shoddy', 'academically immature', 'intellectually dishonest', 'bad faith', 'carping', 'cynical', 'negative', 'arrogant', 'prejudiced', 'partisan', 'indoctrination', and 'travesty'. Their analysis also encompasses interactionism and phenomenology, yet they still claim to be representing the interests of pluralism, that is, 'to have regard for different viewpoints and to teach with an appropriate degree of humble eclecticism' (Cox and Marks, 1982: 83). The irony is that they fail to come up to their own criteria. They are just as prejudiced as the Marxist perspective they denigrate, just as 'intellectually dishonest' and 'arrogant'. Their arguments are rarely supported with hard evidence; irrelevant, controversial, and obscure references are used to <u>appear</u> to support their arguments which would not stand up to critical scrutiny. Furthermore, none of the five conclusions they reach - drastically reduce the number of sociology departments, make sociology a subject taught only at postgraduate or post-experience level (this is particularly patronizing, implying that children and young adults do not live 'real life', as they refer to it, or have 'experience'), appoint only staff with direct experience of work (presumably studying and teaching are not 'real work'), make the courses more relevant (by identifying with the objectives of the profession they are training for), and make the goals the enhancement of the outcomes of professional practice - follows from their previous opinionated discussion.

Having argued that such right-wing views and indeed liberalism are as partisan as those of the left wing, it is not my intention to prolong this debate, because it is my contention that it is a 'red herring'; value freedom and value neutrality are myths. But those who argue for its possibility and desirability do need to have their own axiomatic assumptions questioned in order to demonstrate that they too have ideologies.

FROM SOCIOLOGY TO PRAXIS

It has been a theme of this chapter that those who have sought to criticize the place of sociology in the curricula of professional training courses have often been right, but for the wrong reasons. I have agreed with some of McNamara's analysis, but for different reasons from those he based his arguments on. The debate about bias in the Open University and the 'radical right' critique have all been fundamentally correct in their attack on sociology, but again for the wrong reasons. I conclude by outlining an alternative critique of sociology in professional training.

As Cox and Marks argue, sociology can be useful to ·the professions, provided it is made relevant and remains at the level of technique. The majority of sociological perspectives - and in this I would also include interactionism and phenomenology - can and do assist the aspiring professional to legitimate their practice. As I have argued elsewhere (Armstrong,.1980), sociology can give spurious legitimacy to professional practice and in that sense serves to contribute to the conferment of status and prestige. Furthermore, that prestige is the basis of a power relationship over those without such prestige. In this sense sociology can be used to legitimate and reinforce inequality in access to power. Others have taken this argument further and suggested that professionals are agents of the state, or even direct agents of capitalism; in short, agents of social control. It is beyond the scope of this chapter to review such arguments. Suffice it to say that unless the sociological perspective adopted is a consistent, coherent, and critical one such analyses will be neglected, and students of sociology will be unaware of their role in the reproduction of social inequalities. It is also possible that if a plurality of sociological perspectives is provided student teachers may become so confused that their action is hindered.

Teachers need to act in a conscious and deliberate way, whether it is because they wish to reinforce the status quo because they believe it essentially worth supporting, or because they deliberately and consciously seek to contribute towards changing the society in which they work and live. Both these require a commitment to a consistent theoretical perspective, and moreover require action that is informed by that consistent theory. In Marxism the notion of praxis has been reserved for describing the dialectical relationship between thought and action so that when we engage in practical activity we have theoretical consciousness of it, and whilst engaged in the activity are able to reflect upon it (Armstrong, 1987). This focus on praxis and its significance for those in education and adult education not only has practical significance but also cuts across academic disciplines. Part of the difficulty we were having with the debates in this chapter is that they were boundaried by false parameters - namely, academic disciplines. Having argued that the second constraint, the issue of bias, was built around a myth, we conclude by suggesting that the epistemological issues discussed earlier in this chapter are equally mythical, and that the question of whether to teach sociology or not is another 'red herring', for what we should all be engaged in is praxis.

NOTES

1   Among these are M. Apple, Ideology and Curriculum (London: Routledge & Kegan Paul, 1979), P. Bordieu and J. C. Passeron, Reproduction in Education, Society and Culture (London: Sage Publications, 1977), S. Bowles and H. Gintis, Schooling in Capitalist America (London: Routledge & Kegan Paul, 1976), H. A. Giroux, Ideology, Culture and the Process of Schooling (Lewes: Falmer Press, 1981), M. Sarup, Marxism and Education (London: Routledge & Kegan Paul, 1975), R. Sharp, Knowledge, Ideology and the Politics of Schooling (London: Routledge & Kegan Paul, 1980), G. Whitty and M. Young (eds), Explorations in the Politics of School Knowledge (Nafferton: Nafferton Books, 1976), P. Willis, Learning to Labour (Aldershot: Saxon House, 1977), M. Young and G. Whitty (eds), Society, State and Schooling (Lewes: Falmer Press, 1977).

2   For a commentary on the relationship between sociology and Marxism see M. Shaw, Marxism versus Sociology (London: Pluto Press, 1974).

REFERENCES

Anderson, Alan (1979) 'Sociology in the health visitors' training', Health Visitor 52: 185-7.

Armstrong, Paul F. (1980) 'Servicing the Professions: Spurious Legitimacy in the Development of Vocational

Training', paper delivered to the British Sociological Association annual conference, University of Lancaster, April; reprinted in P. Abrams and P. Lewthwaite (eds), Development and Diversity: British Sociology, 1950-1980, London: British Sociological Association.
——— (1987) 'Praxis in adult education: a synthesis of theory and practice', in M. Zukas (ed.), Papers from the 1987 Standing Conference on University Teaching and Research in the Education of Adults, Leeds: University of Leeds.
Banks, Olive (1968) Sociology of Education, London: Batsford.
Barber, C. Renate (1968) 'The role of sociology in the curriculum of the health visitor course', Health Visitor 41 (4): 185-7.
Bower, G. H., and Hilgard, E. R. (1981) Theories of Learning, Englewood Cliffs, N.J.: Prentice-Hall.
Chambers, D. (1966) 'Some reflections on sociology in the colleges of education', Education for Teaching 71: 42-5.
Cox, Caroline, and Marks, John (1982) '"What has Athens to do with Jerusalem?": teaching sociology to students on medical, nursing, education and science courses', in C. Cox and J. Marks (eds), The Right to Learn, London: Centre for Policy Studies.
Craft, Maurice (1963) 'Why sociology for teachers?', Education for Teaching 62: 30-8.
Culley, L., and Demaine, J. (1978) 'Sociology of education and the education of teachers: a critique of D. R. McNamara', Educational Studies 4 (3): 221-7.
Dale, Roger, Esland, G., and MacDonald, Madeline (1977) 'A political campaign', Times Educational Supplement, 18 February.
Demaine, Jack (1981) Contemporary Theories in the Sociology of Education, London: Macmillan.
Durkheim, Emile (1956) Education and Sociology, New York: Free Press.
Eggleston, John (ed.) (1979) Teacher Decision-making in the Classroom: a Collection of Papers, London: Routledge & Kegan Paul.
Elsey, Barry (1986) Social Theory Perspectives on Adult Education, Nottingham: Department of Adult Education, University of Nottingham.
Freeman, H. (1976) 'Is there a Marxist bias in the Open University?' Times, 10 December.

Gould, Julius (1977) 'Scholarship or propaganda?' Times Educational Supplement, 4 February.

Halsey, A. H. (1965) 'Sociology for teachers', New Society 157: 26-7.

Heraud, Brian (1979) Sociology in the Professions, London, Open Books.

Hirst, P. H. (1963) 'Philosophy and educational theory', British Journal of Educational Studies 12 (1): 51-64.

—— (1965) 'The two cultures, science and moral education', Education for Teaching 67: 6-12.

Jackson, P. W. (1968) Life in Classrooms, New York: Holt Rinehart & Winston.

Jarvis, Peter (1985) The Sociology of Adult and Continuing Education, London: Croom Helm.

—— (1987) Review of Social Theory Perspectives on Adult Education, by Barry Elsey, International Journal of Lifelong Education 6 (3): 263.

Jones, R. Kenneth (1984) Sociology of Adult Education, Aldershot: Gower.

Kornreich, Robert (1977) 'The relevance of sociology to health visiting - which type of sociology?', Health Visitor 50: 264-5.

Lukacs, G. (1923) History and Class Consciousness, trans. R. Livingstone, 1971 edition, London: Merlin Press.

McNamara, D. R. (1972) 'Sociology of education and the education of teachers', British Journal of Educational Studies 20 (2): 137-47.

—— (1977) 'A time for change: a reappraisal of sociology of education as a contributing discipline to professional education', Educational Studies 3 (3): 179-83.

Macrae, D. (1977) 'In support of Professor Gould ...', Times Educational Supplement, 4 March.

Musgrave, P. W. (1965a) 'Sociology in the training of teachers', Aspects of Education 3: 41-54.

—— (1965b) 'Syllabuses and teaching methods for sociology in colleges of education', Education for Teaching 68: 53-8.

—— (1965c) The Sociology of Education, London: Methuen.

Noble, Trevor (1976) in Sesame (Open University newspaper), June/July.

North, Maurice (1975) 'Why sociology?', Health Visitor 48: 113-14.

Otley, C. B. (1966) 'Sociology in the college of education', Education for Teaching 69: 56-8.

Ottaway, A. (1963) Education and Society, London: Routledge & Kegan Paul.

Owen, Grace (ed.) (1977) Health Visiting, London: Ballière Tindall.

Reid, Ivan (1974) 'Sociology in colleges of education: some considerations', in Reid and Wormald (eds), op. cit.

—— (1978) Sociological Perspectives on School and Education, London: Open Books.

—— and Eileen Wormald (eds) (1974) Sociology and Teacher Education, Sociology Section of the Association of Teachers in Colleges and Departments of Education.

Robinson, P. (1981) Perspectives on the Sociology of Education, London: Routledge & Kegan Paul.

Roucek, J. S. (ed.) (1961) Readings in Contemporary American Sociology, New York: Peter Owen.

Ruddock, Ralph (1972) Sociological Perspectives on Adult Education, Manchester: University of Manchester Monographs, No. 2.

Shaw, Roy (1980) 'Attacking the liberal tradition', Times Higher Education Supplement, 5 December.

Shipman, Marten D. (1974) 'Reflections on early courses', in Reid and Wormald (eds), op. cit.

Taylor, William (1966) 'The sociology of education', in J. W. Tibble (ed.), The Study of Education, London: Routledge & Kegan Paul.

Thompson, Jane (ed.) (1980) Adult Education for a Change, London: Hutchinson.

Westwood, Sallie (1980) 'Adult education and the sociology of education: an exploration', in Thompson (ed.), op. cit.

Young, Michael F. D. (ed.) (1971) Knowledge and Control, London: Collier-Macmillan.

Youngman, Frank (1986) Adult Education and Socialist Pedagogy, London: Croom Helm.

Chapter six

CULTURAL STUDIES, CRITICAL THEORY AND ADULT EDUCATION

Colin Griffin

The aim of this chapter is to introduce and consider the implications of critical theory for the construction of adult education knowledge. Increasing professionalization has indeed had the effect of raising the epistemological issues as well as the consciousness of a distinctive body of thought (Jarvis, 1987). At the same time, following Freire, a 'critical pedagogy' has been developed which poses a radical challenge to conventional theory construction in adult education and, indeed, questions the possibility of constructing education knowledge in conventional terms at all (Freire and Shor, 1987; Livingstone, 1987). But the radicalism of Freire, or Gramsci or Habermas, has been conceived too exclusively in social and political terms, and not sufficiently in terms of the challenge it poses to conventional epistemological paradigms. From a critical perspective the whole debate around the fields or the forms of knowledge, or rationalism or positivism, reflects a mistaken view of knowledge itself. It is a perspective which challenges the validity of the so-called 'source disciplines' and the whole idea of the separation of theory and practice which this way of thinking about adult education knowledge reinforces. It questions the validity of 'applying' theory to practice in any case, whether this be the application of Habermas's emancipatory theories to adult learning or Freire's liberating pedagogy to the inner cities of the industrialized countries. It also confronts head-on the adoption of the kind of 'instrumental rationality' or pragmatic and process-oriented methodology which characterizes so much North American thinking about adult eduation and which, from this perspective, represents a mistaken view of both theory and practice and the relation

121

between them. All knowledge, from the perspective of critical theory, is in some sense a social and cultural construct, and there is no possibility of an ideologically indifferent theory or practice. The underlying epistemological principle of critical theory is that theory and practice are indivisible. What it challenges, therefore, is the assumption that there are abstract bodies of knowledge which somehow await 'application' in the real world of education: all such knowledge is a construction of social life and cultural practice. If this were true, there never could be an 'adult education discipline' any more than a primary education discipline or a further education discpline. In his brief but not unsceptical introduction to critical theory and education Rex Gibson has set the debate about education theory against wider intellectual trends:

> 'Educational theory' is precarious, disputed and discounted. The earlier confidence that philosophy, sociology and psychology provided a firm foundation for the rational justification of practice has been eroded to such an extent that these disciplines have virtually disappeared from many courses of teacher education. The tide of anti-intellectualism, always a feature of British life, has rarely run more strongly. Does critical theory have a part to play in countering that tide, in re-establishing a firm intellectual grounding for schooling? [Gibson, 1986: 169]

In the case of adult education these issues may be addressed in the first place by considering the significance of Freire's critical pedagogy for theory construction and its origins in a particular school of Marxist thought. There are some fairly obvious senses in which Freire is not a Marxist thinker. The most obvious is that he does not appear to be concerned with specific historical forms of capitalism and with forms of oppression expressed in capitalist relations of production (Youngman, 1986). Moreover, in his book The Politics of Education (1985) Friere succeeds in discussing aspects of culture, power, and liberation with little or no reference to the state and its role in reproducing capitalist or any other historic forms of oppression. Nor is Freire the only liberation theorist from Latin America to have drawn upon existential, Catholic, and Marxist philosophy (Dussel, 1985). Nevertheless, his work in the construction of a critical pedagogy remains one of the very few serious challenges to traditional construction of adult education knowledge as instrumental rationality or as the 'application' of theory to practice.

In the first place, Freire is concerned with education as such, not with culturally contingent categories of adulthood: when he speaks of critical pedagogy he does not mean critical andragogy. He is also concerned with theorizing education in cultural and political terms as a product of the lived experience of oppression and resistance. To a remarkable extent, theory construction in the social sciences has disregarded the experience of women, of ethnicity, of human creativity. Only more recently have we been witnessing the development of a cultural and political analysis of familiar elements of adult education discourse such as personality (Leonard, 1984), ageing (Phillipson, 1982), and leisure (Clarke and Critcher, 1985). These studies, together with the Marxist strand of feminism (Delphy, 1984), are all conducted from a perspective of critical social theory which owes, as does Freire, something at least to a certain tradition of Marxist thinking. This, however, is not in the tradition of economic and historical determinism but rather in that of humanism and freedom: beyond class and economism, as it is sometimes put:

> Classical Marxism has never taken seriously the categories of culture, ideology, and the lived experiences of everyday life. Trapped within the belief that the mode of production is the structuring force of human societies, classical Marxism has relied on a notion of power that sees domination as an outgrowth of capitalist economies governed by the dynamics of commodity production and history as a process primarily informed by contradictions rooted in the forces and relations of production. [Aronowitz and Giroux, 1986: 123]

In classical Marxism conflict, struggle, and oppression are conceived exclusively in terms of class relations under capitalism, a process which implicates the state as an instrument, and there is no sense in which Freire could be described as taking this line. But later developments of Marxism, such as that which has come to be known as critical theory, have focused less upon class and economism and much more upon issues of knowledge, theory, and ideology, and Freire's critical pedagogy can be located much more confidently in this neo-Marxist tradition.

In fact, there never was a single tradition of critical theory, and it is particularly resistant to summary (Connerton, 1976: 22-39). Nevertheless, it is possible to speak of a central core of issues which identify it as an intellectual movement, and the origins of critical theory are generally located in the establishment in 1923 of the Institute of Social Research associated with the University of Frankfurt. The 'Frankfurt school' were primarily represented in the work of Max Horkheimer, Theodor Adorno, and Herbert Marcuse, whilst the later work of Jürgen Habermas continued the tradition in a renewed and modified form. These four are usually taken to be 'the central figures of critical theory' (Held, 1980: 15). As for its central features, these have recently been summarized by Gibson (1986: 3-16) in the following terms:

1. Critical theory is a diverse rather than a unified tradition so that it would be more accurate to speak of critical theories.
2. Critical theorists are preoccupied with theory and theory-construction for its own sake and continue to analyse the possibilities, nature, and status of social theory as such (e.g. Acourt, 1987).
3. Critical theorists reject scientific 'naturalism' and insist that, whatever else they may or may not be, social theories are different from theories in the natural sciences, which are concerned with what is 'given' in nature: 'Critical theory argues that in human affairs all "facts" are socially constructed, humanly determined and interpreted, and hence subject to change through human means.' Critical theory, unlike scientific theory, recognizes and acknowledges relativity and subjectivity in its object and methods.[1]
4. Critical theory claims to be a source of enlightenment, disclosing the true interests of individuals and groups, and revealing the irreconcilable conflicts of interest which characterize social life underneath a veneer of harmony.
5. Critical theorists are concerned with autonomy and the possible liberation and emancipation of oppressed individuals and groups. Its concern for emancipation 'marks out critical theory's true distinctiveness'.
6. Unlike classical Marxism, it postulates the relative autonomy of the education system (and other cultural forms) from the economic basis of society and the

relations of production which inhere in it.

7. It is critical of instrumental rationality, which is concerned with means rather than ends, with methods rather than purposes: 'Instrumental rationality limits itself to "How to do it?" questions rather than "Why do it?" or "Where are we going?" questions. It is the divorce of fact from value, and its preference, in that divorce, for fact.'

8. Critical theory is very much concerned with the study of culture, to which it accords 'a high degree of autonomy and independence from economic factors'.

9. Also in contrast with aspects of classical Marxism, critical theorists emphasize the individual and individual purposes, stressing 'the creative, active, meaning-seeking, need-fulfilling aspects of men and women, seeing them as potentially free and capable of achieving their self-set goals'. In this connection, critical theory is much concerned with ideology, by which is generally meant not so much abstract systems of ideas and beliefs as the ways in which it permeates everyday 'commonsense' life: 'they stress its very ordinariness, its familiarity, its manifestation in the taken-for-granted asssumptions of family, classroom, workplace and friendship relationships'.

10. Critical theory is concerned with aesthetics and the arts, unlike orthodox Marxism, again placing stress upon human creativity and its role in culture, which is at once social but relatively autonomous from the economic basis. Creativity is held to be an expression of emancipation whilst at the same time reflecting patterns of domination in society.[2]

11. Critical theorists have been influenced by Freud, to such an extent that psychoanalysis constitutes 'a central resource of critical theory'. The study of personality in relation to social behaviour is a mirror-image of the study of society itself, in which conflict and disharmony lie barely concealed under an impression of order and rationality.

12. Critical theory claims to operate at different levels of explanation, the personal/interpersonal, the institutional, and the structural, and to link all three of these. Gibson is sceptical of this claim, though, arguing that critical theory has operated overwhelmingly at the structural level and therefore with a confused concept of the 'relative autonomy' of culture.

13. Language is an important focus of critical theory, on the understanding that 'language is central to the conduct, determining and understanding of all social life'. Not surprisingly, critical theorists tend to employ a language of their own in which to express and communicate their ideas.

One of the most important epistemological implications of the critical theory perspective is the 'non-disciplinary' nature of knowledge. In this it differs from traditional theory. As Horkheimer put it:

> Theory for most researchers is the sum-total of propositions about a subject, the propositions being so linked with each other that a few are basic and the rest derive from these. The smaller the number of primary principles in comparison with the derivations, the more perfect the theory. [in Connerton, 1976: 206]

In other words, traditional theory construction tends to reflect the division of labour as it exists in any society at any given time: thus science and the scientific model of theory come to be thought of as somehow timeless and as existing independently of the social relations of production. For critical theorists, however, all the forms of human understanding, not excluding that of the natural world itself, are socially constructed in the course of the development of relations of production. Moreover, in attempting to illuminate Freire's critical pedagogy in the light of critical theory, it is possible to view knowledge not only as socially constructed but as the basis of social action. As Henry Giroux put it, it is necessary to move beyond the phenomenological perspective to one that is critical:

> A dialectical notion of knowledge represents a transition from a contemplative analysis of constructed meanings to the transformation of socio-economic structures which narrowly define and legitimize such meanings. The means for such a transition rests, in part, with the development of a pedagogy of critical thinking, a pedagogy which helps students link knowledge to power and human interest. [Giroux, 1981: 81]

Here again we may observe how Freire's own perspective seems to incorporate phenomenological and Marxist elements whilst at the same time not reflecting either phenomenology or Marxism in their classic forms. Believing that knowledge of any kind is a reflection of human interests, but that it is also implicated in power and powerlessness, Freire moves beyond phenomenology to a critical, social action approach. At the same time, there is none of the historical analysis of the relations of production in Freire which would lead him to regard all knowledge as an ideological function of class relations in classical Marxist terms. Most of Freire's basic assumptions about knowledge reflect a 'critical theory' analysis, to the effect that it is a reflection of human interests (not necessarily class interests) and that it is intimately connected with the possibility of human liberation (not necessarily in revolutionary terms).

Similarly, the centrality of culture for Freire reflects fairly exactly its significance for the critical theorists: the idea of culture as merely a function of economic relations or class interests is rejected in favour of a dialectical view of culture as a site both of oppression and of resistance. His view of the culture of silence, 'born in the relationship between the Third World and the Metropolis', typifies Freire's view of 'true' science as the discovery of the connection between human knowledge, human interests and power relations:

> The only authentic points of departure for the scientific knowledge of reality are the dialectical relationships between men and the world, and the critical comprehension of how these relationships are evolved and how they in turn condition men's perception of concrete reality. [1985: 86]

If we take culture to stand for, among other things, the source of our perception of concrete reality, and if knowledge is so closely related to human interests, then its significance for the politics of oppression or liberation is immense. There is a vast literature of critical theory in one form or another which treats cultural production and reproduction as a primary analytic category of (generally capitalist) relations of production. Freirean concepts of cultural action and cultural power lie squarely in this critical tradition. It is a tradition perhaps best represented in Britain by the work of the Centre for Contemporary Cultural Studies at the University of Birmingham, particularly in this present context the treatment of ideology (Centre for Contemporary Cultural Studies, 1978). Freire's own dialectical view of culture lies very much along these lines: 'To the extent...that interiorization of the dominators' values is not only an individual phenomenon but also a social and cultural one, ejection must be achieved by a type of cultural action in which culture negates culture' (Freire, 1985: 53). More recently (Freire and Shor, 1987: ch.1) liberating pedagogy has been located in a more analytic treatment of elite and mass cultures.

Many themes of critical pedagogy are those of critical theory itself, although it has been those writers of a more classical Marxist persuasion who have focused upon historical and economic analysis. The objects of analysis, both of critical pedagogy and of critical theory, defy the possibility of theoretical knowledge as the 'sum-total of propositions about a subject'. This is not only because the idea of a 'subject' is a cultural product but because theoretical knowledge is itself the expression of human interests: in this sense, all such knowledge is not so much true or false as critical or not. Theoretical knowledge, which is produced in the course of the division of labour by those whose function is to 'produce' knowledge, takes for granted the 'naturalness' of the social and political order, as though it were of the same order as the natural universe. When Freire insists on dialogical education 'starting from the students' comprehension of their daily life experiences' he believes this to be the genuinely scientific or theoretical enterprise. All our understanding must incorporate our understanding of our selves and our interests: 'If I am no longer naïve, it means that I am no longer acritical' (Freire and Shor, 1987: 106). Horkheimer put the same point in the language of critical theory:

> The classificatory thinking of each individual is one of those social reactions by which men try to adapt to reality in a way that best meets their needs...The world which is given to the individual and which he must accept and take into account is, in its present and continuing form, a product of the activity of society as a whole...The facts which our senses present to us are socially preformed in two ways: through the historical character of the object perceived and through the historical character of the perceiving organ. Both are not simply natural; they are shaped by human activity,

and yet the individual perceives himself as receptive and passive in the act of perception. [in Connerton, 1976: 213]

With this perspective on knowledge, critical theories of education have focused not upon 'education' as a subject in its own right so much as upon schooling and the experience of schooling in relation to various aspects of social control, the state, the curriculum, cultural and economic reproduction, and so on. Certainly this is the radical education tradition: the social construction of 'the classificatory thinking' of individuals in capitalist societies leads 'naturally' to a radical conceptualization of any discussion of education in relation to class, ideology, and the state (Apple, 1982). But it is also a certain tradition of thinking about knowledge formation and theory construction itself, as a more recent example makes clear:

> Central to the concerns of the authors in this book is an attempt to situate historically the construction of experience as it is mediated through the particular practices of gender, race, and class specific ideologies. More to the point, the concept of experience, the notion of social forms, and the category of transformation are specifically viewed as instances of cultural productions which only become intelligible when seen in relation to systems of power that point to both the persistence of oppressive structures and ideologies and the possibilities for struggle and social change. [Livingstone, 1987: xv]

In their recent book, which was dedicated to Freire, Stanley Aronowitz and Henry Giroux have directly dealt with the relation between critical theory and education (Aronowitz and Giroux, 1986: ch. 6, 'Radical pedagogy and the legacy of Marxist discourse'). Reviewing the failure of classic Marxist categories to address late twentieth-century social issues, the authors suggest that 'the theoretical scalpel wielded by the Frankfurt theorists cut deep into the body of Marxist doctrine'. This is especially the case with regard to their development of a theory of culture, in contrast to the crude economism of classical Marxism. The idea of a relatively autonomous culture which nevertheless served to legitimate the values of instrumental rationality was an important, if flawed, one. Nevertheless the authors share Gibson's view that the Frankfurt school, although innovative in some respects, 'remained wedded to the original theory'. The implications for education are fairly clear, though: the boundaries of schooling or the 'education system' must not be too tightly drawn nor its political significance overemphasized; radical educators should therefore identify themselves more closely with other groups striving for progressive change around broader educational issues; they should adopt a strategy of 'critical literacy and cultural power', making clear the connection between knowledge and power, and presenting knowledge as 'a social construction linked to norms and values' and serving 'very specific economic, political and social interests'. Critical literacy would also focus more upon developing the self-knowledge of individuals and their awareness of 'how knowledge gets produced, sustained, and legitimated'.

The contribution of critical theory and cultural studies perspectives to the kind of radical pedagogy associated with Freire is enormous, and it is important to understand that his ideas can be traced to a well established intellectual tradition which first gained its identity in Europe and the struggle against Nazism and fascism during the 1930s (Held, 1980: ch. 1). The epistemological position which is represented by critical theory and cultural studies can also be traced back much further in the history of philosophy than Marxism, industrialism, and the rise of modern science. The positivistic concept of science and social science, which is based upon a historical objectivity and the dichotomies of facts and values, subject and object, theory and practice, is rejected by critical theorists such as Horkheimer, Marcuse, and Adorno in favour of a much more dialectical approach. Although not presenting a monolithic account (Held, 1980: chs 6, 7 and 8), they place consistent stress upon a concept of reality and our knowledge of it which is constructed from the historical and social experience of individuals, and in which facts and values, subject and object, and theory and practice are simply aspects of a single reality. The idea of science and scientific knowledge is itself the construction of a specific historical form of the division of labour: in short, science itself takes on the aspects of ideology, serving identifiable human interests in what Freire calls 'the oppressor's world'. True scientific knowledge, for critical theorists and radical pedagogues alike, is represented by an act of transformation: it is in acting upon rather than understanding the world that true scientific knowledge is gained.

To sum up, critical theory is critical of received categories of knowledge, including scientific knowledge, because they tend to reflect a positivistic separation of facts and values and of theory and practice, and because they purport to be ahistorical and universal categories. Above all, any conception of knowledge which fails to locate it in relation to the social relations of production and to oppressive social structures fails thereby to provide a complete account of it. Of course, scientific theory is a source of genuine knowledge (and one which has been progressive in the course of history) but if it is taken as the paradigm of all knowledge, or if its categories are taken to be absolute rather than relative to human interests, then from the perspective of critical theory its claims are not made out. In which case science has an ideological aspect, and its taken-for-granted categories become incorporated into the uncritical 'commonsense' assumptions of scientist and non-scientist alike.

The implications of Freire's views for radical adult education practice are too familiar to rehearse here. But if his work is located in the tradition of critical theory, then the picture changes. From this point of view the whole idea of 'applying' Freirean theory to practice becomes problematic, if not actually contradictory, given the actual identity of theory and practice for critical theory. Admittedly, Freire hardly works out theory with the same self-conscious rigour as did Horkheimer, Adorno, Marcuse, or Habermas. Nevertheless, it clearly follows from his views of knowledge and cultural action that 'received' categories should be analysed in relation to historical and specific social relations of production and structures of oppression. The question is not perhaps so much one of whether practice can be influenced by Freirean ideas, since it demonstrably can and has been, as whether such practice could be authentically Freirean in terms of their origins in critical theory. There is an important distinction to draw, therefore, between 'influence' and 'application' in this context. Many of Freire's ideas, such as the culture of silence or conscientization are relative to specific historical conditions: they are analytic categories of Third World practice rather than purported universal or 'scientific' categories of radical pedagogy.

The real challenge posed by Freire's ideas, in so far as they express a version of critical theory, is not that of 'applying' them in different social and historical conditions, but rather the challenge they represent to received categories of adult education knowledge. The danger lies in neglecting the epistemological significance of his work for theory construction in adult education whilst 'applying' his theories to adult education practice. In the end Freire's ideas may be in danger of incorporation into an instrumental rationality of radical professional practice, which would be directly contrary to the spirit of critical theory which informs so much of his thinking.

The challenge of Freire and of critical theory is to any attempt to construct adult education as a discipline at all, regardless of arguments about 'source disciplines' or 'forms' or 'fields' of knowledge. From a critical perspective these are not genuine theoretical categories at all, but rather an attempt to construct a body of professional knowledge through the application of abstract or 'scientific' theory to practice. Source disciplines, such as philosophy, psychology, sociology, or management theory, are uncritically accepted as sources of knowledge itself. From a critical perspective, however, they stand for 'classificatory thinking' on the part of individuals who occupy a definite position in the social relations of production. The whole idea of 'subjects' and 'disciplines' reflects a view of knowledge divorced from the relations of production or from the expression of human interests in the form of ideology. Professional adult education knowledge, in so far as it reflects such 'disciplines' at all, uncritically reproduces the old dichotomies of fact and value, subject and object, theory and practice, which Freire and the critical theorists consistently deny. The models, categories, and typologies of emergent adult eduation theory, together with the elevation of 'common-sense' distinctions between childhood and adulthood or pedagogy and andragogy to 'theoretical' status are, from a Freirean or critical perspective, a typical instance of the way in which knowledge itself is 'constructed' around human interests: ideology in the guise of science.

The 'needs-meeting' ideology attributed to adult education (and other emergent or semi-professions) is a classic instance of the instrumental rationality of groups seeking their place in the division of labour in society. Because 'needs' are a constructed category, their significance for professionals is ideological rather than theoretical, regardless of the vast philosophical literature which accumulates around abstract concepts such as these.

Other concepts familiar to professional practitioners, such as andragogy or personal growth, are also uncritically constructed with little or no reference to the human interests they stand for or the way in which they are located in specific historical conditions or social relations of production; on the contrary, they are presented as having the universal and timeless character of scientific theory. That they are, however, genuine ideologies is proved by the fact that they can be put to any ideological use: andragogy is an effective learning system as much for business managers under capitalism as for the encouragement of socialist citizenship, whilst 'needs-meeting' is such a procrustean concept that it could be embraced by governments of any ideological persuasion. What the critical theory perspective strongly suggests is that theory construction and the knowledge base of adult education must, in the final analysis, reflect professional interests in the division of labour in society. Furthermore, issues around 'source disciplines' and the disciplinary status of adult education knowledge itself are spurious intellectual exercises whose prime function is to help create an illusion of objectivity and scientific status for good professional practice. In short, in their present state, all the 'disciplines' of adult eduation constitute uncritical theory. If Freire's ideas, such as conscientization, or even ideas of andragogy or perspective-transformation, were to be implemented as accounts of how knowledge is actually generated in society they would all have authentically radical implications for oppression and liberation: they would express a genuinely critical theory of society. However, in the course of their 'application' as theoretical ideas they are simply being incorporated into the instrumental rationality of radical adult education practice: in the form of professional ideology they are capable of serving a whole range of interests and of furthering the cause of either oppression or liberation. It cannot be without significance that the state, of whatever political and ideological form, has never taken more interest in the nature and content of adult learning.

It was suggested that Freire cannot be regarded as adopting a Marxist approach, especially in view of his neglect of the state and its role in maintaining and expressing diverse forms of oppression. Radical pedagogy has generally analysed the role of the state in terms of alternative Marxist traditions to that of critical theory, especially with reference to Gramsci, Althusser, and

Poulantzas (Apple, 1983: ch. 3), and the well known study of Bowles and Gintis (1976) was conducted from a perspective far removed from that of critical theory. It has to be said that the state was not a major preoccupation of the critical theorists, which is one of the factors which distinguish them from other Marxist schools of thought. Habermas, for example, rejected the overwhelming importance attached by Marx to the evolution of social and political systems, whilst Horkheimer, Adorno, and Marcuse were more concerned with knowledge, ideology, theory, and culture. But as neo-Marxists they were inevitably concerned, indirectly perhaps, with the role of the state, particularly under fascism (Held, 1980: 52-65).

It seems inevitable that a critical theory of adult education knowledge should be concerned with the role of the state, whether this is in capitalist societies or not. Especially is this the case with liberal democracies, where the state's role with respect to creating the conditions of individual freedom is particularly problematic. In a critical theory approach, too, the issue of ideology is central, and here there is much more by way of analysis than in the case of the state. In relation to the sociology of knowledge, the theory of ideology has a complex position: not only does it stand for the ways in which ideas express class interests and create the conditions of hegemony in society, but ideology can also stand for the way in which social reality itself is constructed through ideas, as Stuart Hall puts it: 'There is no objective reality - and hence there can be no "scientific" knowledge of it. These are only the different "takes on reality", lodged in the different perspectives which social actors bring to the world' (Centre for Contemporary Cultural Studies, 1978: 21). On the whole, the critical theorists rejected this philosophical position in favour of a dialectical approach which reflected the mutual deter-mination of reality and our ideas about it. But there could be little doubt that they would regard attempts to formulate universal and abstract bodies of knowledge about the non-natural world as falling within the first broad meaning of ideology, namely, as interests in the guise of science. This is illustrated in their critique of the rise of instrumental rationality as the dominant ideology of Western society:

> They shared Weber's view as to the probability of the continuing expansion of rationalization and bureau-cratization. They also shared his pessimism as to the

dangers and risks involved which Weber called the 'iron cage' of a highly bureaucratized division of labour. The extension of formal, means-end rationality to 'the conduct of life' becomes a concern as a form of domination: means becoming ends, social rules becoming verified objectifications commanding directions. [Held, 1980: 65-6]

So a critical theory approach to adult education would incorporate analysis of the ideological processes of bureaucratization and of the ideology of instrumental rationality which underpins it. This is particularly important in view of the centralizing tendencies now at work in society and the tendency of adult eduation to adopt the characteristics of a professional public service. Inevitably, in the course of these processes, adult educators will be set public tasks and priorities to address which will increasingly take on social welfare forms. These tasks will be formulated in 'needs-meeting' and social policy terms, and the professional task constructed around the identification of needs and the development of appropriate and distinctive professional skills to meet them. In the course of this process, which is a process occurring in the division of labour in society, 'uncritical' theory (of adult learning, or needs, or the management of provision, or the curriculum, or whatever) evolves in the form of abstract 'disciplines', 'sub-disciplines', or 'source disciplines' whose sole function is that of application to practice. These theories are 'uncritical' in terms of the several grounds which have been set out above, not least because, from a professional point of view, adult education is a bureaucratic category, not coterminous with adult learning any more than adult learning needs are coterminous with human needs, or education management as such, and so on.

The critical theory perspective construes theory itself as originating in the practice of social relations of production, particularly as - in the form of ideology - it expresses the interests of a dominant group or class. It denies the separation of theory and practice as meaningful, and therefore refutes the whole process of 'applying' abstract or scientific theory to practice as a mistaken belief about the nature of knowledge. At the same time, the critical perspective claims to uncover the true nature of the need for theory in the instrumental rationality of professional practice.

The claims of the critical theorists are not necessarily made out, and they can certainly be challenged (Held, 1980: Part 3), but the general outline of their approach to knowledge, theory, and epistemology does find a clear reflection in the critical or radical pedagogy of Freire and others. And although this line of thought has been mostly developed in the context of schooling, it applies equally well to adult education. Indeed, the efforts to distinguish adult education from schooling are a prime example of the attempt to elevate the 'commonsense' categories of 'classificatory thinking' to some kind of theoretical status: the dichotomy of childhood and adulthood is socially constructed, and finds cultural expression in specific historical societies and within distinctive forms of the social relations of production. The attempt to construct universal categories of adulthood, or indeed of learning or personality or needs, is, from a critical theory perspective, an ideological rather than an authentically theoretical exercise.

So what are the implications for adult education as a knowledge 'discipline' in the light of critical theory, with its distinction between knowledge and ideology and its focus upon the way in which all our analytic categories arise within the social relations of production and cultural reproduction? Perhaps they can best be reviewed by reverting to the central features of critical theory as outlined by Gibson and sketched at the outset here.

Although there are diverse strands of critical theory, all critical theorists were, as Gibson says, intensely interested in theory itself and dismissed any possibility that there could be any such thing as 'non-theoretical' or 'atheoretical' practice. Since no valid distinction between theory and practice can be drawn, it follows that there is no adult education practice that does not express theory and no adult education theory that does not arise directly from adult education practice. The whole business of 'applying' theories to adult education practice which are generated in contexts other than adult education would therefore be ruled out, and the knowledge base would <u>be</u> the practice.

In particular, critical theory rejects the possibility of 'positivist' or 'scientific' theory in adult education as in any other area of social life. The social world is not the 'natural' world and its 'facts' are not 'given' as they are for natural science but inextricably linked to values. It is impossible to construct, for example, a purely factual or 'scientific' account of how adults learn which could then be 'applied' to adult education practice. On the contrary, critical theory discloses the true interests of individuals and groups in society and claims to be emancipatory. Unlike science, critical theory is prescriptive in the true interests of the oppressed, which is the point at which Freire's ideas most closely reproduce this school of Marxist thought. But the wider implications for adult education knowledge are that it could not, as a theoretical discipline, be construed in any other terms than those of struggle and conflict: under capitalism, to present theory as scientific or objective or neutral is to collude with an oppressive system. From a 'critical' perspective therefore, adult education theory is the practice of class struggle or of anti-racist or anti-sexist work. And believing, as these theorists do, in the relative autonomy of culture and education from the economic 'base' of society, adult education may be theorized as a potentially effective source of resistance to incorporation into state or public policy, thereby addressing 'needs' of the political system (or of the profession itself) rather than those of adult learners as such, who otherwise are only the beneficiaries of adult education ideology. At the heart of adult education knowledge, in other words, should be a critical theory of whose interests are really being served and whose needs really met in practice, rather than a 'scientific' theory of interests and needs or a philosophical discourse upon the meaning of the words.

As adult education takes on the characteristics of a profession, with all that implies for the training of adult eduators and the functional requirement for a body of knowledge of 'disciplinary' status in the division of labour, its practices will increasingly reflect an ideology of instrumental rationality. As was suggested, this can be a characteristic of radical as well as of non-radical professional practice, and it seems a very important contribution of critical theory to adult education knowledge. And typically it is a recommendation that authentic knowledge should be reflexive and focus upon the self-awareness of the subject - in this case the adult educator.

Gibson described the critique of instrumental rationality in these terms:

It is the obsession with calculation and measurement: the drive to classify, to label, to assess and number, all that is human. As such, it is the desire to control and to dominate, to exercise surveillance and power over others and over nature. Because of its preference for the intellectual over the emotional, it represents the devaluation and marginalisation of feeling. It is a kind of intellectual activity which actually results in the decline of reason itself, and it therefore stultifies, distorts and malforms individual and social growth. [1986: 7]

There is a danger, therefore, that the professional imperatives of discipline knowledge will conflict with the ideology of adult education practice if these are conceived as separate: the adoption of a professional instrumental rationality may actually negate the aims of individual and social growth which are so often proclaimed to be at the heart of the adult education enterprise. Even reflexive learning itself, if not located in a cultural and social analysis, may be directed to the instrumental purposes of professional practitioners (Schon, 1987). The importance of culture for critical theory cannot be exaggerated, for it stands for everything that is truly human and social and in opposition to the world of nature, which is the only proper object of scientific theory. Our access to culture is, strictly speaking, untheorized and direct. Culture, whether this refers to a high culture, a popular culture, or simply a general way of life, stands in critical theory for all the ways in which society is made real for individuals, and for the critical theorists, as Held says, it was a notion 'closer to Freud's than to classical Marxist and non-Marxist understandings of the term'. In fact the relation between individual and society, and the possibilities for individual freedom and autonomy, were of central importance for them, particularly in relation to ideas of personal growth and development and the ways in which they were related to ideology (reproduced in the individual psyche as authoritarianism, for example). The implications of a critical theory perspective on individual freedom and personal growth for adult education knowledge are considerable: instead of the 'uncritical' categories of individualism and personality, in which these are taken to exist in a cultural and political vacuum, the critical theory of these concepts, and therefore of the learning needs which inhere in them, is firmly located in a social analysis. Conventional or 'uncritical' theory of the 'source disciplines' merely, from this perspective, reproduces commonsense categories of the 'natural' order of society and dresses them up in the trappings of science and purported objectivity.

Even a brief outline of the epistemological principles of critical theory suggests its powerful (if contestable) challenge to the conventional theory/practice paradigm which adult education knowledge increasingly reflects, and the gap which is likely to open up between adult education theory (whatever it turns out to be) and adult education as a form of cultural practice. As the social process of professionalization creates the need for a 'discipline knowledge' of adult education, so the origins of Freirean cultural practice in critical theory become clearer. As a result the gap between emancipation and the instrumental rationality of professional practice widens: the fate of radical pedagogy may yet be to become a form of adult education knowledge.

NOTES

1   Our knowledge of the physical universe, in so far as it is 'given' in nature, is not relative or subjective. But, from the standpoint of critical theory, nothing is wholly relative or wholly absolute, wholly subjective or wholly objective when it comes to human understanding. In so far, therefore, as natural science is a form of human understanding it could not be reduced entirely to a form of absolute and objective knowledge without the loss of some, at least, of the meaning of 'science'. Relativity and subjectivity are categories of our understanding rather than attributes of the physical universe, and natural science is undoubtedly a form of human understanding.

2   The autonomy of culture (and therefore of education systems) from economic systems of production is thus perceived by critical theorists in dialectical terms, so that conventional knowledge reflects both the class relations of production and the creative potential of cultural forms for transcending them.

REFERENCES

Acourt, P. (1987) 'The unfortunate domination of social theories by social theory', Theory, Culture and Society 4.

Cultural studies

Apple, M. W. (ed.) (1982) Cultural and Economic Repro-
duction in Education: Essays on Class, Ideology and the
State, London: Routledge & Kegan Paul.
Aronowitz, S., and Giroux, H. (1986) Education under Siege:
the Conservative, Liberal, and Radical Debate over
Schooling, London: Routledge & Kegan Paul.
Bowles, S., and Gintis, H.(1976) Schooling in Capitalist
America, London: Routledge & Kegan Paul.
Centre for Contemporary Cultural Studies (1978) On
Ideology, London: Hutchinson.
Clarke, J., and Critcher, C. (1985) The Devil makes Work:
Leisure in Capitalist Britain, London: Macmillan.
Connerton, P. (ed.) (1976) Critical Sociology: Selected
Readings, Harmondsworth: Penguin Books.
Delphy, C. (1984) Close to Home: a Materialist Analysis of
Women's Oppression, London: Hutchinson.
Dussel, E. (1985) Philosophy of Liberation, New York: Orbis
Books.
Freire, P. (1985) The Politics of Education: Culture, Power
and Liberation, London: Macmillan.
Freire, P., and Shor, J. (1987) A Pedagogy for Liberation:
Dialogues on Transforming Education, London:
Macmillan.
Gibson, R. (1986) Critical Theory and Education, London:
Hodder & Stoughton.
Giroux, H. A. (1981) Ideology, Culture and the Process
Schooling, London: Falmer Press.
Held, D. (1980) Introduction to Critical Theory: Horkheimer
to Habermas, London: Hutchinson.
Jarvis, P. (ed.) (1987) Twentieth Century Thinkers in Adult
Education, London: Croom Helm.
Leonard, P. (1984) Personality and Ideology: Towards a
Materialist Understanding of the Individual, London:
Macmillan.
Livingstone, D. W. (ed.) (1987) Critical Pedagogy and
Cultural Power, London: Macmillan.
Phillipson, C. (1982) Capitalism and the Construction of Old
Age, London: Macmillan.
Schon, D. A. (1987) Educating the Reflective Practitioner,
San Francisco: Jossey-Bass.
Youngman, F. (1986) Adult Education and Socialist
Pedagogy, London: Croom Helm.

Chapter seven

THE EPISTEMOLOGY OF ADULT EDUCATION IN THE UNITED STATES AND GREAT BRITAIN: A CROSS-CULTURAL ANALYSIS

Stephen D. Brookfield

It is evident from a review of prevailing conceptualizations of adult education, of the range of providing agencies, and of the varying orientations evident towards defining the role of adult educators, that the field of adult education in the United States is characterized by a paradigmatic plurality. Adult education as a body of knowledge, theory, or research can be thought of as multi-paradigmatic or, perhaps even more accurately, as pre-paradigmatic. No agreement exists on a central body of research insights, theoretical tenets, or philosophical axioms. This means that, depending on the agency or practitioner concerned, adult education can be defined as an effort in collective consciousness-raising, a means by which workers can be 'retooled' to help the American economy become more competitive, or a way of assisting people in their personal spiritual development. The best known and influential theorists and researchers in the field (Malcolm Knowles, Paulo Freire, Cyril Houle) and the writers from whom they draw most strongly (Eduard Lindeman, Carl Rogers, Karl Marx, Erich Fromm, Ralph Tyler) operate according to directly antithetical assumptions about the purpose of education and the nature of the wider society within which educational activities are grounded. Given the diversity of settings and agencies involved in helping adults learn in the United States, and the contrasting purposes towards which these efforts are directed, it is no surprise to find such paradigmatic plurality in conceptualizations of appropriate practice. Indeed, in a pluralistic society such as the United States, in which no one centralized statutory governing or providing body for adult education exists, such conceptual and curricular confusion may well be a professional given in the field.

The pragmatic tenor of American culture is as apparent in the theory and practice of adult education, as it is in other areas, and spending time conceptualizing practice is considered to be unnecessary by many in this field. Indeed, some adult educators believe that trying to identify some definitional characteristics which are unique to adult education is a fruitless endeavour. To them, adult education as a field of study or practice does not possess epistemological or methodological distinction. Campbell (1977) declares that trying to impose a single definition on the kaleidoscopic range of activity and approaches comprising adult education is unproductive and tedious. Verduin et al. (1977) observe that adult education is a multi-faceted and complex process, encompassing subject and interest areas as broad as those of the population it serves. Epistemologically, according to this approach adult education does not possess a distinctive, independent theoretical framework; rather, it is conceived in generalist terms. As Knowles (1962) makes clear, the orientation underlying the doctorate in education (the most common degree awarded to doctoral candidates in postgraduate adult education programmes in the United States) is generalist. In his words, 'the adult educational role is essentially interdisciplinary in character, and [that] therefore the bulk of an individual student's program will be directed toward the development of generalized competencies' (1962: 141).

Many practitioners protest that conceptualizing adult education is unnecessary, principally because the activity defines itself in terms of its clientele. Put simply, adult education in the United States is held to be equivalent to the education of adults. This simple semantic inversion (from 'adult education' to 'the education of adults') has considerable epistemological implications. It means that adult education is defined primarily in operational (rather than intrinsic) terms; that is, as the provision of opportunities for adults to acquire skills and knowledge in a systematic, purposeful manner. An example of this operational approach is Long's belief that adult education 'includes all systematic and purposive efforts by the adult to become an educated person' (1987: viii). To many American educators the idea that adult education is equivalent to the education of adults is appealing for its democratic associations. It is a generous, broad and all-encompassing concept of educational provision. It allows for flexibility in terms of format and setting, and is sufficiently generic to include activities as diverse as military education, training in business and industry, adult basic education, recreational programmes, liberal arts discussion groups, and community action initiatives.

Alternatives to the broadly operational approach to the conceptualization of adult education discussed above do exist. One approach grounds the practice of adult education in notions of adultness. This approach presumes that if we can identify the essential characteristics of adulthood, in particular the manner in which adults differ from children and the uniquely adult roles they play in society, then we can derive the essential nature of adult education from a consideration of these characteristics. Derived from this analysis of adulthood, so the argument goes, will come a specification of the curriculum, methods, and purposes of adult education. Sworder (1955), for example, identified the responsibilities of adulthood as participating in political affairs, maintaining economic stability, assuming parenthood status, and providing a cultural and spiritual environment for future generations. Schwertman (1955) believed that adults' accumulation of experience meant that adult education was fundamentally different from secondary education and that the task of adult education was the 'constant expansion of experience in desirable directions' (p. 41). Such directions would be to increase knowledge in general, to develop intellectual skills, and to increase aesthetic and spiritual sensibility.

Verner (1964) defined the adult as a person with responsibility for himself or herself and for others, who had accepted a functionally productive role in the community. He did not, however, develop a curricular agenda based upon the nature and requirements of this responsibility. To Liveright and Haygood (1969) adult education was a process whereby persons no longer attending school on a regular and full-time basis consciously undertook sequential and organized activities to bring about specified psychomotor, affective, or cognitive changes, or to solve community problems. Darkenwald and Merriam (1982) view adult education as a process whereby individuals performing the social roles of adulthood undertake systematic and sustained learning to bring about changes in knowledge, attitudes, values, or skills. These attempts to develop a conceptualization of adult education all suffer from their cultural specificity. What are conceived as the social roles of adulthood, or the cultural characteristics of adultness, are reflective of a particular subcultural milieu. Definitions of adultness which focus on the performance of social roles such as being a parent or holding down a regular job do betray the class and cultural orientation of the definer. According to these ideas, for example, people who are unemployed, who have no children, or who live as single parents, are not fulfilling the social roles of adults. In the United States and Great Britain such a definition would exclude a significant proportion, perhaps even a majority, of the population. This definition of adulthood applies chiefly to members of the middle classes in Western societies, at times of full employment in those societies. It is severely flawed owing to its class and cultural bias.

An alternative approach to conceptualizing adult education is through a form of quasi-functional analysis. Seeking to understand the significance of certain behaviours or institutional structures through an analysis of their functions is a well attested analytic exercise in the social sciences. Functional analysis as developed in anthropology and sociology attempts to ascertain the extent to which an institution, ritualistic behaviour, or system of received codes and values serves to maintain the larger whole of which it is a part. To this extent a functional analysis of an adult education system would explore the manner in which that system sought to inculcate values, transmit knowledge, and develop skills which contributed to the continued and effective functioning of the society of which it was a part. Functional analysis is a post facto approach to conceptualization in which we seek to understand how an institution, set of behaviours, or value system contributes to the maintenance of an existing order. It is both analytic and descriptive and is devoid of prescriptive elements. The purpose of functional analysis is to understand the functioning of social wholes through a fragmentation and compartmentalization of those wholes into their component parts.

Empirical analyses of the functioning of adult education systems, or of the manner in which the adult education system contributes to the maintenance of the social whole, are rare in the North American literature. Instead, a form of quasi-functional analysis is evident in which prescriptive and descriptive elements are mixed together. Hence analysts present as 'functions' of adult education descriptions of purposes for which adult education programmes are established, estimations of actual achievements of programmes, and statements regarding preferred purposes for adult education. An early example of this is Bryson's (1936) analysis. Bryson declared that adult education performed five functions in the pursuit of one overarching purpose defined as 'the enlargement of the personality and the quickening of life' (p. 39). These functions were (1) to provide remedial education so that everyone possessed the minimum skills needed for life in American society (for example, literacy or child care skills), (2) occupational training, (3) relational education, in which the study of emotions, attitudes, and psychological habits would help us to understand ourselves and our relations with others, (4) liberal education (defined as activities pursued for their own sake), and (5) political education, including the study of politics as a subject discipline and training for political action. Bryson saw the performance of these functions as resulting in 'an increase in the student's own power of self-direction ... a constant growth in independent thinking power and in the capacity for the management of one's own program' (1936: 31).

Writing after the Second World War, Paul Essert (1951) outlined a similarly broad-ranging and wholly prescriptive analysis of functions for adult education. Adult education was charged with achieving five purposes, all of which were considered to be innately desirable. It had to enhance adults' sense of occupational achievement so that they took a pride and satisfaction in their work. It had to restore and revive in people the experience of scientific inquiry so that they could enjoy the beauties of their existence. It had to grant the experience of self-government, so that a fundamental task of the adult educator became helping people find or establish laboratories through which they could share in the determination and responsibilities of government. It had to set education within the groups (such as neighbourhood and community groups or work groups) in which adults acquired basic daily behaviour patterns. Finally, it had to encourage the experience of intermittent solitude so that adults could counteract the unwholesome group demands of American culture and build a personal philosophy.

As conceived by Essert, the functions of adult education in America can be seen to be infused with a moral imperative. This same prescriptive spirit informs Hallenbeck's (1960) essay 'The function and place of adult education in American society'. Hallenbeck identified five characteristics of American culture - the rapidity of

145

change, the dominance of technology, the intensity of specialization, the complexity of relationships, and the vastness of opportunity - which framed the way in which adult educators used their special position to develop learners for life in that culture. Specifically, adult educators were (1) to expand adults' communication skills, (2) to develop in students qualities of flexibility for change, (3) to improve human relations, (4) to facilitate people's participation in democratic activities, and (5) to nurture personal growth.

The historically significant analyses of Bryson, Essert, and Hallenbeck are not functional analyses in the technical sense in which this term is used in the social science literature. In most of these cases we might better substitute the term 'purposes' for that of 'functions'. Hence the functions of adult education described are more statements of desired outcomes - favoured aims which the writers concerned feel adult educators should pursue. Even in Hallenbeck's analysis, where these desired purposes are rooted in an analysis of social conditions, the functions outlined are in no sense descriptive of empirical reality. These personal statements are essentially philosophical charters; prescriptive visions of what purposes adult education might serve. A simple change of preposition - replacing 'of' by 'for' - is a more accurate indication of the nature of these analyses. They are statements of functions 'for' adult education (in the sense of being prescribed purposes) rather than analyses of the functions 'of' adult education (in the sense of being empirical assessments of the contributions made by adult education to the maintenance of the social whole). Elements of strong personal preference are evident in these three contributions. Perhaps the nearest to an empirically based analysis of adult education functions in the American literature is Darkenwald and Merriam's (1982:6) declaration that the basic functions of adult education are instruction, counselling, program development, and administration. This analysis, however, is set within the context of a discussion of professional roles. It is a role analysis of adult educators' typical tasks rather than an account of how adult education structures and behaviours contribute to the maintenance of the larger society.

One final point should be made regarding the efforts to conceptualize adult education through functional analysis. Many American writers ascribe to adult education some form of political function, either through adult education assisting adults to make informed, responsible political (primarily electoral) choices, or in terms of participation in adult education classes comprising a training' laboratory for democratic activity. Bryson (1936) described the political function of adult education as being the provision of accurate, trustworthy information to citizens and the creation of opportunities for adults to discuss issues of public concern with other citizens. Teachers of adults were urged to inculcate principles of rational scepticism in their students and to urge them to stand firmly against the winds of doctrine (p. 64). He declared that:

> a constant and stubborn effort to help those students who work with him to acquire a more alert attitude toward' their already accepted and verbalized beliefs, and toward all new things offered them, is the hallmark of a fit teacher for grown men and women. (p. 65).

As a result of their encouraging an attitude of alert scepticism, Bryson warned teachers of adults, they would likely encounter the enmity of political leaders and conventional thinkers. Because rational scepticism served as a corrective to the simplistic solutions and propaganda offered by political leaders, teachers who nurtured such scepticism would be open to the public opprobrium.

Bryson's colleague at Columbia University, Eduard Lindeman (1926, 1945), believed that adult education was integral to the democratic struggle and necessary to counteract the influence of demogogues. Participation by adults in a network of neighbourhood discussion groups examining issues of racial discrimination, the merits of free enterprise, and socialist economic systems, the democratization of educational facilities, and the role of the United States in world affairs, would ensure the future of democracy. More recently Knowles and Klevins (1982: 16) declare that:

> adult education is, or ought to be, a highly political and value laden activity. When individuals are involved in education they tend to expand: their awareness of self and environment, their range of wants and interests, their sense of justice, their need to participate in decision-making activities, their ability to think critically and reason rationally, their ability to create

alternative courses of action, and, ultimately, their power or control over the forces and factors which affect them - this is political action.

ORGANIZING CONDITIONS OF GRADUATE EDUCATION: SOME TRANSATLANTIC DIFFERENCES

In exploring the literature of adult education in the United States and United Kingdom it is impossible not to be surprised and intrigued by the epistemological differences between the two countries. There is an apparent lack of common intellectual frames of reference, and scholars, researchers, and theorists in each country appear to be remarkably ethnocentric, at least where the other's organizing concepts are concerned. These organizing concepts are, at root, embedded in the two societies' political cultures. The history of American adult education as documented in standard texts such as those of Adams (1944), Gratton (1965), and Knowles (1977) is cast firmly within the liberal democratic framework which informs the culture and political system of the country. Adult education is seen as existing to enhance the individual's creative powers, aesthetic capacities, and economic opportunities. This tradition is discernible in Lindeman's (1926) early writings, through the Great Books programme of the 1950s, to the current popularity of the related concepts of andragogy (Knowles, 1984) and self-directed learning (Knowles, 1975). It is striking just how much this latter concern of self-directed learning has dominated the adult education research agenda and occupied the minds of American practitioners (Brookfield, 1985), whereas in the United Kingdom this phenomenon is only rarely researched. The finding that adults design, conduct, and evaluate their own learning in an independent manner free of institutional control is a perfect enhancement to the American ethos of rugged individualism. Not surprisingly, writers, researchers, and practitioners exploring this form of learning have found a ready and receptive audience in the United States.

In Britain, on the other hand, it is much harder to find any kind of consensual agreement as to what activities, concepts, and philosophies comprise any kind of central tradition in adult education. To many the adult education movement is inextricably bound up with the emergence of working-class movements, collective organizations, and structural forms such as trade unions, worker education, and the Labour Party. This tradition is vigorously alive and well in recent works such as those by Thompson (1980), Lovett (1975), Lovett et al. (1983), Youngman (1986), and Ward and Taylor (1986). Some of their intellectual forerunners are Tawney, and the authors of the 1919 report, and they fuse elements of Freire's and Gramsci's ideas with their own community development and community action experience. According to this tradition, adult education should be analysed according to the extent to which it buttresses and reinforces the prevailing wider social structures. Proper adult education practice as advocated by those who locate themselves in this tradition is concerned with assisting oppressed groups in the process of their collective advancement.

A tradition which runs markedly counter to this worker education rationale is that which views adult education as concerned with the development of aesthetic judgements and intellectual capacities. It emphasizes the cognitive outcomes of learning over and above any alterations in wider social structures that might result from adult education participation. As conceived by Livingstone (1945) and more recently by Lawson (1979, 1982, 1985) and Paterson (1979, 1987) this orientation argues that adult educators should remain politically neutral and should refrain from exercising their positions of power to promote collective action on the part of their learners. An attempt has been made to redefine this liberal tradition in such a way that it encompasses those elements in adult education practice in Britain and America which are concerned with challenging dominant cultural values and political ideologies (Taylor et al., 1985). In my opinion (Brookfield, 1986) this is only partially successful and major differences between the liberal and socialist positions remain regarding the proper function of adult education.

Irrespective of the merits of the claims laid by different writers to the correct interpretation of the liberal tradition, it remains clear that the American and British adult education traditions are very different. America has a largely consensual, liberal democratic tradition with no real polarities of opinion or divisions across the field regarding what should be the proper outcomes of adult education. In Britain, by way of contrast, there is a real and fierce debate over the connection between adult education and collective political action. Those who view adult eduction in terms of individual cultural enhancement, and those who see it as contributing to the collective advancement of oppressed groups, hold fundamentally unresolvable beliefs about the proper function of adult educators. No such public debate among those adhering to such clearly differentiated political positions is currently present in American adult education, though there is evidence that this was much more the case some forty years ago (Taylor et al., 1985).

The United States is a culture which values pragmatism and in which a much greater degree of consensuality concerning political values and arrangements is evident than in Britain. There is an overwhelming acceptance of the capitalist ethic as the normal and natural mode of economic arrangements, with the values of free enterprise and entrepreneurial activity accepted almost as unchallenged givens. Although there are policy differences between the Democratic Party's advocacy of higher levels of public spending on public welfare programmes compared to the Republicans' much espoused aim of 'getting government off the people's backs', these differences occur at points along a relatively narrow continuum of ideological orientation compared to that existing between the British Labour and Conservative parties. Both American parties operate within a consensus framework in which the capitalist free enterprise ethic is, essentially, unchallenged. For both parties the capitalist mode is viewed as the embodiment of the American approach to economic management, reflecting the values of individuality and entrepreneurial freedom which lie at the culture's core. One American adult educator who deplored this consensuality was Eduard Lindeman (1926), who condemned the manner in which capitalist ethics had infused the practice of education. To Lindeman, capitalism was a doubtful competitive ethic designed to favour the crafty, strong, and truculent. He warned that the entire American educational system was becoming deter-mined by the need to respond to the needs of business and industry regarding the kinds of skilled workers required for more efficient production. As a major element in the post-World War II reconstruction effort he urged that adult educators focus their energies on prompting adults to explore the suitability of different economic arrangements (such as socialism, capitalism, and the mixed economy) for different societies (Lindeman, 1944).

As well as the virtually unchallenged acceptance of the capitalist, free enterprise ethic, there also exists in the

United States a consensus on the range of ideological debate which is acceptable in the political sphere. America, alone among the members of the Western alliance, does not contain within its political culture clearly articulated polarities of left- and right-wing persuasions. In European societies individuals are used to considering ideas, interpretations, policies, propaganda, and party statements drawn from a broad philosophical spectrum. There are right-wing, left-wing, and centrist groups in every political system and, at different times, ruling groups which subscribe to socialist, social democratic, capitalist, and fascist ideologies. In European cultures, therefore, citizens are used to witnessing intellectual conflict between clearly articulated and opposed ideologies. Governments of different political hues rise and fall, but one enters adulthod with a perspective that there are highly differentiated alternatives available regarding how political and economic structures might be managed and altered. Adults are used at least to viewing, and sometimes to participating in, vigorous debates concerning the merits of contrasting ideologies. They are not unused to, or offended by, the possibility of debate about which of a number of ideologies are better, more humane, or more efficient.

No such tradition of debate concerning a wide range of alternative political ideologies exists for the great majority of adults in the United States. There are, certainly, debates between Democratic and Republican politicians, activists, and followers regarding the degree to which adjustments might be made to the free enterprise, liberal democratic system to ensure that it encourages production, economic growth, and individual enterprise. The basic system, however, and its underlying assumptions are rarely criticized concerning their fundamental ethical validity and economic effectiveness. In contrast to European cultures, it is entirely possible to reach adulthood in the United States with little awareness of any alternatives to the free enterprise system, and with no understanding of, or acquaintance with, alternative political philosophies. In particular, discussion of the merits or validity of socialist and communist philosophies is rejected out of hand as entirely inconceivable and inappropriate to the American democratic tradition. Given the frequency with which socialist parties have comprised ruling groups, or have been members of ruling coalitions, in the governments of the chief European allies of the United States since 1945

(Britain and France), this rejection of alternative political ideologies is often difficult for Europeans to understand.

In contrast to the United States, Britain is a society in which people are used to living under governments which represent clearly opposed political ideologies, even if the policy decisions of those governments have not always reflected their ideologies. Within each of the main parties themselves there is an additional level of debate between right, left, and centrist groupings. Adults living within such a political culture are not as intimidated by considering widely diverging ideological interpretations as those who grow up in a culture which effectively excludes a whole ideological orientation as fundamentally evil or irrelevant, and which regards discussion of the contrasting merits of this orientation as unpatriotic and somehow undemocratic. In Britain the workings of the economy, the distribution of power on a macro-societal level, and the way individuals perceive their life chances will frequently be understood in terms of warring class interests. When people view their society's economic and political arrangements, and perhaps their own biographies, as functions of wider competing class interests, they develop a world-view very different from the consensual perspective so dominant in the United States. They become used to viewing society not as a plurality of mutually complementary sub-cultures in which individual initiative is rewarded with status and money, but as a perpetual arena of class and sub-cultural warfare. In such an arena education is frequently claimed to be a contested site in which alternative ideologies compete through institutional structures and representatives of those structures for the hearts and minds of students. Different activists claim education to be a central element in the struggle for equality, efficiency, revolution, or productivity. In European cultures it is quite usual to view education as a tool of social engineering or reform. Education is assigned a pro-active function; it is seen as contributing to the creation and maintenance of a certain social order, rather than simply being required to adapt to the requirements and demands of free market forces.

HISTORICITY AND ADULT EDUCATION

The term 'historicity' describes people's awareness of how their individual actions are affected by, and located within, past actions, ideas, and developed structures. Those who possess this awareness place their lives, the social structures within which those lives are embedded, and the belief systems informing them in a historical çontext. People with this outlook understand the present in terms of the past. They view contemporary events as being partially determined by previous events, rather than as ahistorical happenings. In British university departments of adult education, lecturers and graduate students exhibit a much greater degree of historicity than is the case in the United States. To American researchers, British academics seem to be preoccupied with investigating the historical origins of the development of adult education. Typical of this view is Boshier's (1977: 232) comment that British adult educators display a 'somewhat compulsive penchant for historical research'.

To what extent is this stereotype of British adult education accurate? In analyses and bibliographies of research undertaken in Britain by Charnley (1974, 1984), Kelly (1974), Legge (1977), Mee (1978), Thomas (1984), and Thomas and Davies (1984) historical research is certainly a major category. Comparative analyses by Guy (1976) and Brookfield (1982) recorded that students and faculty in British university departments of adult education conduct research into the history of adult education much more frequently than do their American counterparts. In terms of historiography, Kelly's A History of Adult Education in Great Britain (1970) is probably the single best known piece of research in the field. A content analysis of the journal Studies in the Education of Adults (formerly Studies in Adult Education) reveals the pre-eminence of historical research. In the last few years papers by Field (1980), Marriott (1981), Marks (1982), Fieldhouse (1983, 1985), McIlroy (1985) have been published in the journal dealing with topics such as nineteenth-century views on workers' education, ideology in English adult education teaching from 1925 to 1950, unemployment and adult education in the 1930s, the Responsible Body tradition, and the TUC education scheme from 1929 to 1980.

This academic concern with researching the historical dimensions of the field is reflected in the relative centrality (compared to the United States) afforded to historical matters in graduate adult education programmes in Britain. It is hard to imagine students leaving diploma, master's, or doctoral degree programmes without some basic awareness of the history and traditions of the field of adult education. Bibliographies such as those of Charnley (1974), Legge (1977), and Thomas and Davies (1984) record the frequency with which historical themes and subjects form the focus of dissertations and theses within graduate programmes. Exposure to the history of the field means that students in these programmes are aware of the connections between workers' education, the development of the labour movement, and the growth of adult education provision. In particular, the political context within which the adult education movement was framed in Britain is emphasized. Students exploring this context can hardly fail to speculate on the political dimensions of adult education. In the most recent bibliography of adult education research (Thomas and Davies, 1984) the category 'History and organization of adult education' has by far the largest number of research projects listed.

It is interesting to note, however, that according to the 1986 Guide to University Courses for Adult Education in the United Kingdom and Eire (SCUTREA, 1986) courses of study in the history of adult education are mentioned less frequently, and with less emphasis as mandatory components of the curriculum, than was the case in the previously published SCUTREA guide of 1983. Analysis of this 1986 guide also reveals a movement towards adopting some of the curricular concerns (and even course titles) of American graduate programmes. There is some ground for believing that the greater exchange of research perspectives occasioned by recent academic exchanges between American and British adult educators is having some real influence on the field. In the last three years there have been exchanges between groups of American and British professors and lecturers who have visited the chief research conferences (AERC and SCUTREA) of each other's countries. A register of the research interests of researchers and academics in each country has been published and distributed in both countries. A British and North American Network for Adult Education (BANANAE) is in place, and 1988 saw the first ever jointly sponsored AERC-SCUTREA conference to be held at the University of Leeds. In the United States, signs of a recent revival of interest in the historical foundations of the field can be seen in the recently created newsletter and journal entitled Historical Foundations of Adult Education: a Bulletin of Research and Information which grew out of a series of

AERC pre-conferences on historical aspects of adult education research. At the main AERC conference itself there has been a marked increase in historical research papers such as those of Craver (1984), Hellyer and Schied (1984), Omolewa (1984), Rockhill (1984), Sisco (1985), Boshier (1985), Gainey (1986), Hellyer (1986), Wallace (1986), Hugo (1987), and Nel (1987). There has been a revived interest in the works of Eduard Lindeman (Brookfield, 1987a; Stewart, 1987).

Notwithstanding the greater exchange of personnel and increase in transatlantic discussion between academics and researchers in adult education, it is still true to say that the majority of professors and graduate students of adult education in the United States do not regard understanding the historical foundations of the field as a major priority. Historical analyses of the development of adult education are rarely undertaken, either as major scholarship efforts by established professors, or for master's or doctoral dissertations. In the years between Brunner's (1959) review of research and Grabowski's (1980) analysis Trends in Graduate Research the emphasis has remained firmly on applied empirical studies. In the 1980 series of handbooks of adult education in the United States issued by the American Association for Adult and Continuing Education, none of the ten volumes published was concerned with tracing the history of the field. The most widely used foundation text of adult education (Darkenwald and Merriam, 1982) omits any discussion of the historical foundations of adult education in the United States. The analyses of adult education research in the United States undertaken by De Crow (1969), Copeland and Grabowski (1971), Hiemstra (1976), and Long (1983) note that 'compared with the British condition, the historical dimensions of adult education in the United States are impoverished' (Long,1983: 264). The ahistorical nature of American graduate adult education was well demonstrated by a study conducted by Day and McDermott (1980) at a large Mid-western university. When graduate students in adult education were asked about significant adult education texts which had appeared over the last seventy years such as the 1919 report, The Meaning of Adult Education (Lindeman, 1926), Ten Years of Adult Education (Cartwright, 1935), Adult Education (Bryson, 1936), Adult Education in Action (Ely, 1936), and Adult Education in a Free Society (Blakely, 1958) they appeared to be generally ignorant of the existence or content of these works. They were also unfamiliar with general histories of the field such as those of Gratton (1965) and Knowles (1977). In a follow-up survey the authors sent their original questionnaire to thirty seven additional graduate adult education programmes in the United States, and found this lack of historicity among graduate students to be confirmed.

POLITICAL CONTEXT AND ADULT EDUCATION

To what extent do lecturers, professors, and graduate students self-consciously place the practice of adult education within a political framework? Do they study the organization and curricula of programmes for the ways in which these reflect the values of dominant groups within society? Are they aware of the connections ·between learning, consciousness change, and political action? Do they analyse participation patterns in adult education for the extent to which classes are disproportionately composed chiefly of learners drawn from certain limited socio-economic groups? Do they view the proper practice of adult education as being that of challenging the status quo, of revealing to learners the structural inequities in their societies, and of prompting the consideration of alternatives of the dominant ideology? Do they see the practice of adult education as centrally located within movements for social, political, and economic change?

These questions are viewed very differently, if indeed they are raised at all, in graduate adult education programmes in Britain and America. In Britain adult education is much more likely to be seen as the educational arm of some movement for social reform. Practice in the field is seen as having some important origins in the growth of the labour movement. Standard histories of British adult education such as those by Harrison (1961) and Kelly (1970) devote a considerable amount of space to discussing the impetus given to the development of adult education through its connection with political movements such as the Labour Party, trade unions, working men's colleges, the Chartists, and the Workers' Educational Association. This political tradition is reflected well in recent works by Thompson (1980, 1983), Lovett (1975, 1988, Lovett et al. (1983), Taylor et al. (1985), Thomas (1982), Youngman (1986), Evans (1988), Cowburn (1986), and Ward and Taylor (1986). In these analyses adult education exhibits a clearly defined political dimension. Adult educators are charged with assisting adults to take control over their personal and political worlds, and to view their own changes in consciousness as occasioned by, and inextricably linked with, collective action. The concepts of liberation, conscientization, and empowerment are placed at the heart of good practice in adult education and these analyses draw strongly on the work of Gramsci and Freire.

In the United States the connection between adult education and political change is, on the whole, ignored, at least if we take the professional and scholarly literature of the field to be at all representative of practice. The ten-volume 1980 handbook of adult education series did not address directly how adult educators could work within the context of existing political movements to advance the interests and conditions of oppressed groups. In the volume in the series in which one might have expected this perspective to be explicitly dealt with - that on Serving Personal and Community Needs through Adult Education (Boone et al., 1980) - no reference can be found to this approach. This absence of attempts to analyse and practise adult education within a political context is difficult to understand, given that until World War II it was placed directly in the mainstream of the American adult education movement. Rockhill (1985) maintains that 'the systematic denial of class in the USA' (p. 187) by dominant groups within the culture represents an exclusion of socialist and radical perspectives from American adult education since the 1930s and that this denial has prevented the development of a separate working-class adult education movement. According to her analysis, socialism 'has been rendered invisible' and 'the liberal tradition in adult education has contributed above all else to the silencing of socialism' (p.207) within American adult education. To Rockhill:

> working class education was delegitimated by the newly emergent profession of adult education. Liberal educational values as they came to be institutionalized in university adult education, provided the basis for the annihilation of working class education as an approach to the education of workers. [p. 208]

In terms of the history of ideas in the field, it is interesting to note that Eduard Lindeman, arguably the

157

single most influential figure in the intellectual development of adult education in the United States, was vilified after World War II for his supposedly socialist and communist leanings. And yet today Lindeman is placed firmly in the progressive educational tradition (Elias and Merriam, 1980) rather than in any radical tradition and is known by most graduate students and professors only through his first book, The Meaning of Adult Education (1926), which is concerned chiefly with methodological and conceptual aspects of adult education rather than with its social and political impact. Through Knowles's (1980, 1984) popularization of certain of Lindeman's ideas, his chief contribution is seen as being in the areas of experiential learning and teaching methods. As recent works (Brookfield, 1987a; Stewart, 1987) have made clear, however, Lindeman's chief concern throughout his life was with the ways in which adult education could contribute to the creation and maintenance of democracy. To Lindeman adult education was irrevocably and undeniably a political activity. At one point he wrote that 'every social action group should at the same time be an adult education group, and I go even so far as to believe that all successful adult education groups sooner or later become social action groups' (1944: 11). The contemporary view which holds Lindeman to be basically a useful source on participatory learning methods is one of the most serious intellectual misunderstandings current within American adult education.

Two other much neglected politically oriented traditions in American adult education deserve mention. The first of these is the Highlander Folk School and Research Center (Adams, 1975; Kennedy, 1981), which since the 1930s has trained community activists to learn from their own, and others', experiences of political involvement. The involvement of Highlander staff in political movements such as the development of labour unions, civil rights campaigns, and land ownership reform represents an important counterpoint to the apolitical element in the American adult education tradition which currently prevails in research and practice within the field. The second tradition is that of the American labour education movement. Apart from isolated papers such as those by Hellyer and Schied (1984) and Hellyer (1986) it is as if, to American scholars of adult education, the labour education movement in the earlier part of this century never existed. Union education programmes and union-management collaborations (such as those between the UAW and the Chrysler or Ford corporations) certainly exist, but their activities rarely form the focus of adult education research.

PHILOSOPHICAL ORIENTATIONS IN ADULT EDUCATION

The absence of a philosophical dimension from discussions which are of central concern to American graduate students, professors, researchers, and theorists in adult education is a surprising conundrum. It is a conundrum because discussion of this sort has in the past been central to the field. Currently, however, the research and professional literature is framed within the context of applications of technique. The habit of debating vigorously alternative philosophical perspectives on the nature and proper purposes of American adult education seems to have been lost. The 1980 handbook on adult education series contained no volume devoted to charting a philosophical mission for the field. In one of the volumes (Kreitlow et al., 1981) some controversial issues were aired and contrasting positions stated in a dialectical fashion. Nowhere, however, was there a sustained analysis of the philosophical rationale which should underly adult education, an explicit attempt to state any fundamental purposes for adult education, or an elaboration of the criteria by which we might judge whether or not those purposes were being realized. Yet as recently as the 1950s a ferment of philosophical discourse bubbled within the pages of the two chief American adult education journals of the time, Adult Education and Adult Leadership. Concurrent with the founding in 1953 of the Adult Education Association of the United States (a successor to the American Association for Adult Education and a precursor of the American Association for Adult Education and a precursor of the American Association for Adult and Continuing Education), the Adult Education journal published accounts of a national debate conducted at the level of living-room discussion groups on the central purposes of the proposed new association. One outcome of this discussion was the publication of seven principles which were agreed on as guiding the American adult education movement (Pell, 1952). Throughout the 1950s and 1960s the Adult Leadership journal featured a column in each issue entitled 'Accent on social philosophy' in which different individuals explored the social relevance of adult education and addressed the kinds of responses adult educators should make to the political issues of the times. The AEA/USA Committee on Social Philosophy and Direction Finding was the most influential committee among the range of different committees existing within the organization in these decades, and it was not uncommon for discussion on the fundamental philosophical purposes of the field to be public and significant.

With the appearance in 1964 of the Commission of Professors of Adult Education's first important professional publication - Adult Education: Outlines of an Emerging Field of University Study (Jensen et al., 1964) - the movement towards greater professionalism and academic respectability for the field of adult education gained momentum. Concurrent with the attempt to define the distinguishing characteristics of adult education as a field of practice (briefly, to establish andragogy as the quintessential adult educational mode), and to discover the unique features of adult learning (briefly, to claim that adult learners are innately self-directed) that have formed the basis of most discussion in American adult education in the last quarter of a century, has been a decrease in philosophical debate regarding central purposes and rationales for the field, particularly politically contentious ones. It is as if the search for academic respectability and the quest for professional identity have effectively depoliticized the field. We have concluded that being seen to engage in public debate about fundamental philosophical questions and issues regarding the proper practice of adult education is unseemly and unprofessional. The search for respectability and professionalism has, in my view, removed much of the politically and socially motivated fire and passion from debate in the field. There is a very real danger of an academic orthodoxy prevailing in adult education which states, briefly, that (1) adults are self-directed learners, (2) andragogical methods are the uniquely adult forms of teaching and facilitation, and (3) adult educators should attempt to meet the felt needs of their learners as their first and overwhelming priority.

This service-oriented rationale is, in effect, an 'espoused theory' of adult education, and while its exclusionary nature has done much to grant a common identity to practitioners from a very diverse range of adult educational settings, it has also effectively removed from

160

the arena of adult educational discourse philosophical debate concerning essential political and social purposes for the field. Monette (1977, 1979) has offered some trenchant criticisms of this service-oriented orthodoxy. The 'felt needs' rationale appears admirably democratic, humanistic, and learner-centred, yet it is one which removes from educators the need to make contentious judgements concerning the merits of alternative curricular offerings. The consummate professional, according to this rationale, is one who accurately assesses what adults want in educational programmes and then successfully mounts courses, workshops, seminars, and other offerings which satisfy these expressed needs. The criteria by which successful adult education is determined which are implicit in this rationale are easily observable, external, and unequivocal. They are the numbers of adults attending courses, the satisfaction they express with their participation, and the revenue they generate.

According to this rationale the responsibility for determining content and curricular direction rests largely with the learner. The educator's role becomes that of facilitating learners acquiring those skills or that knowledge which learners themselves have specified. A good adult educator is seen as one who gives adults what they say they want, who markets programmes which leave learners satisfied, and who generates revenue for the sponsoring agency. One implication of the adoption of this rationale is that educational activities in which learners are challenged, in which their existing assumptions and prejudices are called into question, and in which they are forced to confront aspects of their values and actions they would prefer not to examine, are likely to be avoided. Such activities are likely to be resisted because of the pain and anxiety accompanying many efforts at self-scrutiny. In seeking to offer programmes which leave participants feeling satisfied and pleased with the outcomes, the danger is that learners will never be provoked or challenged for fear of their feeling displeased and not returning with their enrolment monies. A second implication arising from the adoption of this rationale is that any discussion of the merit or worthwhileness of different curricula becomes meaningless and irrevelant. If the overriding purpose is to attract large numbers of learners to programmes, then 'good' curricula for adult education become, to all intents and purposes, those which meet learners' declared wants. We can see, then, that behind the apparently democratic learner-centredness of the 'felt needs' rationale lurks a wholly consumerist justification of how good practice in adult education should be conceived. With only occasional exceptions (Beder, 1987; Cameron, 1987) debates on the philosophical purposes of adult education will probably be seen by most professional adult educators as immature reflections of the last vestiges of amateurism in the field and as peripheral to the central task of creating a professional identity.

In British programmes of graduate adult education, however, such a debate still exists in a very active way. Because the striving for professional identity and academic credibility has not been anything like as strong in Britain as in the United States (British professors frequently combine their academic role with a role as programme developer in extra-mural programmes or continuing education divisions), there has been no sense of embarrassment about admitting in public to very distinctively different philosophical orientations within the field. There are debates concerning the social role of adult education (Joyce, 1973; Paterson, 1973), calls for politics to be put on the agenda of the field (Simey, 1978), and calls for adult educators to attack current priorities in government policy (Ruddock, 1974). Against the radical adult education orientation evident in works such as Thompson (1980, 1983), Lovett (1975, 1988), Cowburn (1986), Thomas (1982), Youngman (1986) Evans (1988), and Ward and Taylor (1986) there is a vigorously argued liberal tradition which holds that the proper purpose of adult education is the development of personhood. In this tradition the emphasis is placed on developing individual qualities of intellectual discrimination, aesthetic appreciation, and moral reasoning, none of which activities is seen as necessarily linked to adult education for social action (Wiltshire, 1976; Paterson, 1979, 1987; Lawson, 1979, 1982, 1985). It is not unusual, then, for graduate students in British university departments of adult education to be asked to consider contrasting philosophical orientations within their academic studies. There is much less of a consensus, or a clearly discernible espoused theory, about what comprises adult education. Instead there are two broadly articulated competing paradigms, representing the radical and liberal traditions in British adult education. Graduate students are exposed to both these traditions and may well try to locate their own beliefs and practice within them. Whilst adherents and advocates of each of these traditions may believe the other's ideas to be fundamentally flawed, they value the debate generated by this polarity of philosophical orientation. A central concern of courses within graduate adult education programmes becomes that of identifying what ought to be the proper purposes of adult education, whether these are seen as the development of discriminatory capacities appropriate to a liberally educated adult, or as working in an adult education capacity with political action movements.

CONCLUSION

Epistemologically, adult education in the United States as a body of theory, research, and practice has little intrinsic coherence. As a recent analysis (Brookfield, 1988) of university postgraduate adult education in the United States makes clear, the curricula of university programmes of professional preparation are diverse and broad. These curricula are oriented towards the improvement of previously defined practice capabilities having to do with planning educational programmes for adults, managing and administering adult education institutions, and improving instructional effectiveness. Topics for research, both that undertaken by professors for their own interest and by postgraduate students for theses and dissertations, are framed by the need to improve practice in these areas (Brookfield, 1982). When the curricula of postgraduate training and the conduct of research in a field are determined by the need to address operational problems of practice, rather than by the need to build an internally coherent body of theory, then we can conclude that the field in question is not epistemologically distinct. This realization is accepted by many American adult educators, particularly those who, like Knowles (1962), conceive the adult educational role as generalist and interdisciplinary.

Methodologically, adult education in the United States is held to be distinct by its commitment to fostering self-directed learning, and by its practice of andragogy. Yet both these commitments are conceptually and methodologically questionable. Research into self-directed learning is class- and culture-specific in its concentration on white, middle-class adults as the sampling frame for such studies (Brookfield, 1985). There are questions concerning the conceptualization of self-directed learning (Brookfield,

1987b), in particular its exclusion of reflective domains of learning (Mezirow, 1985). The proposed separateness of andragogy as a set of practices appropriate only to adults, and not found with children and adolescents, has been criticized as methodologically naive (Hartree, 1984; Pratt, 1984). Knowles himself (1980, 1984) has come increasingly to recognize this and to be less certain and all-inclusive in his claims for andragogy as a discrete and separate adult education method.

Despite, or perhaps because of, this lack of epistemological and methodological distinctiveness, American adult education professors, postgraduate students, and researchers spend a great deal of time debating the intrinsic characteristics of adult learning and trying to build a theory of adult learning (Mezirow, 1981). This may well be interpreted as a sign of the professional insecurity which afflicts those university professors of adult education who find themselves constantly in the position of making clear to their colleagues the nature of their field. It is embarrassing to be asked by a colleague in another educational field to explain or define adult education as a body of research, theory, or practice, and to be unable to give a convincing answer.

Merriam (1987) discerns three broad approaches to theory-building in the area of adult learning: theories based on the supposedly unique characteristics of adults, theories based on adults' life situations, and theories based on adults' development of critically reflective capacities. All these theoretical approaches are characterized by a certain exclusivity, by a desire to focus only on what is uniquely adult, and to ignore capacities and cognitive operations which might be observable throughout the life span. Yet learning as a phenomenon is so empirically complex and conceptually ambiguous that to claim for adult learning some form of empirical or conceptual uniqueness is, in my view, a major mistake, the consequence of which will be that adult education is never taken seriously as a field of study. One does not need to be an expert in child psychology to know that what are claimed as distinctive features of adult education (for example, the adult learner's tendency towards self-directedness) are frequently observable in children. One does not need to be an experienced schoolteacher to know that what are claimed as methodologically unique principles of adult education (for example, relating curricula and methods to learners' past experiences, encouraging group collaboration) are found throughout the schooling system. Indeed, the philosophy behind open classrooms and much primary (in American terms, 'elementary') school teaching is wholly andragogical.

Again, anyone who has taught adults knows that a group of learners does not share some homogeneous character-istics such as all being self-directed learners or all preferring to work in groups. Adult learning groups will contain learners who exhibit great diversity in terms of their personalities, preferred learning styles, cultural conditioning, past experiences, current activities, future expectations, and motives for participation. Even with groups who are culturally similar, or who are drawn from a particular social class, we cannot assume that all learners will share the same preferred learning style. There will be those who think visually, those who are field-dependent and those who are field-independent, those who are convergent thinkers and those who are divergent thinkers, those who think in linear modes and those who think laterally, those who are syllabus-bound and prefer a great deal of external direction and structure, and those who are syllabus-free, preferring to cross disciplines and to disregard artificial, institutional delineations concerning what comprises a body of knowledge. The literature of cognitive science suggests that the mechanisms of cognitive processing are essentially the same throughout the life span. The means by which we code new stimuli, assign meaning to new experiences, interpret events through our perceptual filters, and make sense of the world, does not differ essentially between children, adolescents, and adults at various stages of adulthood. These cognitive mechanisms do not operate in some different way when we are thirty-five, compared to when we are fifteen. Although the meanings we generate, and the insights we come to, are certainly different at the various stages of the life span, the mechanisms by which these meanings are assigned and insights realized are, as far as we know, essentially the same. To claim for adult learning or adult education some kind of epistemological distinctiveness is foolish, given that everyday commonsense tells us that many of what are claimed as adult learning or teaching styles are observable at earlier stages in the life span. Additionally, to claim some generic characteristics for adults as learners ignores the diversity of observable learning styles, personalities, and cultural conditionings. Even to talk of adulthood as a generically separate stage of life, compared to childhood or adolescence, ignores the reality that the years between, say, twenty-one and death exhibit untold complexities, variations, phases, stages, and intricacies.

In place of the obsessive and exclusionary attempt to define adult learning and adult education as an epistemologically discrete and distinctive area of study, researchers and theorists in this field would be better engaged in locating their activities within the broader framework of research into learning and education. Attempting to isolate ourselves from the mainstream of research and theory in learning and education in a quest to discover the unique features of adult learning and adult education serves only to emphasize the sense of marginality which that quest seeks to dispel. We might better conceive of studying learning which occurs in adult contexts, rather than adult learning as a distinctive domain. It is easy to understand and sympathize with the motivation for wanting to generate a uniquely adult theory of learning, for by doing so we would create for ourselves a readily identifiable professional identity. But such a motivation is, in my view, misguided, and will result in the very consequence we are seeking to avoid. By maintaining the obviously false proposition that adult learning and adult education are conceptually and empirically discrete from other forms of learning and education, we make a claim that is unsupportable and that will only serve, in the long run, to reinforce our status as a marginal discipline which does not deserve the serious consideration of other educational researchers and theorists.

REFERENCES

Adams, F. (1975) Unearthing Seeds of Fire, Winston-Salem: John F. Blair.

Adams, J. T. (1944) Frontiers of American Culture: a Study of Adult Education in a Democracy, New York: Scribner.

Beder, H. (1987) 'Dominant paradigms, adult education and social justice', Adult Education Quarterly 37 (2): 105-13.

Blakely, R. J. (1958) Adult Education in a Free Society, Toronto: Guardian Bird Publications.

Boone, E. J., Shearon, R. W., White, E. E., and associates (1980) Serving Personal and Community Needs through

Adult Education, San Francisco: Jossey-Bass.

Boshier, R. (1977) review of Register of Research in Progress (C. D. Legge), Adult Education 27 (4): 231-2.

—— (1985) 'Revolting soldiers: the origins of education in the armies in World War One', Adult Education Research Conference Proceedings, No. 26, Tempe, Arizona: Arizona State University.

Bright, B. P. (1985) 'The content-method relationship in the study of adult education', Studies in Adult Education 17 (2): 168-83.

Brookfield, S. D. (1982) 'Adult education research: a comparison of North American and British theory and practice', International Journal of Lifelong Education 1 (2): 157-67.

—— (1985) 'Self-directed learning: a conceptual and methodological exploration', Studies in Adult Education 17 (1): 19-32.

—— (1986) review of University Adult Education in England and the USA, Studies in the Education of Adults 18 (1): 52-4.

—— (1987a) Learning Democracy: Eduard Lindeman on Adult Education and Social Change, London: Croom Helm.

—— (1987b) 'Conceptual, methodological and practical ambiguities in self-directed learning', in H. B. Long and R. M. Smith (eds), Adult Self-directed Learning: Application and Theory, Athens, Georgia: Department of Adult Education, University of Georgia.

—— (1988) Training Educators of Adults: the Theory and Practice of Graduate Adult Education in the United States, London: Croom Helm.

Brunner, E. (1959) An Overview of Adult Education Research, Chicago: Adult Education Association of America.

Bryson, L. (1936) Adult Education, New York: American Book Company.

Cameron, C. (1987) 'Adult education as a force toward social equity', Adult Education Quarterly 37 (3): 173-7.

Campbell, D. D. (1977) Adult Education as a Field of Study and Practice: Strategies for Development, Vancouver: Centre for Continuing Education, University of British Columbia.

Cartwright, M. A. (1935) Ten Years of Adult Education, New York: Macmillan.

Charnley, A. H. (1974) Research in Adult Education in the

British Isles, Leicester: National Institute of Adult Continuing Education.

———— (1984) 'Research and research documentation in adult education, 1974-1984: a personal view', Studies in Adult Education 16: 58-69.

Copeland, H. G., and Grabowski, S. M. (1971) 'Research and investigation in the United States', Convergence 4 (4): 23-32.

Cowburn, W. (1986) Class, Ideology and Adult Education, London: Croom Helm.

Craver, S. M. (1984) 'Social and economic attitudes in the education of industrial workers in Richmond, Virginia, 1884 to 1904', Adult Education Research Conference Proceedings, No. 25, Raleigh: North Carolina State University.

Darkenwald, G., and Merriam, S. B. (1982) Adult Education: Foundations of Practice, New York: Harper & Row.

Day, M., and McDermott, W. (1980) 'Where has all the History gone in Graduate Programs of Adult Education?' Paper presented to the 1980 National Adult Education Conference, St Louis, November.

De Crow, R. (1969) New Directions in Adult Education Research, Syracuse, N.Y.: Syracuse University Papers in Continuing Education for Adults, No. 139.

Elias, J. L., and Merriam, S. B. (1980) Philosophical Foundations of Adult Education, Malabar, Florida: Robert Krieger.

Ely, M. L. (ed.) (1936) Adult Education in Action, New York: American Association for Adult Education.

Essert, P. L. (1951) Creative Leadership of Adult Education, New York: Prentice-Hall.

Evans, B. (1988) Radical Adult Education: a Political and Philosophical Critique, London: Croom Helm.

Field, B. (1980) 'The Southern Counties Adult Education Society: some nineteenth century views on workers' education', Studies in Adult Education 12 (2): 101-8.

Fieldhouse, R. (1983) 'The ideology ˌof English adult education teaching, 1925-1950', Studies in Adult Education 15: 11-35.

———— (1985) 'Conformity and contradiction in English responsible body tradition', Studies in the Education of Adults 17 (2): 121-34.

Gainey, L. (1986) 'Clandestine learning among slaves: evidence from the Federal Writers Project "Slave Narratives, 1936-1938"', Adult Education Research

Conference Proceedings, No. 27, Syracuse, N.Y.: Syracuse University.

Grabowski, S. M. (1980) 'Trends in graduate research', in H.M. Long and R. Hiemstra and associates, Changing Approaches to Studying Adult Education, San Francisco: Jossey-Bass.

Grattan, H. C. (1965) In Quest of Knowledge, New York: Association Press.

Guy, D. M. (1976) 'A review of articles in three adult education publications, 1970-1974', Continuing Education in New Zealand 8 (2): 48-60.

Hallenbeck, W. C. (1960) 'The function and place of adult education in American society', in M. S. Knowles (ed.), Handbook of Adult Education in the United States, Chicago: Adult Education Association of the United States.

Harrison, J. F. C. (1961) Learning and Living, 1790-1960, London: Routledge & Kegan Paul.

Hartree, A. (1984) 'Malcolm Knowles's theory of andragogy: a critique', International Journal of Lifelong Education 3 (3): 203-10.

Hellyer, M. R. (1986) 'Adult education and government repression in the U.S.; 1919-1920 revolutionary radicalism', Adult Education Research Conference Proceedings, No. 27, Syracuse, N.Y.: Syracuse University.

—— and Schied, F. M. (1984) 'Workers' education and the labor college movement: radical traditions in American adult education', Adult Education Research Conference Proceedings, No. 25, Raleigh: North Carolina State University.

Hiemstra, R. (1976) Lifelong Learning, Lincoln, Nebraska: Professional Educators Publications.

Hugo, J. M. (1987) 'The elegant arts amid the coarser plants of daily necessity: a retrospective view of a women's study club, 1885-1957', Adult Education Research Conference Proceedings, No. 28, Laramie: University of Wyoming.

Jensen, G., Liveright, A. A., and Hallenbeck, W. C. (eds) (1964) Adult Education: Outlines of an Emerging Field of University Study, Washington D.C.: Adult Education Association of the United States.

Joyce, P. (1973) 'Education for social change', Adult Education 46 (3): 170-4.

Kelly, T. (1970) A History of Adult Education in Great

Britain, Liverpool: Liverpool University Press.
—— (1974) A Select Bibliography of Adult Education, London: National Institute of Adult Education.
Kennedy, W. B. (1981) 'Highlander praxis: learning with Myles Horton', Teachers College Record 83: 105-19.
Knowles, M. S. (1962) 'A general theory of the doctorate in education', Adult Education 12 (3): 136-41.
—— (1975) Self-directed Learning, New York: Cambridge Books.
—— (1977) A History of the Adult Education Movement in the United States, Malabar, Florida: Robert E. Krieger. ·
—— (1980) The Modern Practice of Adult Education, New York: Cambridge Books.
—— (1984) Andragogy in Action, San Francisco: Jossey-Bass.
—— and Klevins, C. (1982) 'Historical and philosophical perspectives', in C. Klevins (ed.), Materials and Methods in Adult and Continuing Education, Canoga Park, California: Klevens Publications.
Kreitlow, B., and associates (1981) Examining Controversies in Adult Education, San Francisco: Jossey-Bass.
Lawson, K. H. (1979) Philosophical Concepts and Values in Adult Education, Milton Keynes: Open University Press.
—— (1982) Analysis and Ideology: Conceptual Essays on the Education of Adults, Nottingham: Department of Adult Education, University of Nottingham.
—— (1985) 'Deontological liberalism: the political philosophy of liberal adult education', International Journal of Lifelong Education 4 (3): 219-27.
Legge, C. D. (1977) Register of Research in Progress in Adult Education, 1976 and 1977, Manchester: Department of Higher and Adult Education, University of Manchester.
Lindeman, E. C. (1926) The Meaning of Adult Education, New York: New Republic.
—— (1944) 'New needs for adult education', Annals of the American Academy of Political and Social Sciences 231, 115-22.
—— (1945) 'World peace through adult education', The Nation's Schools 35 (3): 23.
Liveright, A. A., and Haygood, D. (eds) (1969) The Exeter Papers, Boston, Mass.: Boston University Center for the Study of Liberal Education for Adults.
Livingstone, R. (1945) On Education, Cambridge: Cambridge University Press.

Long, H. B. (1983) Adult Learning: Research and Practice, New York: Cambridge Books.

—— (1987) New Perspectives on the Education of Adults in the United States, London: Croom Helm.

Lovett, T. (1975) Adult Education, Community Development and the Working Class, London: Ward Locke Educational.

—— (ed.) (1988) Radical Approaches to Adult Education, London: Croom Helm.

—— Clarke, C., and Kilmurray, A. (1983) Adult Education and Community Action, London: Croom Helm.

McIlroy, J.A. (1985) 'Adult education and the role of the client: the TUC education scheme, 1929-80', Studies in the Education of Adults 17 (1): 33-58.

Marks, H. (1982) 'Unemployment and adult education in the 1930's', Studies in Adult Education 14: 1-15.

Marriott, S. (1981) 'State aid - the earliest demands for government support of university extra-mural education', Studies in Adult Education 13 (1): 28-44.

Mee, G. (1978) 'Research programmes for adult educators', Studies in Adult Education 10 (2): 161-7.

Merriam, S. B. (1987) 'Adult learning and theory building: a review', Adult Education 37 (4): 187-98.

Mezirow, J. (1981) 'A critial theory of adult learning and education', Adult Education 32 (1): 3-27.

—— (1985) 'Self-directed learning: a critical theory', in S. D. Brookfield (ed.), Self-directed learning: from Theory to Practice, San Francisco: Jossey-Bass.

Monette, M. (1977) 'The concept of educational need: an analysis of selected literature', Adult Education 27 (2): 116-27.

—— (1979) 'Paulo Freire and other unheard voices', Religious Education 74 (2): 543-54.

Nel, J. (1987) 'The University of Wyoming's role in the historical development of adult education in Wyoming, 1886-1918', Adult Education Research Conference Proceedings, No. 28, Laramie: University of Wyoming.

Omolewa, M. (1984) 'Neglected themes in adult education historical research in Canada', Adult Education Research Conference Proceedings, No. 25, Raleigh: North Carolina State University.

Paterson, R. W. K. (1973) 'Social change as an educational aim', Adult Education 45 (6): 353-9.

—— (1979) Values, Education and the Adult, London: Routledge & Kegan Paul.

—— (1987) 'Adult education and the individual', International Journal of Lifelong Education 6 (2): 111-23.

Pell, O. A. H. (1952) 'Social philosophy at the grass roots: the work of the AEA's Committee on Social Philosophy', Adult Education 2 (1): 123-32.

Pratt, D. D. (1984) 'Andragogical assumptions: some counter-intuitive logic', Adult Education Research Conference Proceedings, No. 25, Raleigh: North Carolina State University.

Rockhill, K. (1984) 'Between the wars: liberalism and the framing of conflict in the framing of adult education', Adult Education Research Conference Proceedings, No. 25, Raleigh: North Carolina State University.

—— (1985) 'Ideological solidification of liberalism in university adult education: confrontation over workers' education in the USA', in R. Taylor, K. Rockhill, and R. Fieldhouse, University Adult Education in England and the USA, London: Croom Helm.

Rubenson, K. (1982) 'Adult education research: in quest of a map of the territory', Adult Education 32 (2): 57-74.

Ruddock, R. (1974) 'A time to attack', Adult Education 46 (6): 25-31.

Schwertman, J. B. (1955) 'What is adult education?' Adult Education 5 (3): 131-45.

Simey, M. (1978) 'Let's put politics back on the agenda', Adult Education 48 (2): 15-22.

Sisco, B. R. (1985) 'From whence we came: a critical examination of selected historical literature of adult education', Adult Education Research Conference Proceedings, No. 26, Tempe, Arizona: Arizona State University.

Standing Conference on University Teaching and Research into the Education of Adults (SCUTREA) (1986) Guide to University Courses for Adult Educators in the United Kingdom and Eire, Leicester: National Institute of Adult and Continuing Education and Standing Conference on University Teaching and Research into the Education of Adults.

Stewart, D. W. (1987) Adult Learning in America: Eduard Lindeman and his Agenda for Lifelong Education, Malabar, Florida: Robert E. Krieger.

Sworder, S. (1955) 'What is adult education?' Adult Education 5 (3): 131-45.

Taylor, R., Rockhill, K., and Fieldhouse, R. (1985) University Adult Education in England and the USA,

London: Croom Helm.

Thomas, J. E. (1982) Radical Adult Education: Theory and Practice, Nottingham: Department of Adult Education, University of Nottingham.

—— (1984) 'Adult education, research and SCUTREA', Studies in Adult Education 16, 70-7.

—— and Davies, J. H. (1984) A Select Bibliography of Adult Continuing Education, Leicester: National Institute of Adult Continuing Education.

Thompson, J. L. (ed.) (1980) Adult Education for a Change, London: Hutchinson.

—— (1983) Learning Liberation: Women's Response to Men's Education, London: Croom Helm.

Verduin, J. R., Miller, H. G., and Greer, C. E. (1977) Adults teaching Adults: Principles and Strategies, Austin, Texas: Learning Concepts.

Verner, C. (1964) 'Definition of terms', in G. Jensen, A. A. Liveright, and W. C. Hallenbeck (eds), Adult Education: Outlines of an Emerging Field of University Study, Washington, D.C.: Adult Education Association of the United States.

Wallace, R.K. (1986) 'The Americanization movement in the 1920's: a neglected aspect of adult education history', Adult Education Research Conference Proceedings, No. 27, Syracuse, N.Y.: Syracuse University Press.

Ward, K., and Taylor, R. (eds) (1986) Adult Education and the Working Class, London: Croom Helm.

Wiltshire, H. (1976) 'The nature and uses of adult education', in A. Rogers (ed.), The Spirit and the Form: Essays in Adult Education in Honour of Professor Harold Wiltshire, Nottingham: Department of Adult Education, University of Nottingham.

Youngman, F. (1986) Adult Education and Socialist Pedagogy, London: Croom Helm.

Chapter eight

OVERVIEW AND CONCLUSIONS

Barry P. Bright

The major conclusion from the foregoing chapters is that the study of adult education does represent serious epistemological issues and problems and that these are all concerned with its postulated lack of rigour in relation to the conventional disciplines. This, as will be discussed further below, is also the case for Griffin's position, which includes abandonment of the conventional disciplines within adult education. All the contributors can be regarded as focusing upon the current adult education-conventional discipline relationship and regarding it as problematical or deficient in some manner consistent with their different prescriptive interpretations of what form this relationship should take. At this more detailed level the consensus disappears and the differences in the definition and justification of particular interpretations of adult education's problematical epistemology become evident. Within this process deeper epistemological issues and positions are revealed which involve alternative definitions of knowledge itself.

The overall conclusion concerning the debatable status of adult education's epistemology is no accident, since the objective of the book is to draw attention to this, and the different ways in which this conclusion can be reached from several perspectives. Although the focus of the book is the study of adult education and the nature of its epistemology and activity, this can be regarded as being reversed in that, as intimated above, the issues raised by this debate have more than a passing relevance for epistemology itself and the conventional disciplines. This was unexpected, and the manner in which the contributors' analyses easily relate and refer to deep epistemological issues was not anticipated in the original proposal for the book. However, given the inter-disciplinary nature of adult education, it may be no surprise, retrospectively, that discussion of its epistemology encom-passes broader epistemological issues. In this sense, and in contrast to the more usual marginal and secondary status attributed to adult education, it can be regarded as of primary importance. Indeed, it could be suggested that a debate of this kind is possible only within an inter-disciplinary, derived field in which these broader issues may become apparent. Although it is true that a broad spectrum of views exists within any given discipline, it is also equally true that such debates rarely discuss interdisciplinary epistemological issues. In addition to drawing attention to the relevance of the present book to epistemology generally, it must also be noted that, again, although focusing upon the study of adult education, it does have relevance for other derived, interdisciplinary areas in education which may be regarded as experiencing similar epistemological problems and tensions.

A further and obvious conclusion from the present book is that the issues it raises are complex. One reason for this is the book's declared focus upon epistemology, albeit relative to adult education, and the complex nature of knowledge and its possible definitions. A further reason is the variety of opinions and views represented by the contributors, all of which vary in either contrasting terms (e.g. Paterson and Griffin) or subtle and relative terms (e.g. Armstrong and Usher), which are, none the less, important and instructive. This interpretive variety was an objective of the book in raising the debate on adult education's epistemology, in contrast to others which blandly modulate a common theme. Another source of complexity is that, although several contributors refer to the concept of 'praxis' and a fundamentally intrinsic practical orientation within adult education (e.g. Armstrong, Usher, Griffin), they do so in theoretical terms. This is obviously inevitable, given the nature and objective of the present book as a forum for, and method of, disseminating alternative views. This source of complexity indicates the conceptual difficulty of the theory-method relationship itself, and is instructive to that extent. Yet another reason for the complexity of the debate is that differences between some of the contributors (indeed, all the contributors, but more explicitly between Paterson and Griffin) can be regarded as fundamental differences in terms of logic. None of the contributors explicitly discusses these logical differences in a directly comparative manner, although implicit reference is obvious in Paterson's, Usher's, and Griffin's chapters. There is therefore a need to outline these differences in approach to logic in order to comprehend more fully the views they are based on. The current author is cognisant of the conceptual minefield this particular area may represent and is apprehensive upon entering it; however, such an undertaking would appear necessary.

A further and final source of difficulty is that recognition and understanding of the problems and issues alluded to by the contributors is inhibited or prevented by the unrecognized existence of those problems and issues within adult education. Thus the contributors' objective in drawing attention to the problems in adult education as they see them may fall on deaf ears precisely because of the existence of the problems to which they draw attention. In addition, professional insecurity, which is created and manifested by these problems, produces a resistance to views which suggest the need for major changes, especially those which suggest that adult educators need re-educating. Also, the subject specialist ethos adult education conveys, as one example of its conventional interdisciplinary nature, obfuscates the necessity for, or the means by which, such a deeper understanding may be contemplated or acquired. This may create a Catch 22 position and possibly finds its most direct and obvious manifestation in the present chapter, which attempts to interpret and compare the different views at a relatively deep level, but which necessarily draws the author into unfamiliar and conceptually complex epistemological terrains. As indicated in chapter one, however unnerving, threatening, or inadequate such epistemological excursions may be, they are necessary and crucial to a more fundamental understanding of the epistemological nature of adult education. To whatever extent the views presented in this book can be regarded as accurate, they require recognition and consideration as part of the further understanding and development of the study of adult education.

Finally, it must be noted that in offering interpretive frameworks within which the different views presented in this book may be placed, some degree of extension and elaboration of those views is inevitable. This may involve unintended errors and misrepresentation of some of the contributors' views and positions, especially in connection with aspects or issues which, for space limitation reasons, were not discussed or only briefly so. An attempt will be made to draw the reader's attention to particular instances of such extension and elaboration as they occur. It must also be borne in mind that the whole of the present chapter itself can be regarded as representing extension and elaboration with which some of the contributors (if not all) may disagree. Despite the author's attempts to remain neutral and offer a balanced account of the views presented, some contributors may object to the approach adopted and its inherent assumptions. Such are the degree and depth of contrast between some of the contributors that a 'neutral' position is often impossible, since the manner in which a problem or issue is conceptualized can be held to betray underlying assumptions.

THE CENTRAL PROBLEM: ADULT EDUCATION'S LACK OF RIGOUR IN RELATION TO THE CONVENTIONAL DISCIPLINES

As indicated above, the views presented in the book indicate a consensus of opinion concerning adult education's lack of rigour relative to the views adopted of the conventional disciplines. That is, the different views concerning the nature of adult education's epistemological problem are a function of and are defined by views the contributors hold concerning the conventional disciplines. Although they differ, all the contributors hold views of the conventional disciplines which lead to the recognition of a problem in adult education's epistemology. Obviously, the nature of the problem varies, depending on the particular view of the conventional disciplines held. More deeply, the different views held concerning the conventional disciplines can be regarded as alternative and competing definitions of knowledge, since the latter can be expected logically to lead to the former. The views concerning the definition of knowledge and the conventional disciplines can, therefore, be regarded as epistemological source reference points by which the definition of rigour and adult education's lack of rigour gain meaning and elaboration. The differences between the contributors in terms of their definitions of knowledge and their views of conventional disciplines will be discussed further below. At this point, however, it may be useful, as a gentle introduction to a complex set of issues, to outline briefly the three major attitudes adopted by the contributors towards the conventional disciplines and adult education's relationship to them. At a relatively simple level this will be achieved by indicating whether these views regard adult education as conforming or not conforming to the conventional disciplines. Within this approach, it will be apparent that one view (Griffin) regards conformity with the conventional disciplines as indicating a lack of rigour relative to the definition of knowledge adopted.

1. Adult education lacks conformity with conventional disciplines

Paterson, Brookfield, and Bright, in order of degrees of strength, would appear to suggest that adult education should conform to and reference itself more closely to the epistemological content and methods of the conventional disciplines. Within this view, adult education's current relationship to the conventional disciplines is fractured, decoupled, hypocritical, and tenuous, which renders it liable to be uninformed, uneducated, irrational (Paterson), guilty of epistemological vandalism (Bright), confused, and creating an inability for it to be taken seriously as an area of academic study (Brookfield).

Several points concerning this view require elaboration. First, Paterson is the strongest adherent of this view, and although his discussion of the currently problematic role of philosophy in adult education finds a correlate with other disciplines (e.g. Bright, Armstrong), his claim that philosophy's contribution to adult education is mainly, but not exclusively, in the form of logical criticism as an epistemological method may place it in a different relationship compared to other disciplines. Indeed, precisely the same claim could be made of philosophy in relation to other disciplines. Second, although Bright points to the lack of conformity of adult education to current psychological knowledge and suggests the need for a greater degree of conformity in this respect, he also accepts the need for a practical definition of adult education rather than an exclusively theoretical one based on discipline knowledge. Third, while Armstrong and Usher recognize the current lack of conformity of adult education to the conventional disciplines, they do not recommend or accept the possibility of an increase in the level of this conformity. It must also be noted that Brookfield suggests both a return to conventional approaches to learning, presumably within psychology, and a return to education, which he regards as a more intrinsic epistemological source than adult education.

2. Adult education represents total conformity with the conventional disciplines

Griffin is the main proponent of this view, within which adult education does not represent a fractured, tenuous, hypocritical, or illogical relationship with the conventional disciplines. Rather, it represents exactly the same scientific model of logical analysis, approach, assumptions, methods, and type of content typically found within the disciplines. More particularly within this view, it is the disciplines themselves which are regarded as being fractured, tenuous, hypocritical, and illogical. The false dichotomies, epistemological vandalism (Bright), tendency to irrationality, and uneducated status (Paterson) attributed to adult education are regarded as a logical extension of these that the conventional disciplines themselves represent. The vertically segregated independent discipline structure of the conventional epistemological system is regarded as representing a set of false dichotomies which fractures and divorces knowledge from reality, to the extent that this system itself cannot be taken seriously. In short, adult education is a mirror image of the conventional epistemological system, which is regarded as erroneous. Given this, Griffin suggests the need to move the entire debate concerning adult education, and, indeed, the definition of knowledge itself, outside the conventional epistemological system.

Although Griffin suggests this general view of adult education, it must not be interpreted as suggesting that it utilizes all the knowledge in the disciplines or that its epistemological concerns and concepts are identical. The false dichotomies and concepts attributed to adult education are different in substantive content from those attributed to the disciplines, although they are identical in their pseudo-scientific methods and ideological objectives. In this sense, there are two interrelated levels of false dichotomies: the higher level represented by the disciplines and the division of knowledge within and between these, and the lower level represented by adult education. Also, it must be noted that although Griffin has been credited with being the major proponent of this view, Armstrong seems to indicate agreement with its ideological and epistemological stance in its application to education. Similarly, Usher would also appear partly to accept the epistemological but not the ideological position entailed by the current view within education. This may appear contradictory, given the above stated agreement of both Armstrong and Usher with the earlier interpretation that regards adult education as lacking conformity to the disciplines (see 1 above). This apparent contradiction will be discussed and clarified in the following sub-section. In terms to be discussed in a later section, Griffin would discount the distinction between epistemological and ideological concerns as illogical and evidence of a further false dichotomy typical. of the conventional approach to knowledge.

3. **Adult education attempts but fails to conform to the conventional disciplines**

Armstrong and Usher indicate that adult education is informed by a conformist intention, indeed a necessity within conventional definitions of education, with regard to the disciplines, but that it consistently fails to match the academic and epistemological model represented by them. They accept that adult education is fractured, illogical, dishonest, pseudo, and vandalistic in regard to the disciplines, but suggests that this is inevitable and unavoidable because the conventional discipline model, and its 'theoretical' orientation, are inappropriate within education. As such, and in contrast to Paterson, Bright, and Brookfield, adult education cannot conform to the disciplines in terms defined by those disciplines. Usher and, implicitly, Armstrong accept the epistemological status of the disciplines as theoretical bodies of knowledge outside education, but both also accept a role for discipline-based knowledge within education, though not in the exclusive terms of the conventional discipline model. Like Griffin, they suggest the need to move the debate about education and its epistemology and definition beyond the restrictive influence and problems of discipline-based theory. They suggest the need to redefine education and the role of discipline-based knowledge within it, in practical terms rather than the 'application of formal theory' sense conveyed by conventional epistemology. Unlike Griffin, they do not suggest the need to define knowledge in terms totally outside the conventional epistemological system.

This view contains both the conformist and the non-conformist elements present within the previous two perspectives. Adult education is regarded as attempting the former because it is identified too closely with the disciplines, institutionally, professionally, and epistemologically. (Griffin and Armstrong would either add 'ideologically' to this list, or submerge institutional, professional, and epistemological affinities within this term.) In contrast, the reality of its activity and epistemology, i.e. the products of its attempt to conform, reveals a considerable lack of conformity and a failure to equal the discipline model. Armstrong and Usher suggest that this is due to the inadequacy of the discipline model within education and is inevitable, given that adult education continues to operate and function exclusively within its terms. Bright also refers to adult education's inappropriate adoption of the intrinsic, theoretical discipline model and its insecurity within this, in terms of establishing a balanced and mature relationship between its epistemological dependence and independence. Usher's and Armstrong's views can be regarded as an attempt to renegotiate this relationship, and, although appealing for a greater degree of accuracy and education in adult education's use of discipline knowledge (i.e. an improvement in level of conformity), Bright also suggests that this could occur within the approach to education adopted by Usher and Armstrong.

From the above discussion it is apparent that the first two views (1 and 2 above) represent totally opposed interpretations of adult education's relationship to conventional disciplines and the nature of its problematical relationship to them. The third view (3 above) represents an interpretation which, in qualified terms, includes aspects from both the previous views. In doing this it invokes a distinction between the role and status of the disciplines outside and within education and necessarily entails a redefinition of education. It accepts the current epistemological problems of adult education and its declared lack of rigour relative to the discipline model as inevitable, and regards them as fruitless and meaningless for education. It is precisely this type of epistemological debate that this view is seeking to avoid and is consequently regarded as, to use Armstrong's phrase, a 'red herring' owing to the restrictive adoption of an incorrect epistemological model.

Overview and conclusions

Again, it must be noted that although the above perspectives are suggested as summaries of the general positions of the contributors, each of the latter can be regarded as relative and continuous rather than discrete and clear-cut. In one sense the general framework adopted 'forces' contributors' views within it and may create inaccuracies or misrepresentation of detailed points and differences.

EPISTEMOLOGICAL REFERENCE POINTS: THREE DEFINITIONS OF KNOWLEDGE

As indicated, the different views of adult education's relationship to the conventional disciplines really amount to different views and definitions of knowledge itself. Similarly, these views can be logically held to lead to different definitions of education. Indeed, it may be suggested that, if Paterson and Griffin could accept the initial premises of each other's position, they would agree with the consequent definition of education they each suggest, as a logical conclusion. In terms of the relationship between the definition of knowledge and the related definition of education, it may be suggested that these represent two epistemological reference points, with the latter embedded within the former. It may also be suggested that, given this relationship, anyone involved in education is also engaged in a view of epistemology and that this has a direct bearing on his/her professional activities.

In order further to progress analysis and understanding of the contributors' views presented in this book, it will be necessary to examine the different interpretations and definitions in relation to the epistemological reference points of the definition of knowledge and education. Not surprisingly, bearing in mind the previous discussion, three such views may be identified. It is suggested that these views may be located within two categories of orientation, the ontological and the epistemological. The use of the latter term may be regarded as a source of confusion, and therefore a brief discussion of the distinction between ontological and epistemological will ensue. The current author's decision to incorporate two of the previous three views within a single category of orientation (i.e. Paterson and Griffin within the ontological category) suggests that, in the fundamental sense to be discussed, both these views, although opposite and contradictory in many ways, are identical in this fundamental sense. (Again, neither of the contributors may necessarily agree with this approach.)

An ontological orientation involves a substantive' claim that the categorical view of the world which a particular perspective, theory, or interpretive position specifies corresponds with reality and 'the nature of things'. The picture of the world it conveys is regarded as fundamental and possessing an essential existence and givenness within nature. It implies that such phenomena and their categories are naturally occurring (idiomorphic), intrinsic, and absolute accounts of the real nature of the world. In contrast, an epistemological orientation regards all knowledge as tentative, temporary, and metaphorical approximations of real phenomena, the accuracy of which is uncertain. Within this view, knowledge is a paradox, since it represents attempts to understand the world in the full recognition of its own temporary status and the unknowability of the world. All knowledge is regarded as derived and secondary in the sense that the human observer of the world and generator of knowledge about the world is also a participant within the world and cannot, therefore, obtain an objective and detached account of it. A good example of this distinction is the problematical status of chance within accounts of the real world. Some deterministic accounts attribute an epistemological status to this concept but not an ontological status, i.e. they do not accept that chance is a real phenomenon within nature and regard it as a temporary epistemological category which will ultimately be replaced by an ontological, deterministic explanation. Conversely, the epistemological view regards all knowledge, including supposedly ontological knowledge, as inevitably and logically epistemological, i.e. tentative, uncertain, and subject to change.

In the context of the present book, it is suggested that Paterson's and Griffin's views can be located within the ontological orientation. Although they would both accept (indeed, Paterson would appear to insist) that a current body of knowledge (e.g. the content of conventional disciplines) will be superseded by later advances, they appear to imply that this is highly unlikely in terms of their particular views concerning the methods, structure, and objectives of knowledge, which they regard as veridical and pertaining to the real nature of the world. In contrast, Usher and

Overview and conclusions

Armstrong appear to adopt a fundamentally derived and relativistic epistemological approach in their attitudes to both the conventional disciplines and the definition of education. Intradisciplinary epistemological problems and issues are regarded as simply that, and should not be imported to adult education, which should concern itself with using this knowledge at a general, not detailed, level whatever its status within the disciplines, in an instrumental rather than intrinsic sense. Similarly, their defintion of education also permits an epistemological relativism and openness focusing upon practical rather than fundamentally intrinsic knowledge.

Ontological definitions of knowledge and education

Paterson and Griffin, as indicated above, adopt totally different perspectives concerning their views of the relationship between adult education and the conventional disciplines. Yet, in the ontological sense discussed, they both claim the idiomorphic and veridical status of their respective views. Although Griffin objects to the categorical and classificatory mode of the conventional disciplines and the scientific model of rationality underlying them, it can be argued that he, too, and necessarily so, invokes dialectically logical categories and classes by which his criticisms may be expressed. Similarly, he takes issue with the notion of objective knowledge of the kind presented by Paterson, but then proceeds, in a manner which betokens objectivity and an absolute orientation, to proclaim all knowledge to be ideological. In this sense the differences between Paterson and Griffin can be regarded as a conflict between fixed opposing systems of categorization. Although both Paterson's and Griffin's objective is to enhance and increase the level and range of conceptual discrimination, demarcation, and understanding, they suggest that this is only possible within the framework of their respective positions. Neither pre-empts possible substantive content within his approach to knowledge (e.g. Paterson's statement that philosophy is totally presuppositionless), but Paterson specifies the method by which this content can be acquired (logical criticism) and Griffin specifies the objectives to which all knowledge is directed (ideology). Conflict occurs because Griffin believes methods are ideological and produce ideologically infused content, while Paterson believes that, although methods do entail objectives which define content, these objectives refer to a critical epistemology and are totally distinct and separate from ideological and political objectives or concerns.

The conventional view

Paterson accepts the conventional epistemological system as represented by the major disciplines, which he regards as representing epistemologically sovereign, fundamental, and indisputable ways of understanding the world, relative to the derived, socially contingent, and small-scale nature of 'fields' of knowledge, such as adult education. Such fields will always be in a position of epistemological debt, since the origin of their informing principles and concepts occurs within the major disciplines. In these terms the required improvement of adult education's current lack of academic rigour is defined by greater adherence to the content and methods of the current epistemological system and its disciplines. Thus Paterson suggests the need for adult education and its educators to be accurately informed of psychological, anthropological, social, moral, logical, and epistemological questions which will develop and lead to an intellectually and academically acceptable level of logical criticism. This view generally interprets adult education's current epistemological problems and, more important, their resolution in terms defined by and within the conventional epistemological system, and does, therefore, adopt an orientation internal to that system, thus illustrating the determining influence and importance of it. Bright and Brookfield also suggest a similar need in the area of psychology, although Bright heavily qualifies this in relation to a practical definition of education within which this greater academic rigour could occur. Brookfield, although referring to this general position at the end of his chapter, does not discuss it in detail, since his major concern is with comparative issues between the United Kingdom and America.

Endemic within Paterson's approach is the importance of formal theory and the crucial role of logical method and criticism in the formulation of theories, concepts, and interpretive frameworks. In this regard he invokes the distinction between substantive content and logical method, and suggests that philosophy's major contribution to epistemology is in terms of the latter; indeed, he refers to the role of philosophy in maintaining 'the flame of rationality'. He is highly critical of adult education and its educators because of their logical ineptitude and imprecision, which result in an uneducated and narrow-minded orientation to the extent of threatening their legitimacy and ability to fulfil the role of educator. One example of this is the tendency of adult educators to accept uncritically 'belief packages' such as scientific naturalism, Marxism, and their internally defined concepts of social praxis, the social construction of knowledge or social change, all of which, he argues, require searching, logical analysis to illuminate grave logical errors in their formulation as theories and legitimate perspectives. (The concept of praxis and the social construction of knowledge view represent major arguments within the positions of other contributors, i.e. Usher, Armstrong, and Griffin respectively. Paterson's objections to these will be considered later.) When discussing several views current in the 1920s and 1930s claiming a political function for adult education in America, Brookfield refers to Bryson's view that adult education should be concerned with the provision of accurate and trustworthy information, and that teachers should inculcate the principles of rational scepticism to counter doctrinaire political views and encourage students to be critically aware of their accepted beliefs. Such a view would appear to conform closely to that of Paterson.

Although accepting the relatively fixed, secure, and ontological status of the conventional disciplines, Paterson does accept that logic and empiricism, as investigative tools, and the substantive content of the disciplines are open to change and progress. In this sense he accepts the tentative and approximate nature of knowledge and the impossibility of perfect knowledge. From this perspective, and possibly in the manner of the philosophy of science (e.g. Popper), logical criticism and empiricism play a crucial and verificatory role in the identification of knowledge. It is precisely because knowledge is tentative, approximate and imperfect that logical and empirical methods are important in delineating what can be classed as 'knowledge' in contrast to unsubstantiated and illogical beliefs. Indeed, Paterson would appear to accept the definition of knowledge as beliefs validated by logical and empirical methods. By these methods, intellectual, social, and cultural understanding and progress may be attained. Similarly, the conceptual categories and classes that formal epistemology critically acknowledges as knowledge are essential in order to make sense of the world, since without them the world would be experienced as a chaotic and disordered entity, or, more likely, our interpretations of order would be characterized by an immature and animistic sublimation rather than by a mature and civilized rationality. The latter, and the critically examined and accepted status of knowledge it leads to, are regarded by Paterson as represented and defined by the conventional disciplines.

Paterson's acceptance of the tentative nature of knowledge can be regarded as an indication that he does not adopt an ontological position, since he accepts that the substantive content of knowledge and its methods have changed in the past and will continue to change in the future. However, he does regard the conventional disciplines as ontologically given, albeit in a fundamentally relative sense (i.e. with the exception of physiological death, nothing is absolutely certain). In addition, although recognizing that the methods by which knowledge is pursued and attained are changeable, his emphasis upon logical criticism implies an equal and restrictive emphasis upon formal logic, which excludes the validity of dialectical logic. For Paterson, the distinction between formal and dialectical logic is meaningless, since the latter is regarded as a pseudo-logic which breaks the rules of formal logic and renders it illogical. The issue of formal versus dialectical logic is instructive, since several contributors (Griffin, Armstrong, Usher, Bright) refer to concepts such as dialectical relationships and praxis, which have a direct reference to dialectical logic. Of more immediate concern is Paterson's insistence on formal logic as an example of his ontological position, since, although it does not preclude any substantive content (e.g. Paterson's statement that philosophy is totally presuppositionless), it could be argued that it precludes alternative ways of regarding and interpreting phenomena, whenever these embody self-contradictions. In this sense, formal logic is being insisted upon as the only logical and veridical method through which the world may be interpreted.

The emphasis upon formal logical method is not intended or designed to lead to a monistic and fixed interpretation of the world. Indeed, Paterson is at pains to draw attention to the need for adult educators to widen their interpretive frameworks beyond those currently available, especially those represented by standardized 'belief packages' and unexamined value judgements. Similarly, the products of critical academic study, i.e. general theories and concepts, are accepted as general statements which take a unique and complex form within a detailed local context; however, the validity and power of such concepts and theories reside in their relevance to a large number of such heterogeneous situations and events. If the pursuit of knowledge were directed to the understanding of each unique local event or context, it would become mere description rather than the useful product of critical analysis.

As indicated above, and as an example of the use of logical criticism and his general view, Paterson offers several instances within adult education of illogical positions. The concept of praxis is criticized because it sometimes assumes that the social consequences to which it leads are a validation of the theory, and that such validation is provided by exemplifying political, economic and/or social theories which are external to it. Paterson points out that the theory of social praxis involves more than mere social prediction, since the essence, and therefore the test, of the theory are the processes it should specify and by which social outcomes occur, i.e. praxis is a theory about processes not outcomes. He goes on to doubt whether the theory of social praxis can sufficiently differentiate and identify the specific social consequences by which the theory may be verified, and asks the rhetorical question, 'Is true an honorific title?', by which he obviously infers that the status of truth and knowledge cannot be attributed to theories of such inadequate logical and empirical calibre. Clearly, Paterson regards logical criticism and empirical verification of theories as our best guarantors of truth and reliable knowledge.

Another example cited by Paterson, which reveals his view of the disciplines, his belief in non-political objective knowledge, and indicates his definition of education, is the social construction theory of knowledge. His suggestion that the view that all knowledge is socially constructed and that, therefore, objective knowledge does not exist (Griffin's view) really amounts to no more than an allegation that social systems can engender weak and false sets of beliefs. This view is regarded as an appropriate empirical question within sociology. It could be argued (e.g. by Griffin) that Paterson has thus removed the political content of the theory, and thereby missed the point of it, by reducing it to an empirical and objective question of whether the beliefs propogated by social systems are true or not. Paterson would not accept that this 'reduces' the theory in any sense, but merely subjects its hypotheses to logical and empirical analysis in order to verify or falsify their truth. From Griffin's perspective it could be argued that this approach is itself ideological, since logical and empirical methods are themselves ideological and are designed and intended to protect, express, and maintain social and economic interests, including those of the proponents of these methods. (More of Griffin's view later.)

Of more immediate interest is Paterson's referral of the question to sociology and his denial of its special relevance to education. He defines education as the transmission of knowledge and regards the latter as referring to 'beliefs which are true, reasonably representative and validly based on adequate grounds'. In these terms education, which includes adult education, has a remit and a responsibility to transmit or communicate only beliefs which are accredited the objective status of 'true' and 'knowledge' by the use of logical and empirical methods within the disciplines. This is consistent with the epistemological sovereignty of the disciplines and adult education's epistemologically derived and inferior status. In this sense, education is an epistemological distribution centre serving the disciplines and the knowledge they identify and produce, and, presumably, legitimate educational theory is concerned with issues relating to the effectiveness of this transmission process. The curriculum in this sense has been set by the disciplines and the knowledge they produce, although education will also be concerned with questions of balance and adequate and accurate coverage of this material and theories of instruction. As Paterson points out, the former will involve reasoned value judgements and localized operational and management restraints. Brookfield suggests that American graduate programmes in the study of adult education are characterized by a preoccupation with operational problems of practice such as course planning, administration of courses, and instructional effectiveness. Brookfield is critical of this approach and regards it as demonstrating a lack of epistemological distinctiveness both in its failure, in its own terms, to achieve a coherent and uniquely adult form and content, and in its failure to draw upon substantive content from the conventional disciplines and education. In addition, Bright, Usher, and Armstrong draw attention to the curricular selection and coverage problems in adult education entailed by this definition of education. Brookfield does not recognize these problems explicitly, although Paterson does, but not in detail; and both of these, together with Bright, but to a lesser extent, could be regarded as accepting the possibility of an adequate resolution of them.

Having defined education in these terms, Paterson draws attention to the problematical nature of the often referred to objectives of adult education to promote social change, and the definition of adult educators' role as agents of social change. The point here is that if political objectives are admitted into education, then so, too, must the concepts of political responsibility and political mandate apply to educators, which, of course, they currently do not. The role of 'educator' is to educate and instruct others in the major types of knowledge and the methods by which knowledge can be identified, as defined by the disciplines. As will be discussed below, Griffin's approach to the definition of knowledge is couched in diametrically opposed terms.

Brookfield notes the recent demise of philosophical and political debate within American adult education in comparison with the historically earlier period of the 1920s and 1930s. At that time a political function for adult education was clearly discernible and was defined and justified in terms of the need for rational and informed scepticism within a democratic society. In making this point, Brookfield implicitly draws attention to the distinction between education, which has political objectives, and educational objectives, which include the necessity of discussing and rationally analysing political positions. Although the latter entails the objective of a democratic society, this can be regarded as politically 'open' in the specific political forms in which it may be achieved, none of which is prejudicially favoured or disadvantaged a priori, by the methods of rational analysis and criticism. In this sense Brookfield and Paterson (1979) concur, with the latter representing an earlier position in American adult education.

The radical view

Griffin is the major proponent of this view, although, as indicated earlier, Armstrong and Usher appear to agree differentially with the epistemological and ideological aspects it entails. The Frankfurt school's critical theory and Freire's critical pedagogy are drawn upon as the major interpretive framework, which, Griffin points out, have important epistemological implications and ramifications. Both these approaches suggest that knowledge is not homogeneous in the sense conveyed by the categories (i.e. disciplines, theories, concepts) of the conventional epistemological system. Rather, knowledge is heterogeneous, in that history, geography, politics, psychology, and sociology, for example, interact and overlap in the 'real' world, as opposed to the highly abbreviated, abstract and overly specialized, and therefore 'unreal', accounts found within the academic disciplines. Thus, for example, an individual person or event may be regarded as a simultaneous manifestation of physical, chemical, biological, psychological, sociological, historical, political, economic, cultural, and geographic phenomena. This approach to knowledge can be regarded as a 'holistic' account in which real phenomena and events comprise complex and reciprocally interactive clusters of intersecting experiences and aspects, which render the conventional epistemological categories derived, detached, and simplistic. In this respect, Bright's and Armstrong's references to the high levels of abbreviation and simplification of discipline-based knowledge within adult education, are regarded as more pertinent to the conventional disciplines themselves. In contrast to the view suggested by Griffin, conventional categorization of knowledge, and the real phenomena it is held to refer to, can be regarded as reductionistic, in that it attempts to summarize and reduce an essentially heterogeneous and complex manifold of events within limited and homogeneous categories. As such, so Griffin argues, it is essentially unreal, since it represents a division between what are regarded as 'legitimate' accounts of reality, which are unreal in this heterogeneous sense (i.e. they dichotomize and divorce knowledge from reality by imposing pre-formed categories upon it in a restrictive and abstract manner). From this perspective, the conventional disciplines are not regarded as corresponding to knowledge in any meaningful sense, and consequently they are discounted as erroneous. On epistemological grounds, therefore, the radical view rejects conventional disciplines as representing admissible and legitimate knowledge. Epistemologically this view can be regarded as falling within that termed 'contextualism'

191

(Pepper, 1942) in which, for example, all events and objects (including individual humans) are regarded as public (heterogeneous) rather than private (homogeneous) events because of their embeddedness within a multitude of contextual intersections. This can be applied to epistemology itself, such that the concept of a singular and independent 'psychological' fact or event, for example, is meangingless given the embeddedness of such events within social, economic, political, historical, and a host of other epistemological contexts. This finds its direct application within the study of adult education, which is interdisciplinary, and which raises the relationship between, and the validity of, the conventional homogeneous categorial disciplines. It may be suggested that for this reason it is no accident that approaches such as critical theory are attracted to adult education.

The conventional view would, obviously, have reservations about this approach and would suggest that although the approximate nature of conventional categories of knowledge is recognized in relation to complex localized contexts, the power of these general categories has been repeatedly demonstrated to be relevant and highly informative. This applies no less to the disciplines themselves, which have formed the major interpretive frameworks of the world, with an impressive and valid historical epistemological pedigree. In addition, the conventional approach would suggest the impossibility of studying the real world in the holistic and heterogeneous sense suggested by the radical view because of the complexity of the world - i.e. in order to comprehend the real world in an ordered, logical, and insightful manner, a degree of abstraction and categorization is necessary and, indeed, inevitable. This type of debate is very reminiscent of the 'holistic' versus 'molecular' (i.e. the sum of the parts is equal to the whole) debate frequently found within science generally and developmental psychology particularly (Lerner, 1976).

In addition to suggesting the false dichotomization between knowledge and reality, the radical perspective also suggests the existence of several other types of epistemological dichotomies which are propagated and entailed by the conventional approach to knowledge, and which result in this separation between knowledge and real events. Thus it is suggested that the conventional system imposes an absolute distinction between theory and practice in which the former is produced by one group of individuals in one context and is 'applied' by another group of individuals within a host of localized and heterogeneous contexts and situations. Griffin and Usher regard adult education as one obvious example of the 'application' of such formal theory. Similarly, and in order partly to support this distinction, subjective and objective are also regarded as distinctly separate such that the myth of 'objective' knowledge as the only valid knowledge is created and sustained. By this process and the logical and empirical methods it involves, the status of 'knowledge' is accorded only to those statements and views which conform to its methods and criteria and which can claim to be 'objective' because of them. The major villain in the creation of these false dichotomies is positivist logical and empirical method, or what Griffin refers to as 'instrumental rationality', which treats human and social issues in the same manner as science treats inanimate physical objects. Griffin accepts the use of the scientific model within the scientific domain, but rejects it within the sphere of human and social concerns and knowledge systems which attempt to describe and interpret these. For him, the social sciences are pseudo-scientific because they invoke and apply the scientific and positivist model, which he interprets as inappropriate. This is also Usher's and Armstrong's position, but is applied more in relation to adult education's use of conventional knowledge than in relation to the total abandonment of that knowledge. The radical view can be located within the reciprocal interaction school which draws the distinction between unidirectional models in physical science and reciprocal and circular models of interaction in the social sciences (Hultsch and Hickey, 1978, Lerner, 1978, Riegel, 1979). The latter invokes the ontologically inevitable interaction of the observer with the object of his/her observation, and the presence of a complex of inter-connected reciprocal interactions within and between numerous variables and dimensions, which confound categorical identification of events or phenomena. The conventional view may recognize the interconnected and reciprocally interactive nature of events, but would still insist upon the necessity and reality of formulating a logical understanding and conceptual categorization of such events, which defines the general nature of these events and their patterns of interaction.

In contrast to the 'false' dichotomization of subjective/objective, theory/practice, and knowledge/reality relations,

Overview and conclusions

Griffin suggests that these are dialectically related and fundamentally interconnected in a reciprocal and reflexive manner. Within this view, it is meaningless, epistemologically, to separate theory from practice, since formal theories themselves are the result of practice, and practice, whether or not informed by formal theory, contains -indeed, would be impossible without - some informal theoretical assumptive basis. This is also Usher's and Armstrong's position with regard to acknowledging informal knowledge as a vital, and, from their view, more important, source and definition of knowledge. Griffin, Usher, and Armstrong all suggest the value of 'praxis' in conceptualizing the dialectical relationship between theory and practice and the greater emphasis upon the latter as both a source of knowledge and an informing principle within education. Similarly, subjective/objective relations are relative, not absolute, concepts, since claims concerning the 'objectivity' of knowledge are relative to the interpretive and methodological assumptions underlying such claims. Again, this demonstrates the dialectical relationship between them. Usher and Paterson reflect, to some extent and with qualifications, this view when they both draw attention to the way in which socially and culturally accepted beliefs influence and form part of individuals' cognitive maps and beliefs. However, Paterson would argue that this demonstrates a logical rather than a dialectical relationship (in some sense which 'transcends' logic), since the distinction between individuals' subjective interpretations of cultural beliefs is easily and logically recognizable.

The radical view does not and cannot, within its own terms, base its objections to conventional epistemology solely upon epistemological criteria. A further, but crucial, extension of the epistemological implications stemming from this view involves the assertion that the conventional epistemological system is ideological in structure, content, and purpose. Within this view, knowledge is regarded as a function of the social context which produces it and whose objectives it represents and fulfils. Objective knowledge is discounted, all knowledge being regarded as relative to the context in which it occurs. Knowledge produced within a given context can have relevance only for that context and cannot be 'applied ' to other external contexts. A dialectical relationship is held to exist between a body of knowledge and its context such that knowledge expresses, legitimizes, and maintains the cultural perception and practices of the social and economic relations within that context. Knowledge is therefore regarded as a crucial determinant of cultural perceptions and expectations concerning the definition of reality within given contexts.

Griffin suggests that one of the most insidious dichotomies of the conventional system is that between means and ends, which, because it emphasizes means at the expense of ends, leads it to regard all objective formal knowledge as non-political. Within this view, the conventional adoption of the scientific model and its exclusive emphasis upon 'how' questions rather than 'why' questions have produced a type of epistemology within the social sciences which is concerned only with means and processes. Obviously, science and the social sciences are filled with 'why' questions, but these are framed in terms defined by the conventional system and the scientific model within which the alleged existence of 'objective' knowledge renders irrelevant the political and ideological. The application of this model to the social sciences has produced 'why' questions directed to the mechanistic explanation of events and their processes, which are politically and ideologically decontextualized and neutered. In this sense the 'why' questions of conventional epistemology are after, rather than before, the ideological and political fact. Within the dialectical and contextualist definition of knowledge, the radical view suggests, ideological influences are inescapable, and indeed are dominant in determining the method, content, objectives, and structure of the knowledge a given context must produce. The major part of a context, which can produce only knowledge relative to it, is defined by the ideological interests and objects residing within that context, and which the knowledge that is produced by it serves. In a manner reminiscent of Armstrong when discussing the hypocritical stance of some sociologists proclaiming the need for a 'humble' eclecticism with the proviso that it does not include Marxist sociology, Griffin suggests that conventional epistemology claims to be ideologically and politically neutral but is, in fact, ideological, precisely because it claims not to be. In other words, a non-ideological epistemology is impossible and the conventional system achieves a higher level of ideological power because it denies this by insisting upon 'objective' truth in the form of abstract, formal theories and perspectives. The villain of the piece within the radical view is 'instrumental rationality' (Griffin) in the guise of formal logic and positivist empiricalist methodology, which produce abstract and supposedly objective categories of 'legitimate' knowledge. Griffin suggests that the conventional epistemological system and its knowledge content reflect, legitimize, and perpetuate capitalist social and economic relations in the general sense that the disciplines and the role of formal, generalized theories and concepts embody the capitalist principle of the division of labour and its attendant unequal social and economic relations. Thus 'legitimate' knowledge is 'produced' by an elitist group of individuals for 'consumption' by another group of individuals of, presumably, inferior status. Similarly, the notion of a restricted number of 'sovereign' bodies of knowledge or concepts within which other phenomena can be interpretively forced, thereby manipulating cultural perceptions of reality, also finds its correlate in unfair social and economic relations.

Adult education is criticized by Griffin for representing the ideological assumptions and objectives of the conventional system. Although Griffin does not give an explicit definition of education, it would appear obvious that he regards education as necessarily concerned with exploring and identifying the ideological assumptions of the knowledge it uses, in the first instance this being directed to the conventional disciplines. For Griffin, the definition of being 'educated' is understanding the ideological basis of conventional epistemology and thereby the political forces and interests which shape not just conventional knowledge but a multitude of cultural and social phenomena. His suggested use of 'praxis' involving the dialectical relationship between all the dichotomies of the conventional system as a means of revealing social and economic interests is, therefore, an ideological praxis, informed by his general interpretive stance. As will be discussed further below, Usher likewise advocates 'praxis', but in epistemological rather than ideological terms. In this ideological sense, Griffin suggests that all theories must be reflective in examining and identifying their ideological interests and assumptions. The role of education is to engage in this reflexive process.

There are several criticisms which can be levelled at Griffin's view. First, the approach seems hypocritical and self-contradictory, since, in its own terms, the only legitimate area of study, application, and comment it can offer is in relation to itself. Whatever context generated the theory, the theory can have relevance only for that context and no other, the logical conclusion being that proponents of critical theory should employ their activities in reflexively exploring the ideological assumptions and interests of the theory itself and its proponents. To apply it to another context could be regarded as breaking its own rules. Griffin does recognize this problem and invokes the distinction between the direct but inappropriate application of a theory (e.g. Freire's critical pedagogy applied to the inner cities) and a theory having 'influence' upon another context. This could be regarded as a convenient 'ad hoc' and 'post hoc' addition to the theoretical structure in an attempt to avoid the criticism of reneging on its own principles.

Second, although the theory eschews formal theory and restrictive categorization, it represents, in this sense, the object of its own criticism, since recategorizing conventional epistemological dichotomies in terms which avoid their segregation is itself replacing one set of formal categories by another. Also, and as discussed above, this approach can be regarded as ontological in the sense that the alleged ideological basis of all knowledge is an absolute position. There is no reference to the possibly tentative nature of the theory or the possibility that it could be overtaken by future theories which may overcome the problems it identifies, within its own terms.

Third, although the objective of the approach is to abandon the conventional disciplines, it is interesting to note that Griffin emphasizes the need to focus upon the disciplines, albeit in order to reinterpret them. Although possibly superficial, this criticism would suggest that, rather than abandon the disciplines, this approach would emphasize them, but in a totally different manner to that suggested by the conventional approach.

Similarly, and fourth, it could be suggested that, to the extent that critical theory represents a position within conventional sociology, the radical view is internal, not external, to the conventional disciplines. Although Griffin does not discuss this, it may be assumed that critical theory would be defended as a non-disciplinary approach, or at least that its status within sociology is debatable.

Fifth, it can be argued, as intimated earlier, that this approach is itself ideological, the content, purpose, and structure of which it does not recognize. Paterson suggests this when discussing some objections to the social construction view of knowledge. He also suggests that, as an ideological and political theory, it has no political mandate or responsibility within education. In this sense both Griffin and Paterson are accusing each other's position of being ideological whilst maintaining the non-ideological nature of their own views. This may be truer of Paterson than Griffin, although the latter does not really discuss the ideological assumptions of the position he advocates. Logically, Griffin would have to accept that all theories and systems of knowledge are ideological, in which case, whilst Paterson eschews ideology within legitimate knowledge, Griffin would regard it as a given in all forms of knowledge, formal and informal, conventional and radical. The final criticism of the critical theory view of epistemology is that, although it is critical of what it regards as pseudo-science within the social sciences, it too could be criticized as such, since it is based on assumptions about logical method, i.e. dialectical logic. As indicated, Paterson regards this as a pseudo-logic which violates the principles of standard logic to suit its own ideological and epistemological interests, and is a further example of the critical sloppiness of much that is currently fashionable within the study of adult education.

Griffin clearly regards conventional epistemology, and the current conformity of adult education to it, as manifesting a deceptive and hypocritical paradox in the sense of eschewing political and ideological intentions whilst simultaneously expressing them. As indicated earlier, Brookfield and Paterson draw a distinction between political objectives in education and educational and epistemological objectives, which include the need for rational debate of political positions. Griffin would regard this as a further example of conventional political hypocrisy, since it is precisely because conventional epistemology divorces knowledge from reality that it can admit any subject for discussion. By imposing a detached, objective, abstract, and theoretical system of categories and criteria upon real phenomena it effectively disarms and neutralizes the real status of these phenomena within the world, and simultaneously maintains the view of the world it assumes. Political debate can readily be admitted within education precisely because the real force and importance of politics have been removed by placing them within an abstract, categorical, and depoliticized framework. The conventional view regards political positions as belief systems which, like all other beliefs, must be subject to rational scrutiny within education. If a political view demonstrates a logical origin in the strength of its arguments it may be accepted as valid epistemology. What others of a political inclination do with this particular view in the political sphere is not, and cannot be within this view, regarded as a concern of education, because it has no political mandate. The radical view would fully accept the necessity of political responsibility, but would insist that it can only be on the basis of a full and honest political agenda which includes the currently hidden political assumptions and objectives of conventional epistemology.

In discussing the demise and consequent absence of philosophical and political debate in American adult education, Brookfield indicates that this debate is very much in evidence within British adult education. The above discussion, and, indeed, the present book as a whole, would appear to testify to his conclusion. Brookfield suggests that although professional necessities lead to the view that such a debate signifies amateurism and immaturity, which contradict professional status, such a view itself is a product of a cultural ethos which specifies a narrow philosophical and political consensus. Pragmatism and capitalist, free-market politics and economics are the major interpretive frameworks within which adult education operates and which it expresses. In one sense, American adult education is a dramatic and stark demonstration of the radical view's claim that the political dimension infuses and informs the epistemological, to the extent of rendering political debate, as an epistemological and logical exercise, irrelevant. For the reasons discussed above, the radical view would regard either the presence or the absence of political debate, defined in these terms, as depoliticized, and therefore ideological, which renders British and American adult education identical. However, whilst the ideological may be more demonstrable within the American system, the British approach appears to raise political issues. Indeed, Brookfield suggests that because of the greater philosophical and political openness within the British system and Europe generally, a wider diversity of views and a greater receptivity to such diversity are present compared to the American system. Of course, the radical view suggests that such diversity is politically deceptive. Like Brookfield, Paterson would lament the absence of philosophical and political debate within American adult education on epistemological and educational, not ideological, grounds.

Brookfield would appear to define the radical view within British adult education as corresponding to the need, via adult education, to correct social and economic injustices characteristic of disadvantaged and oppressed groups in society. This is clearly present within Griffin's and Armstrong's references to unequal economic and social relations, although it could be suggested that the remit of the radical view, and its categorization of social groups as 'oppressed' via oppressive knowledge, extends to include a much wider population. For example, to the extent that the radical view can be accepted, although academics and intellectuals may gain social and economic advantage from adopting the conventional view of knowledge, they are also, by definition, oppressed epistemologically and politically. Indeed, more so, since they are attributed and come to regard themselves as experts in knowledge, yet they remain ignorant of or indifferent to, or critical of the alleged political bias of knowledge. Similarly, the middle-class managers of a capitalist, free-enterprise system, although gaining economically and socially, are also politically and epistemologically oppressed. It may be interesting to note that because of the presence of political debate within British adult education, Brookfield regards the latter as demonstrating a greater awareness of such issues in comparison to America. The radical and conventional views would appear to differ in terms of what they regard as demonstrating 'awareness' and in their definitions of a 'critical' debate.

In passing, it may also be pertinent to note that Brookfield regards the debate between the conventional and radical views in adult education as fundamentally irresolvable. As intimated earlier, this conclusion appears to have informed both Usher's and Armstrong's suggestion that adult education should redefine itself in terms of the practical rather than the exclusively theoretical.

Epistemological definition of knowledge

As indicated above, the third view of knowledge adopts a fundamentally more relativistic and tentative view of knowledge in comparison to the previous two views discussed. This may be because this position would appear not to be concerned (for good reasons rather than indifference) with the kind of debate represented by, or, to some extent, the total claims of, the earlier views. The position to be discussed below is one that corresponds mainly to Usher's view, although Armstrong and Bright, to a lesser extent, hold related positions. This view also corresponds to that which is critical of the conventional disciplines, but which suggests a modified role for them within education, generally, and in terms defined by a redefinition of education itself. This entails a redefinition of knowledge which admits both formal, conventional discipline knowledge and the informal knowledge residing within localized practice in heavily contextualized situations.

Usher is broadly sympathetic with Griffin's criticism of the inappropriate nature of the scientific model, but rather than criticize this in terms of its implications for conventional disciplines and knowledge, he restricts these criticisms to indicating the relative inappropriateness of such knowledge within education. Thus he is in full agreement with Griffin's view that conventional epistemology erroneously reserves the status of 'legitimate' knowledge to that produced by the conventional disciplines, which imposes a false epistemological dichotomy between formal, theoretical knowledge and its 'application' to other contexts. One such 'applied' context is education, which, by definition, is regarded by the proponents of the conventional system as possessing no other major source of knowledge to guide its activities. Correction of the latter assumption is one of the objectives, if not the major objective, of Usher's chapter. Similarly, Usher agrees with, and indeed offers a very interesting and illuminating exposition of, the dialectical relationship between contexts and the knowledge they produce, demonstrating the applicability of the theory/practice relationship within both conventional, formal epistemology and informal knowledge. However, this is directed towards establishing the presence of informal knowledge within localized practice in educational situations rather than demonstrating the inadequacy of conventional knowledge per se.

Usher is concerned with the problems that the conventional discipline model (i.e. the technical rationality model) creates for education, rather than with the broader epistemological and ideological issues they represent, as in Griffin's approach. However, it would be naive to assume that Usher is either unaware of or indifferent to these broader issues. Indeed, it could be suggested that because Usher envisages a future role for the disciplines within education and regards them as illustrating the theory-practice contextual relationship in terms of formal theory, he regards them as valid in their own terms and epistemological context, and would disagree with Griffin's ideological interpretation.

Usher does agree with Griffin that conventional definitions of formal theory are detached and divorced from reality, even though they are assumed by their proponents to reveal the nature of the world. Usher suggests that formal theories cannot be 'mapped' on to practice and context-ualized situations, because they are decontextualized and abstract. Within this position, Usher emphasizes the role of value judgements in defining localized practical contexts and the inability of formal, discipline-based knowledge to take account of these. To this extent Usher agrees with Griffin, but not with the latter's extension of this position into a comprehensive societal and cultural level of ideological and political invasion. Also, unlike Griffin, Usher accepts formal knowledge as a source of useful paradigms, sensitizing concepts and metaphors within education, and thus accepts their utility in a general and allegorical, rather than a literal or 'foundational', sense. He suggests that the conventional interpretation of the role of the disciplines within education in this foundational sense produces problems. One of these is the selection problem referred to by Bright, and represented by the large degree of intra-disciplinary eclecticism of theories and interpretations, all of which suggest competing and often contradictory definitions of what are the relevant 'facts'. Another problem is represented by the interdisciplinary nature of education and the competing eclecticism this produces in terms of a collection of independent disciplines, all of which claim the intrinsic merit of their particular orientation towards the world. Armstrong also raises very similar issues when he discusses the complex nature of sociological theory and the difficulty of teaching this level of complexity within education. Also, the interdisciplinary nature of education causes problems in the demands made upon students to become socialized in several complex disciplines when the students typically do not possess a basic familiarity with any of them. Similarly, Armstrong raises the selection issue within sociology and its attendant problem of alleged bias from different academic quarters within it, thus demon-strating the inherent problems of attempting to import and 'apply' discipline knowledge in a direct manner. In addition, and perhaps more important, Armstrong suggests the view that an academic and critical mode of thinking is incompatible with the practice and activity represented by education, thus further questioning the validity of discipline-based knowledge within education. This is also a theme within Usher in his emphasis, following de Castell and Freeman (1978), upon education as a field of practice rather than a 'field' of knowledge within the conventional system. Usher also draws attention to the pseudo-scientific character of the social sciences and the methodological criticisms of ecological invalidity, unrepresentativeness, and lack of objectivity. These criticisms further demonstrate the divorce of discipline-based knowledge from reality and practical contexts which involve action in the world rather than knowledge of the world. This is also a major theme of Griffin's analysis and critique of conventional epistemology. However, Griffin interprets informed action in the world in an exclusively ideological sense; Usher is more concerned with action within localized contexts.

An interesting point of difference which emerges from Usher's chapter is that, although he suggests that the adoption of the conventional epistemological model has resulted in an imbalance between rigour (i.e. defined by adherence to the conventional model) and relevance (i.e. practical relevance) in which the latter has been sacrificed for the former, this would appear to contradict the views of Paterson, Bright, and Brookfield, who suggest the lack of academic rigour within adult education. If these views are seen collectively, adult education could be regarded as lacking both rigour and relevance, which could be regarded, in Bright's terms, as indicating adult education's uncertain, ambivalent, and hypocritical stance in relation to its own definition as either a theoretical or a practical activity. Usher is correct, although adult education could be interpreted as more oriented in intention, rather than products, towards academic rigour.

The major point of Usher's position is that it admits into the domain of 'legitimate knowledge' both conventional epistemology and informal knowledge which is necessarily found within local, practical contexts, with the obvious emphasis being upon the latter within education. A major distinction is drawn between theoretical and practical knowledge. The former is defined in scientific and universal terms which offer insights into the nature of the world, whereas the latter is defined by the need to act appropriately in the world. Invoking the theory-practice dialectical relationship, any action in the world must involve information and knowledge. Conventional discipline knowledge, by definition, is abstract, general, and decontextualized in terms of heterogeneous operational circumstances and value judgements within and relative to local situations. Therefore, informal knowledge must reside within local contexts and is, indeed, defined and produced by those local contexts which ensure its relevance and appropriateness. An important characteristic of practical knowledge, and echoing a theme of Griffin's, is that it is reflexive and hermeneutic. Unlike theoretical knowledge, its outcomes cannot be predicted and are therefore fundamentally subject to revision because of the importance of the social consequences and outcomes they necessarily lead to, and also because each local practical situation is different from others and represents a differential set of factors and considerations. The contextual dependence of knowledge renders informal knowledge heterogeneous and contingent, which necessarily prevents application of informal knowledge in one context to another and which entails the need to review and reformulate appropriate knowledge on each occasion. The application of bland formulae and categories emanating from the conventional disciplines is also inadequate. In addition, Usher suggests that the 'application' of universal laws and principles to practical situations is never literal, since the latter always mediate the former, and to this extent the universal is always changed as a result of its application to the particular. Within this Usher suggests a reciprocal interaction between the universal and the particular, thus indicating a qualified relevance for theoretical knowledge, but not a foundational one, within practical situations. In one sense, Usher seems to be suggesting that theoretical knowledge has its place as such and its declared objective of 'theoretical' understanding is valid and useful. However, its relevance in practical situations and the real world, characterized by the need for committed, informed, responsible, but fundamentally contextualized action, is very limited. The distinction between an ivory-tower 'theory for its own sake' position, and that suggesting the need for practical and responsible action in the real world dealing with the complex operational and moral dilemmas it often entails, is evident. Also, it is not just practical knowledge which is characterized by reflexivity and a hermeneutic imperative, for theoretical knowledge can also - indeed, should - be interpreted within this approach in order to understand the nature of contexts that produced it, and to understand more fully the nature of the knowledge it represents. Usher, later in his chapter, suggests that such an approach to conventional theoretical knowledge is relevant within education as a further illustration of the contextual dependence and dialectical relationship between theory and practice and knowledge and their contexts. This echoes a theme found within Griffin, but again does not entail the ideologically informed abandonment of the disciplines. Similarly, and in contrast to Armstrong, Usher appears to accept the retention of the categories represented by the disciplines within the approach he suggests. Armstrong can be regarded as advocating a similar approach in his reference to the need for 'praxis' but suggests that this would 'cut across' traditional discipline boundaries.

Both Usher and Armstrong advocate the need for a 'praxical' definition of education. Usher defines this in terms of the dialectical relationship between informal theory and practice residing in practical situations. He also, as indicated above, recognizes the existence of this relationship within formal theory but suggests that, although this relationship can be used to understand the origin of formal theory, the latter cannot be 'applied' to practical situations in a literal sense. Informal theory and practical knowledge, in contrast to formal theory, are applied directly to local situations, and a 'praxical' approach to education involves identifying the informal knowledge that practitioners use and its relationship to the context which generated it and to which it is applied. Within this process formal theory can be analysed in a similar 'praxical' manner and can be used to inform, in a metaphorical sense, interpretation and understanding of informal knowledge. Armstrong also suggests the need for a 'praxical' approach to education, and although he does not elaborate this concept, it may be assumed that he does agree with the general statements of Usher with regard to the dialectical nature of 'praxis'. In addition, Armstrong clearly indicates that the type of theoretical debate concerning the conventional role of disciplines within education is misplaced and irrelevant within education defined in a practical manner. However, Armstrong also clearly accepts Griffin's view concerning the ideological nature of the conventional disciplines and the manner in which this is reduced to a technicist profess-ionalism. Usher also recognizes this when he distinguishes between practical knowledge and technical knowledge, the latter conforming to the conventionally accepted direct application of formal knowledge. In this sense Usher is seeking to redefine education from technical knowledge to practical and 'praxical' knowledge. Armstrong agrees with this; however, his close affinity with Griffin's ideological interpretation suggests an ideologically based 'praxis' in which the objective would be to remove discipline based boundaries within education. This may refer only to the need to adopt meta-discipline paradigms and/or the total indifference to discipline labels in education when using formal knowledge. Conversely, it may refer to the ideological interpretation and definition of education which Griffin suggests. Such considerations point to the different definitions of 'praxis' and suggest a distinction between an ideological praxis and a practical praxis. Griffin would discount this distinction as meaningless, since for him all practice is ideological. An alternative approach to these differences is to suggest either that praxis can be defined differentially in relation to its objectives (political versus non-political) or in relation to the scale of its remit (social, cultural versus local).

Having outlined the nature of this approach to the definition of knowledge and education, it may be pertinent to consider some of the criticisms that can be made of it. First, there is the need to bear in mind Paterson's objections to the theory of social praxis discussed earlier. Of particular note is the view that the essence of praxis resides in the processes it refers to, i.e. the dialectical interrelationship between theory and practice. None of the contributors offers a detailed account or detailed examples of these processes. Although subject to the criticism of conventionalist terminology and approach, it may be suggested that if the theory of praxis is a valid theory, it could reasonably be expected to demonstrate the recognition of some broad categories by which this process could be identified and understood. Although the content of informal knowledge within local, practical contexts is necessarily contingent and unpredictable, the method by which their relationship and process are revealed could be expected to display some continuities, albeit in broad and general terms. The counter-argument to this criticism is that it demonstrates the conventional approach and imposes a dichotomy between content and method. Griffin's and Usher's view that conventional epistemology and its methods result in a process and prediction-oriented ethos has relevance here.

Presumably the essence of praxis is that it is not only the content of informal knowledge and its context which are contingent, but also the detailed processes by which their dialectical relationship finds expression, and hence cannot be identified or stipulated a priori.

Another type of criticism of the current view is that, although it advocates the necessity of a 'practical' and 'praxical' approach, it does so in formal theoretical terms. Although the view recognizes the existence of practice underlying formal theory, it stipulates the relative lack of relevance of formal theory to practical situations, which must involve the simultaneous and reciprocal existence of informal knowledge and action. In this sense it may be regarded as contradicting its own position, or at least suggesting the further distinction between a theoretical approach to praxis and a practical approach to praxis. The latter approach may be recommended on logical consistency grounds, and also because a 'theoretical' approach to praxis becomes embroiled within theoretical arguments and distinctions so reminiscent of formal theory and the conventional disciplines. The advocates of praxis may wish to circumnavigate this type of debate, which they may regard as obscuring and preventing the truly practical approach to education they suggest.

A futher criticism of the present view is that it may accelerate current tendencies within adult education towards a technicist professionalism. These tendencies are recognized by Usher, Griffin, and Armstrong within the terms of the conventional adoption of the theoretical discipline model within education, within which formal theories and perspectives are regarded as an educator's tool kit with which learning problems may be 'diagnosed' and corrected. If this is happening with theoretical knowledge, as Armstrong, Griffin, Usher, and Bright suggest, how much greater is the danger of its happening within a praxical education which focuses upon practitioner informal theory and local contexts. Usher, Armstrong, and Griffin all suggest that the praxical approach is an attempt to prevent the further development of professionalism defined in technicist terms, and although this approach will focus upon heterogeneous situations and knowledge, it is suggested that this may result in formal and generalized statements concerning informal knowledge and local contexts, which could then form the basis of a more informed and consequently dangerous technicism. Griffin is the only contributor who recognizes the technicist danger to the incorporation of critical theory within the conventional approach, which would reduce it to another item on the technical-rationality curriculum. This, presumably, is one reason why he suggests the total abandonment of the conventional model.

As indicated, Paterson disagrees with the validity of the theory of praxis on logical grounds. In addition, he would also appear to take issue with the notion that his view effectively ignores local operational and contextual circumstances as important sources of influence and knowledge. Whilst formal knowledge from the disciplines may be regarded as primary, its mediation by local factors is accepted, as is, indeed, the possibility that such alteration may lead to or suggest new discoveries in formal knowledge.

Brookfield refers to pragmatism as a culturally pervasive informing ethos within American society generally and adult education particularly. He also regards the curricular content of graduate programmes in adult education as essentially concerned with operational problems of practice. Given the above discussion of 'praxis' and practical action, what relation does this have to American pragmatic practice in adult education? Brookfield suggests a thoroughly political instrumental account of pragmatism within American adult education practice. The major result and manifestation of this is the consumerist and operational definition of adult education in which 'adult education' is inverted to mean the 'education of adults' and within which adult education is defined by its clientele. This admits and represents a service-oriented and 'felt needs' rationale, which expresses the capitalist themes of humanistic individualism, democracy, and quantitative measurement of customer satisfaction and professional efficiency. The theoretical and methodological underpinning of this approach is andragogy (Bright and Griffin suggest the predominance of humanistic psychology within this), with its definition of adults as self-directed learners, and participatory and independent learning methods, the result of which is the negotiated curriculum. From this perspective, the practice of adult education has largely been transferred to the student/s, the tutor's role being defined as that of facilitating individual and collective student learning needs. Consequently, curricula within American graduate adult education programmes reflect organizational and administrative functions, although some curricular content is devoted to instructional effectiveness, which, presumably, comprises andragogical principles. Brookfield's reference to the greater organizational and administrative role of American adult educators, in comparison with British adult educators, may be correct, although he seems to imply that this is a cause of operational curricula rather than a result of it. In the British context it is interesting to note that Paterson refers to adult education surrendering the curricula to students in terms of optional modules from which students select course structures. This is an order of magnitude removed from the American negotiated curriculum, but is informed by the same question concerning the role of adult educators and the nature and status of the epistemology they draw upon. Paterson and Brookfield, from their respective cultural and epistemological positions, both suggest the need for greater reference to, and inclusion of, more substantive epistemology within adult education as defining the practical educational activity of adult educators and adult education.

The pragmatism of American adult education seems to represent a paradox. On the one hand, its conceptual and methodological base is very narrow, and indeed, this is possibly the major point of Brookfield's chapter. On the other hand, it is characterized by a pluralistic and heterogeneous manifestation of forms, types, and objectives. The radical view would possibly suggest a solution to this paradox in the terms of Marcuse's (1974) notion of repressive tolerance and the distinction between apparent but specious external forms and fundamental, internal forms.

From the perspective of Usher's and Armstrong's suggested need for a 'praxical' and practical approach within British adult education, American pragmaticism appears antithetical to the intention of examining and exploring the nature of the informal theory practitioners use within localized contexts. As Brookfield suggests, American adult educators appear to be reluctant to consider the need to examine their practice, which they interpret, paradoxically, as unpragmatic and unprofessional. In this sense American adult education practice represents a self-fulfilling prophecy either because the principles of practice (i.e. andragogy) are regarded as inviolate and/or because those principles justify a pluralistic methodology which justifies the impossibility and irrelevance of examining practice. Another aspect, of course, is that the consumerist orientation abandons not only curricular content but also practice, since, as Brookfield suggests, the definition of good professional practice is to give students (customers) what they want.

COMMON THEMES

It may be suggested that within the above discussion four common themes are evident. The contributors adopt different perspectives within these, but they may represent useful dimensions and 'pegs' by which to identify the major positions of the contributors. The suggested four themes are: (1) internal versus external orientation relative to conventional disciplines, (2) formal theory versus informal theory and praxis, (3) political versus non-political, (4) formal logic versus dialectical logic. In view of the lengthy discussion of the first three dimensions represented by the present chapter up to this point, it is proposed to restrict current discussion to the topic and dimension of logic. As indicated earlier, the writer is aware of the conceptual complexity this area represents and his own lack of knowledge within it. However, because of its importance to the positions adopted by the contributors, it is necessary to outline briefly what seem to be the major differences in their approaches to logic which themselves, and axiomatically, define their approaches to knowledge.

As indicated above, the conventional view insists upon the need to identify homogeneous categories in a formal manner, which involves the formulation of theories and categorization of phenomena in a logically and empirically acceptable manner. This involves the law of identity within formal logic and specifies that A cannot simultaneously equal non-A, which it regards as a logical contradiction. Although it necessitates the stipulation of criteria by which homogeneous groups of phenomena, concepts, and laws may be identified, tested, and accepted, it does not insist that such group membership, concepts, or laws are exclusive, and readily accepts that membership of other groups and the relevance of other concepts and laws may also apply to a given phenomenon. What it does insist upon is that the relevance of other categorical criteria do not contradict the criteria governing the original categorization. Thus, for example, it would be illogical to accept the statement that 'All rich men are fat,' if the associated definitions of 'rich' and 'fat' were constructed to contradict and exclude each other. However, in the absence of such or any definitions of these terms, the statement is logical, since its content does not specify any grounds for substantiating a logical contradiction. The law of identity seeks to discover and remove logical contradiction by necessitating and examining clearly stated properties, concepts, and inferences. This is prevalent within the physical sciences and social sciences, where theories are required to demonstrate logical cohesion and consistency such that derived hypotheses are correctly based upon logical premises and propositions and do not involve self-contradiction or circularity of definition.

In contrast to formal logic, dialectical logic suggests the necessity to consider all phenomena as containing contradiction. This is based on the assumption that all phenomena demonstrate and are characterized by inevitable and dynamic change, which logically suggests that things do not remain static and are thus continually contradicting their previous identities. This contravenes formal logic's law of identity. Thus an individual human being is not exactly the same today as he/she was yesterday, or even a moment ago, since the large number of biological and chemical processes taking place within the human body will continuously, albeit marginally, change the chemical and biological profile of the individual. Similarly, psychological, social, and physical (e.g. weather, climate) influences are all regarded as interacting and changing the individual on a continuous basis. Within this approach, contradiction is an inevitable characteristic of all phenomena, animate and inanimate. Thus the moment an individual's life begins is also the moment he/she begins to die, the relationship between life and death being regarded as reciprocal, interactive, and relative. A similar view is adopted of the dialectical relationship between an individual and the various contexts within which he/she exists, in which each influences the others and therefore represents an indivisible complex of continuous interaction within which identifiable boundaries between self and context are meaningless. Similarly, theory and practice, means and ends, content and method, and subjective and objective distinctions are regarded as hopelessly interconnected such that each implies and defines the other. They contradict each other, yet mutually and simultaneously coexist and cannot be separated because of their interdependence and reciprocal relationship.

211

Overview and conclusions

As indicated earlier, Paterson regards dialectical logic as a pseudo-logic or rhetoric which professes to break the rules of formal logic in order to admit the political and ideological within epistemology, to serve the ideological interests of its proponents. It could be argued that the 'dialectical' relationships suggested by this type of logic are recognizable as logical rather than dialectical relationships within formal logic. The latter does recognize their relational existence, but in terms which deny their mutual contradiction and relative definition, and which insist upon independent definitions of each of them whilst recognizing their logical relations to other concepts. Formal logic would also accept that, although change is continuous, in many respects the scale (e.g. molecular) or rate (e.g. geological) of change is such that to all intents and purposes it can be ignored, and that in a fundamental sense the law of identity and the continuity and homogeneity of identity is retained and demonstrable within phenomena.

Griffin and Usher (Armstrong also, implicitly) adopt a negative attitude towards technical and instrumental rationality and the formal logic which underlies it, because of its epistemological divisiveness and homogeneous categorization of knowledge. As indicated, Usher accepts formal logic and its products in the theoretical disciplines, but takes issue with its direct application to education, which he regards as inappropriate.To the extent that Usher and Armstrong advocate the redefinition of education in praxical terms, a concept which is based on dialectical logic and the reciprocal relationship between informal knowledge and practice, they accept dialectical logic. However, Usher also accepts a role for formal logic and formal theory within education, and so he would appear to accept both types of logic. Griffin would appear to accept dialectical logic only within the social sciences, although he accepts the value of formal logic within the physical sciences. In addition, Usher's acceptance of both formal and informal knowledge and their interaction within the social sciences could be regarded as demonstrating a truly dialectical perspective, since he recognizes their mutual contradiction in some senses (e.g. theoretical/practical, means/ends, universal/ particular, objective/subjective), and he also recognizes their interaction and similarity (e.g. context-dependent, emerged from practice, interpretive).

OTHER MAJOR ISSUES

The discussion so far has attempted to locate the contributors' views of adult education within a general framework, which has involved the definition of knowledge, education, and the role of the disciplines within and outside education. Within this approach some attempt has also been made to suggest both stark and subtle contrasts, contradictions and similarities between the positions adopted by the contributors. There are, however, several remaining areas of importance to adult education which, although often mentioned in passing, are either implicitly or explicitly referred to by the contributors and which, therefore, require comment and discussion. These areas comprise the following issues:

1   Adult education: a clash of disciplines?
2   Professionalism within adult education.
3   Adult education for adult educators?

Each of these areas will be discussed in turn, after which the present chapter will conclude with an outline and discussion of each of the contributors' suggested future directions which adult education should adopt.

Adult education: a clash of disciplines?

The title of this sub-section is prompted by the notion that although the study of adult education is generally accepted, at least as it is currently constituted, as an inter-disciplinary area of study and practice, it could be suggested that some views within the present book represent the competing positions of different disciplines both within and external to adult education. This may, indeed, be predictable within the conventional, vertically independent structure of the disciplines, and has been alluded to earlier. In more detail, however, it may be suggested that Paterson and Griffin represent the competing and conflicting interests of philosophy and sociology, respectively, with the different types of logic subsumed within these loyalties. Of course, this position is too simplistic, since there may be branches of philosophy and sociology that Paterson and Griffin, respectively, would not wish to be associated with. For Paterson this would correspond, presumably, with that

213

philosophical orientation which is sympathetic to the dialectical interpretation, and for Griffin, by his own admission, functionalist sociology would not appear to be a feasible option. In addition, as discussed, there is some doubt concerning the status of Griffin's view within sociology; however, as a tentative indication of its discipline location, critical theory is taught in British universities in departments of sociology. It may also be pertinent to repeat that Paterson's claims concerning the pre-eminence of logical criticism in adult education could equally apply to all the disciplines. Similarly, Griffin's ideological epistemology view would also apply to all the disciplines. It should also be noted that Griffin is particularly critical of the predominance of psychology, albeit one type of psychology (i.e. humanistic), within current adult education and suggests the need for sociological and political analysis.

From this brief consideration emerges the possibility that adult education, precisely because it is inter-disciplinary, is subject to epistemological competition and tension among the different disciplines, and that some of the views presented above reflect this. Paterson would reject this, since his major claim for philosophy is in terms not of substantive content but of logical method, and in the example given earlier concerning his view of the social construction of knowledge theory he obviously feels that he can accurately and logically discriminate between philosophical and other discipline terrains. In this sense, Paterson also indicates his view that critical theory concerns sociological issues. Griffin would, presumably, discount the suggestion that critical theory is a sociological theory, preferring to regard it as a non-disciplinary theory within which the irritating and irrational epistemological conflicts produced by the false homogeneous categorization of knowledge by the conventional disciplines are avoided. Armstrong, too, would appear to suggest a similar orientation in his view that praxis within education would 'cut across' discipline boundaries. Both these positions, however, may represent perspectives informed by sociology.

This issue again raises the questions of the definition of knowledge and its relation to education. More particularly, it suggests that adult education imports epistemological conflicts and issues endemic within any definition of knowledge adopted. The conventional, radical, and mixed (i.e. Usher and Armstrong) views define the nature of the problems currently experienced by adult education's epistemological constitution differently, but all would admit the existence of epistemological tensions and problems within the view they advocate. From their different perspectives, the nature and scale of the problems avoided are obviously regarded as infinitely superior to the problems inherited by adoption of their views.

Professionalism within adult education

Paterson and Brookfield appear to suggest a prescriptive definition of the 'professional' within adult education in intellectual and academic terms in relation to the role of an 'educator' as one who is educated and who educates others in substantive epistemological content and method based within the conventional disciplines. Brookfield regards this as a necessary remedial response to current definitions in American adult education, which emphasize a consumerist and narrowly based technicism which largely excludes substantive or comprehensive epistemological content, and leads to the absence of informed and critical debate. Indeed, Brookfield explicitly states that the emergence of profess-ional institutionalization with the formation of the Commission of Professors in Adult Education in 1964 meant the demise of philosophical and political debate within the profession, and a concomitant rush towards a questionable conceptual and methodological position, which was more acceptable to the demands of a pragmatic profession within a pragmatic culture. Paterson, too, regards British adult education as representing the adoption of many questionable positions; however, this is within the context of the presence of philosophical and political debate, rather than, as in the American case, its absence. In this sense, Paterson is critical of the level and accuracy of debate, whereas Brookfield is critical of the absence of debate. More particularly, Paterson is critical of the current level of debate within British adult education because it already displays consumerist tendencies within its epistemology in the guise of 'belief packages' and fashionable dogma.

Bright, too, adopts something of this approach, and seems to suggest that, at university level, part of the professional role definition of an educator must involve a detailed and informed familiarity with formal theoretical knowledge and its methods in some recognized epistemo-logical area. He goes further and suggests that, because

215

adult education is interdisciplinary, there is a case for extending this professional epistemological remit beyond a single discipline, possibly in the area of epistemology itself, which may offer metadisciplinary frameworks within which some common, but general, frameworks may be available. However, Bright regards this as only part of the definition of the role of an adult educator, and accepts the position suggested by Usher and Armstrong concerning the need for a 'praxical' approach which focuses upon informal practitioner knowledge. In the latter approach, although there is a role for formal theoretical knowledge, the emphasis is upon the redefinition of education and adult education as a practical activity which involves a complementary and crucial body of knowledge at the informal, practical level. Although this approach could be regarded as an 'easy' option, one which surrenders the curriculum to the students in the manner that Brookfield and Paterson are critical of, and which runs the risk of becoming technicist and consumer-oriented, it can be argued that it will become technicist only if it attempts to diagnose practical problems in a fixed and restrictive manner. The major point of the praxical approach is that it seeks to encourage practitioners reflexively to identify the relationship between informal knowledge and practical activity within a given situation and to recognize that each situation is different. In this sense it seeks to make explicit, elaborate, and expand the cognitive 'maps' and informal theories practitioners use in local situations. It attempts to do what Paterson suggests concerning the need to elaborate and differentiate between a larger number of world-views, but does so in practical, informal, rather than formal, theoretical terms. It also attempts to draw a parallel between the theory/practice relationship in both formal (i.e. conventional discipline-based theory) and informal contexts. In addition, as Usher notes, much of practitioner informal knowledge and the practice it leads to may be relatively rigid and habit-formed. This suggests the possibility, and difficulty, of creating a deeper understanding and realization of alternative ways of interpreting situations, establishing newer and more appropriate informal theories, and formulating a richer repertoire of possible practical activities within given situations. Within this whole process the 'professional' status of the teacher may not be very apparent; indeed, in attempting to draw the parallel between formal and informal knowledge, this approach seeks to remove the superiority of the teacher implicit in the conventional technical knowledge definition of education. However, the 'praxical' approach is not another version of the American negotiated curriculum. Although it may contain an explicit emphasis upon the experience of the students, this relates to their professional rather than personal lives. Similarly, although the 'praxical' approach may not be able to specify a curriculum in detail because its content is dependent upon the practical problems focused upon by the practitioner students, it can specify informal practitioner-based knowledge and action as its focus and is, therefore, not totally open-ended.

Armstrong agrees with the 'praxical' approach to the definition of adult education and the professional role within it, although it is not clear precisely what he means by this in comparison to Usher's approach. However, Armstrong makes an interesting point when he suggests that critical mode thinking, the objective of Paterson, Brookfield, Bright, and even Griffin, is incompatible with the professional execution of teaching activity. The general distinction suggested is that teachers act, then think, whereas critical thinking involves thought, then action. The extreme interpretation of this view would suggest that all theoretical knowledge should be abandoned within education, and that prescriptive practical teaching skills should be specified and competence levels enforced within the profession. Armstrong does not suggest this, and he can be regarded as accepting the 'praxical' approach, with its practical emphasis. It is worth noting that Armstrong sees the role of formal theory within education defined practically and as ignoring discipline boundaries, thus indicating he pre-eminence of practical problems within education and the totally unhindered and unrestricted use of any formal theory which can help either further understanding, or resolution, of the problem irrespective of its status within conventional formal knowledge.

In similar terms to that discussed of the 'praxical' approach, the radical view would also dispute the label 'professional' on ideological and epistemological grounds. Within this approach, the sole purpose of individuals working within education, and the sole purpose of education itself, is to reveal and examine ideological and political interests that are served, maintained, and legitimated by knowledge. Griffin suggests, for example, that adult education could exercise its educational function more responsibly by analysing the social and economic interests of the propagators of andragogy and the way these were served, maintained, and legitimated by that theory.

Adult education for adult educators?

All the contributors and their different views clearly and strongly point to the need for adult educators to be better informed and educated with respect to the positions advocated. As indicated earlier, this may be difficult either to accept or to realize, given the professional insecurity that appears to pervade adult education in both Britain and America. Whether adult educators should take courses in philosophy, psychology, sociology, the theory of 'praxis' within education, or epistemology is an open question. But the necessity for a change in orientation within adult education, and the logic of establishing it upon firmer epistemological and methodological grounds than is currently the case would appear to be inevitable.

REFERENCES

de Castell, S., and Freeman, H. (1978) 'Education as a socio-practical field: the theory/practice question reformulated', Journal of Philosophy of Education 12: 13-28.

Hultsch, D.F., and Hickey, T. (1978) 'External validity in the study of human development: theoretical and methodological issues', Human Development 21: 76-91.

Lerner, R. M. (1976) Concepts and Theories of Human Development, Reading, Mass.: Addison-Wesley.

—— (1978) 'Nature, nurture and dynamic interactionism', Human Development 21: 1-20.

Marcuse, H. (1974) One-dimensional Man, London: Abacus.

Paterson, R.W.K. (1979) Values, Education and the Adult, London: Routledge & Kegan Paul.

Pepper, S.C. (1942) World Hypotheses, 1961 edition, Berkeley, Cal.: University of California Press.

Riegel, K.F. (1979) Foundations of Dialectical Psychology, New York: Academic Press.

Chapter nine

REJOINDERS AND FURTHER COMMENTS

R.W.K. Paterson, Paul F. Armstrong, and Robin S. Usher

SOME REMARKS ON LOGIC

R.W.K. Paterson

As a professional philosopher and public teacher of philosophy, I find that there is a widespread misunderstanding of the nature and scope of logic. Thus religiously oriented members of extra-mural classes will often comment, on some ordinary logical point in the philosophy of religion, 'Ah yes, but these matters [e.g. God's apparent toleration of innocent suffering] are above human logic.' I cannot count the occasions when, teaching some topic in ethics or social philosophy, I have heard otherwise intelligent people say, 'Yes, but life isn't logical, is it?' or 'No doubt, but you are forgetting that people aren't always logical.'

Perhaps this is because (unlike, say, algebra) clear thinking does not figure as an identifiable subject on the curriculum of most schools. At any rate I now know better than to reply that logic is not about the divine plan, or about life, or about people, since such a reply leaves the hearer in his cosy assumption that logic is quite irrelevant to his cherished beliefs on these topics. I now reply, plainly and correctly, that logic is the study of the consistency of beliefs, whether the beliefs in question concern God, life, human nature, or whatever, and that the only way to avoid logical criticism is to abstain from holding or stating beliefs. This seems to be a self-denying ordinance which few of the critics of logic are willing to put into practice. Indeed, it is noticeable that, when logic appears to favour their beliefs, they welcome it as an ally; but, when it appears to threaten their beliefs, they denounce it as sterile, narrow, and artificial.

The yoke of logic is in fact a very gentle one. Basically all it requires of us is the acknowledgement that at least one of two mutually inconsistent beliefs is false. Of the two propositions, 'The richest 10 per cent of the population are currently paying less tax than they were five years ago' and 'The richest 10 per cent of the population are currently paying more tax than they were five years ago', at least one must be false. Of course they might both be false, since the people in question might be paying exactly the same amount in tax today as they were five years ago. If the original propositions had read '... are currently paying less tax ...' and '... are not currently paying less tax ...', we would have known, not only that one of the propositions must be false, but also that one of them must be true. And that is virtually all that logic has to tell us about these propositions. Logic alone cannot tell us which of them is true. For that we need the empirical knowledge of the economist or the fiscal expert.

Nor can logic tell us which of the separate propositions given above are false. However, if we combine pairs of these propositions to form compound propositions, logic can tell us which of these compound propositions are necessarily false. For example, 'The richest 10 per cent of the population are currently paying both more tax and less tax than they were five years ago'. This proposition is necessarily false because it is self-contradictory. If I follow the statement that 'Peter is paying more tax than in 1984' by the statement that 'Peter is paying less tax than in 1984', the effect of the second statement is simply to cancel out the first, leaving no coherent statement on the table for intelligent discussion. Either statement on its own is self-consistent and therefore, as far as logic is concerned, may be either true or false. But the compound statement formed by combining these mutually inconsistent statements is self-contradictory and hence, by logic alone and without knowing anything whatsoever about amounts of tax actually paid in 1984 and 1989, we can know that it cannot possibly be true, that it is necessarily false.

Obviously, in declaring the proposition, 'The richest 10 per cent of the population are currently paying both more tax and less tax than they were five years ago', to be self-contradictory, I am assuming that the terms used in the proposition do not change their meanings in the course of the proposition. If 'pay more tax' meant 'pay a greater total amount of money in tax' while 'pay less tax' meant 'pay a smaller proportion of their income in tax', the whole proposition might still be empirically false but it would no longer be self-contradictory. Although 'Both p and non-p' enshrines a formal contradiction, there is no logical contradiction whatever in asserting 'Both p^1 and non-p^2'. Because ordinary language (unlike the notations used in symbolic logic) is often fraught with highly ambiguous terms ('freedom', 'equality', 'democracy', 'education', and so on), it is often the case that seeming contradictions are not really contradictions, and also that seemingly consistent sets of propositions embody hidden contradictions. For this and other reasons an important task of philosophy - as the application of logic to beliefs typically expressed in relatively informal language - is to try to state our moral, political, religious, and other beliefs with as much logical clarity as possible, so that unavowed assumptions and concealed implications can be brought into the daylight and tested for their overall mutual consistency.

What is styled 'dialectical logic' is commonly referred to by its apostles as if it were some kind of alternative to, or rival of, standard logic. Now indisputably there are problematic topics in the more advanced spheres of logic, as there are in mathematics; and undoubtedly logicians can make mistakes, as can mathematicians. But these problems need to be resolved, and the mistakes rectified, using the procedures appropriate to formal logic and mathematics. There is no place here for 'dialectical logic' any more than for 'dialectical arithmetic'. 'Reasoning' by 'dialectical logic' would deserve the same suspicion - indeed, indignation - which we would show towards a crooked financier who, using 'dialectical book-keeping', tried to convince us that £5 million and £5 million equalled £20 million. To revel in logical contradictions demonstrates that the reveller is deeply muddled, irresponsibly careless, or downright dishonest.

However, there may well be a place for something misnamed dialectical 'logic', which is in no sense at variance with standard logic because the 'contradictions' which it highlights are in no sense logical contradictions. When Lenin and Mao spoke of the 'contradictions' between the peasants and the urban proletariat, they were simply using a fundamentally misleading Hegelian terminology. There is just no formal contradiction involved in the proposition that different groups have opposed class interests. Nevertheless, to interpret social processes in terms of class conflict may well yield important social insights and in general produce a much deeper understanding of the roots of social change. So construed, a 'dialectical' perspective may be invaluable as an investigatory method, as a heuristic. But the most excellent conceivable heuristic, far from superseding standard logic, must partly depend on standard logic, since otherwise it could not even consistently frame its distinctive principles of method or coherently state whatever new insights or better understanding it claimed to achieve. And when Engels spoke of the dynamic tensions, the interactions, polarities, collisions, attractions, and repulsions which, he claimed, pervade all natural processes, he was of course free to call these 'contradictions'; but if Marxists equate these 'contradictions' with logical contradictions, the consequence is that they are debarring Engels from stating his fairly interesting (if scarcely very original or profound) views about the workings of Nature. For if the proposition, 'All things in Nature interact dynamically with their opposites', were to be exempted from the logical Law of Contradiction, Engels's statement would entail its own contradiction ('No things in nature interact dynamically with their opposites'), with the result that he would have succeeded in saying precisely nothing about Nature and its workings. Indeed, anyone who says, 'I reject the logical Law of Contradiction', is on his own showing simultaneously saying, 'I accept the logical Law of Contradiction.'

Of course the actual Engels did not reject formal logic, but explicitly affirmed, in Socialism: Utopian and Scientific, the enduring need for formal logic as an indispensable intellectual tool. It is modern Western Marxists or neo-Marxists, particularly the adherents of the Frankfurt school, who are so hostile to formal logic. The Horkheimers, Adornos, and Marcuses regard formal logic as 'an instrument of social control and domination'. But if formal logic, and with it the logical Law of Contradiction, is rejected, in favour of 'dialectical logic', which welcomes contradictions, the proposition, 'Logic is an instrument of domination', entails the proposition, 'Logic is not an instrument of domination', and once again precisely nothing is being asserted. It is staggering that such distinguished thinkers, who have exerted such influence in so many areas of modern social theory, appear to be so ignorant of the very nature of the discipline they are attacking. After exposing some of the confusions in Marcuse's criticisms of formal logic, MacIntyre (1970: 78) puts the point very well:

> Marcuse's own high-handed scorn about those [logicians] whom he criticizes makes it not inapposite to remark that the arguments which I have been deploying are very elementary ones, familiar to every student with the barest knowledge of logic. The suspicion is thus engendered that not only Marcuse, but also Adorno and Horkheimer, actually do not know any logic and it is certainly the case that, if they do know any, all three have taken some pains to conceal their knowledge of the subject which they are professedly criticizing.

The relevance of all this to theorizing about adult education is as follows. In chapter two I suggested that academic philosophy has a distinctive contribution - only a contribution, but an indispensable contribution - to make to the study of adult education. We all hold beliefs about the nature and proper aims of adult education, and many of us try to integrate these beliefs into organized belief-systems which, among much else, claim to display the importance of adult education for the life of the individual and the well-being of society. Any belief about adult education will logically depend on various assumptions, often in widely distant spheres of human concern; it will have logical relationships of consistency and inconsistency with other beliefs simultaneously asserted; and from it there will logically follow yet other beliefs, perhaps unstated or unrecognized. It is the task of philosophy to identify and clarify the logical assumptions and implications of our beliefs about adult education, and to test the latter for their mutual consistency. If we profess to hold two beliefs which, perhaps indirectly and at several removes, turn out to be contradictory, one or both of those beliefs must be either given up altogether or revised in whatever slight or drastic degree is necessary to remove the contradiction. If a cherished system of beliefs turns out to secrete internal logical inconsistencies, that system of beliefs must be either given up or subjected to conceptual surgery which will remove the sources of inconsistency. The more cherished and deeply held the system of beliefs the greater will be the psychological pain of the surgery. But we must make no mistakes about this: if the logical surgery is needed, but not carried out, the belief-system in question is dead. It survives, not as a genuine system of beliefs, but merely as a set of verbal ceremonies, incantations, or fetishes. Logic alone cannot possibly tell us what to believe, about adult education or anything else. But its diagnoses, when correct, can certainly tell us when our verbal deliverances actually express beliefs about adult education, its meaning and purpose, and when they are merely pretending to do so.

Reference

MacIntyre, A. (1970) Marcuse, Modern Masters series, . London: Fontana.

HISTORY AND PRAXIS: EXTENDING THE DISCUSSION

Paul F. Armstrong

Critical reflection is a dynamic and on-going practice. This is a welcome opportunity to reflect on both my own chapter and how it has been perceived in the context of the book, as outlined in chapter eight. Earlier I argued that the epistemological relationship between adult education and sociology is problematic. I recognized that the epistemological status of sociology is in itself problematic and cannot be taken for granted. But, upon reflection, I would not wish to support the claim that the lack of congruity between adult education and sociology prohibits the illumination of adult education theory and practice. To make it plain, one does not need a degree in sociology in order to grasp a sociological perspective on adult education. Indeed, one does not need a lengthy study of psychology, philosophy, or whatever before one can apply a psycho- logical or philosophical perspective to adult education. Disciplines have socially and politically as well as epistemologically constructed boundaries, which are not permanent and rigid. The boundary between sociology and psychology is not always clear; nor is the boundary between philosophy and psychology, nor that between philosophy and sociology, and so on. In an ideal typical way, it would be possible to distinguish disciplines on the basis of the axiomatic assumptions that they make about the world, so that - for example - a sociologist is typically interested in social structures and collective action, whereas psychology has its focus on individual behaviour. Now, this is a gross simplification, for within sociology, as I have attempted to show, there are a plethora of perspectives, often with fundamental differences between them in the kinds of assumptions they make about the world, so that to talk in terms of conventional disciplines is unnecessarily restrictive. It should be clear, however, that I am not concerned to reject conventional disciplines. This would appear to be a side track, which inevitably will turn out to be a blind alley. The point is to be critical of whatever one is engaged in, and sociology provides but one vehicle for the development of critical reflexiveness.

Within chapter eight, the editor has raised many issues of contention. In this response I shall restrict myself to elaborating the notion of praxis, with which I concluded chapter five, and broaden out from praxis to encompass history, which this book has appeared to neglect, both as a conventional discipline and as a vehicle for critical analysis.

The concept of praxis has been introduced into adult education literature largely since 1970, when Freire's Pedagogy of the Oppressed was published in English. Freire was using praxis to refer to 'reflection and action upon the world in order to transform it' (Freire, 1970: 28). Thus, in the process of liberation, praxis becomes central, in the dialectical relationship between thought and action. This distinguishes theory for its own sake, on the one hand, and pure action or activism, on the other:

> The insistence that the oppressed engage in reflection on their concrete situation is not a call to armchair revolution. On the contrary, reflection - true reflection - leads to action. On the other hand, when the situation calls for action that action will constitute an authentic praxis only if its consequences become the object of critical reflection. In this sense, the praxis is the new raison d'être of the oppressed; and the revolution, which inaugurates the historical moment of this raison d'être, is not viable apart from their concomitant conscious involvement. Otherwise, action is pure activism. [Freire, 1970: 41]

Whilst there is no transformation without action, 'if action is emphasised exclusively to the detriment of

225

reflection, the word is converted into activism' (Freire, 1970: 60), and, according to Freire, this negates 'true praxis' and makes dialogue impossible.

For Freire praxis is distinctively human. Herein lies the difference between human beings and animals, for humans can act creatively on the world and their history:

> Only men are praxis - the praxis which, as the reflection and action which truly transform reality, is the source of knowledge and creation. Animal creativity, which occurs without praxis, is not creative; man's transforming activity is. [Freire, 1970: 73]

Using Freire's own words, we can summarize his position on praxis by reporting that he begins:

> by reaffirming that men, as beings of the praxis, differ from animals, which are beings of pure activity ... men's activity consists of action and reflection: it is praxis; it is transformation of the world. And as praxis, it requires theory to illuminate it. Men's activity is theory and practice; it is reflection and action. [Freire, 1970: 73]

Moreover, education plays a key part in liberation as praxis, for liberation cannot accept a mechanistic concept of consciousness as an empty vessel to be filled, as some forms of education conceive it. Education must be 'problem-posing' so that people can 'develop their power to perceive critically the way they exist in the world with which and in which they find themselves' and 'education is thus constantly remade in praxis' (Freire, 1970: 56). Teachers and students unite in their efforts to overcome 'authoritarianism and alienating intellectualism', as 'teacher-student and student-teachers reflect simultaneously on themselves and the world without dichotomising this reflection from action'. In this way the process of education can establish 'an authentic form of thought and action'.

Freire's usage of praxis emphasizes the dialectical, reciprocal, simultaneous, and creative relationship between reflection and action, between theory and practice, which he links to social transformation, or 'revolutionary praxis which must stand opposed to the praxis of dominant elites' (1970: 96). Thus Freire's notion of praxis has both a dialectical and an ideological nature. It is true that such a conception contains its paradoxes, as the editor points out in chapter eight. But the critical engagement in praxis raises contradictions and paradoxes to the surface so that they can be exposed to critical analysis, rather than hidden away from view. It is also true that as described here such an analysis would appear to be abstract and theoretical rather than emergent from practice. Again, this is a contradiction inherent both in praxis and in the discussion of praxis, but in facing up to the contradiction the genuinely dialectical nature of praxis becomes apparent. Ideological criticisms of praxis are fair, but when addressed in terms of formal logic are not, unless the underlying ideology of the critique is equally exposed for analysis. In chapter eight the editor summarized one of the contributing authors' critique of praxis. The critique is addressed to the theory of praxis. In reality, and in terms of praxis itself, such a distinction is meaningless, and can make sense only in terms of formal logic. Praxis can be tested out only in practice, not from within formal logic. As the critique suggests, praxis is always socially, culturally, and historically located. Given that praxical action is contingent, it must be understood in those terms, not those of abstract theorizing or logical analysis. It cannot be justified in terms of formal theoretical knowledge. In so far as a theoretical approach and a practical approach to praxis can be distinguished, then this reflects the inherent contradiction, which can be resolved only through praxical action. The separation of theory and practice, even for analytic purposes, comes from outside, not within, praxis.

Nevertheless, although praxical action must be both the point and the test, we should still be able to think analytically and critically about the concept of praxis. For this clearly has an intellectual tradition, which Freire tends to neglect. The historical and intellectual heritage of the concept of praxis are never fully discussed by Freire, and adult educators have borrowed the concept, carried along by the excitement of his message, without critically analysing what Freire actually means by liberation, by social transformation, and ultimately, by praxis.

One recent book has recognized this, and its author, Frank Youngman, seeks to relocate the concept of praxis in its intellectual history, and attempts to rescue the concept, if it is not too late, from eclecticism. As he points out, the concept of praxis is not exclusively nor even originally Marxist, but has a long intellectual history which extends back to ancient Greece. However, Youngman (1986: 55) wishes to reserve the concept for its non-mundane meanings, since 'The utilitarian connotations of "practice" simply as doing or action are unhelpful when discussing exactly what "practice" means within the Marxist tradition.' For Youngman, praxis is an integral part of Marx's philosophy and is central to his reflection theory of knowledge, in what is a distinctively human activity, as Marx discusses it in his writings, particularly in his early works. These writings of Marx reflect a humanistic interpretation which counters the more deterministic versions of Marxism, which tend to fit more closely people's commonsense notions of Marxism.

This discussion, stemming from the criticism that Freire has ignored the intellectual tradition of the concept of praxis, has begun to root the concept back into its history. It may be worth while to pause at this point to examine briefly the ideas of some of those within this tradition who have been referred to in the discussion, such as Gramsci, Lukacs, and the Frankfurt school, not all of whom are referred to explicitly by Freire, and yet his writings reflect that he is aware of their ideas. The influence of Gramsci on Freire is clear to see. Like Gramsci, Freire stresses human agency or the potential for a conscious, critical, reflective dimension to human agency. They both share a notion of human agency in which critical and systematic thought is interwoven with action in the creation and continuous re-creation of the social and material conditions of life. What Freire calls 'conscientization' has its parallel mode of thought and action in the work of Gramsci, who stressed the need for ideological critique at the level of consciousness. An important aspect of praxis and the relationship between consciousness and praxis is the notion of relative autonomy,[1] and actually to engage in and work with people in a historical analysis of the nature of that relative autonomy is an important activity. Through that kind of analysis it is possible to change the degree of autonomy. Now, admittedly, awareness alone is not sufficient to change the objective conditions in which we live. However, a critical analysis together with an examination of the nature of those objective conditions does bring about the possibility of change.

Gramsci, from whom the notion of relative autonomy is derived, realized that generally people engaged in practical activity have no theoretical consciousness of it. Indeed, a person's theoretical consciousness can be historically opposed to his or her activity:

> One might almost say that he has two theoretical consciousnesses (or one contradictory consciousness): one which is implicit in his activity and which in reality unites him with all his fellow workers in the practical transformation of the real world; and one, superficially explicit or verbal, which he has inherited from the past and uncritically absorbed. [Hoare and Nowell Smith, 1971: 333]

Such a contradictory state of consciousness, Gramsci argues, does not permit action, but rather encourages ' a condition of moral and political passivity'. Here Gramsci sees consciousness as part of what he calls 'hegemony' - one of his major concepts - to refer, among other things, to rule or domination by consent rather than coercion. In terms of 'social reproduction' theories of social control, hegemony is a most useful idea which relates to praxis in so far as it is through praxis that counter-hegemonies could be constructed. It is here that Gramsci explicitly sees a role for the educator of adults, primarily through political action, to engage in uniting theory and practice to transform society, and at the same time transforming the principle of hegemony. However humanistic these ideas may sound, hegemony can be interpreted in a quite deterministic way, suggesting that our domination at the level of ideas is so powerful that even our common sense reflects the interests of the ruling classes. A critical passage in Marx's own writings that reflects this ambiguity is to be found in The German Ideology:

> The ideas of the ruling class are in every epoch the ruling ideas, i.e. the class which is the ruling material force of society is at the same time the ruling intellectual force. The class which has the means of material production at its disposal, has control at the same time over the means of mental production, so that thereby, generally speaking, the ideas of those who lack the means of mental production are subject to it. [Marx, 1845: 64]

Here we return to the issue of determinism, in so far as it appears that the means of production, whether material or mental, determine consciousness and ideas, and that the economic base of any society determines the ideological superstructure. Whereas Marx and Engels remained largely ambiguous on this, for Gramsci this apparent contradiction is best understood as a dialectical relationship, and, like Freire, he rejects outright any notions of determinism, although his own concept of hegemony conveys a similar paradox.[2]

Gramsci was an activist as well as a theorist. He was engaged in political action, including various socialist movements in Italy during and immediately after World War I, and he was one of the founders of the Italian Communist Party, of which he was subsequently elected leader. He was imprisoned for his political beliefs and actions. For him the study of socialist ideas was for the possibility of bringing about a socialist transformation of society, not for mere academic interest. He said that the class struggle must be waged at the level of ideas and find itself in political action, not in libraries or universities.

Lukacs, a Hungarian Marxist, was a contemporary of Gramsci, who held similar ideas and interpretations of Marxism.[3] In his classic text, History and Class Consciousness, Lukacs's central and underlying concept was praxis. Like Gramsci, Lukacs was concerned to repudiate a fatalistic economic determinist version of Marxism in favour of a commitment to creative action; but, again like Gramsci, he was aware of the practical constraints on this in contemporary Europe, reflecting upon the role of working-class social movements during and immediately after the World War I. He argued that consciousness of the proletariat is history made conscious of itself at a particular stage of development. History is never deterministic, but, along with Gramsci, there is a commitment to the idea of historical necessity, referring to Marx's classic statement in The Eighteenth Brumaire of Louis Bonaparte: 'Men make their own history, but they do not make it just as they please; they do not make it under circumstances chosen by themselves, but under circumstances directly encountered, given and transmitted from the past' (Marx and Engels, 1950: 225).

A contemporary of Lukacs and Gramsci, Karl Korsch, writing in his 1920s, argued similarly that Marxism was both a 'theory of social revolution' and a 'revolutionary philosophy' based on the principle of the unity of theory and practice, or more precisely on the unity of 'theoretical criticism' and 'practical revolutionary change', the two conceived as 'inseparably connected actions' (Korsch, 1923). However, Korsch was more satisfied than either Lukacs or Gramsci with more orthodox interpretations of praxis, especially following Engels's ideas, which he quoted with approval. Engels is often held responsible for the rather narrow view of praxis based on the idea of 'the proof of the pudding', or the testing of theory against reality. Korsch tended to see praxis more as 'pudding eating' or testing theory than did either Lukacs or Gramsci.

Whatever their interpretations of praxis, all three provided a great stimulus to the further discussion and examination of the concept of praxis from the 1920s onwards. The concept was also independently elaborated by Marcuse, who saw Marxism as a 'theory of social activity, of historical action'. More specifically, he elaborated the concept to encompass labour, which is related to 'doing' and is therefore a specific form of praxis. All these interpretations have found their way into the thinking of the Frankfurt school, for whom the relation between theory and praxis has always been a major concern, although they have probably focused more on theory (i.e. critical theory) than praxis. Habermas attempted to formulate the concept of praxis in a different way by distinguishing 'work' or 'purposive rational action' and 'interaction' or 'communicative action'. According to Habermas, social praxis as understood by Marx included both 'work' and 'interaction', though Marx had a tendency to reduce it to work or labour.[4]

Apart from Freire and Gramsci, none of these writers had very much to say about praxis in adult education. Inevitably, therefore, such conceptual discussions are rather abstract and not reflective of the concept of praxis itself. In a book of this nature it would be hard to convey the notion of praxis in anything other than abstract and conceptual terms. However, it is hoped that this rejoinder has clarified the direction of my earlier chapter, and conveyed my commitment to an approach to adult education for social change which is overtly ideological, dialectical in nature, critical in practice, confronting both contradictions and paradoxes, and freed from the constraints of epistemological debate. In doing so, the significance of a historical dimension to analysis has been demonstrated. In accordance with the position set out earlier, a praxical approach to adult education can draw on knowledge and perspectives originating from any of the conventional disciplines, provided there is both ideological and epistemological consistency. The boundaries between, say, history and sociology are themselves ideological constructs that require critical analysis.

Notes

1 For a discussion of this concept see C. Fritzell, 'On the concept of relative autonomy in educational theory', British Journal of Sociology of Education 8 (11), 1987: 23-35.

2 For a further discussion of these ideas and their application to the education of adults see H. Entwhistle, Antonio Gramsci: Conservative Schooling for Radical Politics (Routledge & Kegan Paul, London, 1979), and P.F. Armstrong, 'L'Ordine Nuovo: the legacy of Antonio Gramsci and the education of adults', International Journal of Lifelong Education, 7(4), 1988 249-59.

3 For an introductory and comparative discussion of Gramsci and Lukacs, see R. Kilminster, Praxis and Method: a Sociological Dialogue with Lukacs, Gramsci and the Early Frankfurt School Routledge & Kegan Paul, London, 1979).

4 For discussion of the Frankfurt school and the work of Marcuse and Habermas see Kilminster, op. cit., and D. Held, Introduction to Critical Theory: Horkheimer to Habermas (Hutchinson, London, 1980).

References

Freire, Paolo (1970) Pedagogy of the Oppressed, Harmondsworth: Penguin Books.

Hoare, Q., and Nowell Smith, G. (eds) (1971) Selections from the Prison Notebooks of Antonio Gramsci, London: Lawrence & Wishart.

Korsch, Karl (1923) Marxism and Philosophy, 1970 edition, London: New Left Books.

Lukacs, G. (1923) History and Class Consciousness, trans. R. Livingstone, 1971 edition, London: Merlin Press.

Marx, Karl (1845) The German Ideology, ed. C.J. Arthur, 1970, London: Lawrence & Wishart.

—— and Engels, Frederick (1950) Selected Works I, London: Lawrence & Wishart.

Youngman, Frank (1986) Adult Education and Socialist Pedagogy, London: Croom Helm.

DECONSTRUCTING FOUNDATIONS, RECONSTRUCTING THE PRAGMATIC

Robin S. Usher

The aim of my chapter was to 'theorize the practical' and by so doing show how the practical is a realm of knowledge in its own right with associated modes of understanding and reasoning. This enables us to see practice differently. But theorizing the practical inevitably raises issues concerned both with the nature of the knowledge found in the practical and its relationship with the knowledge contained in the disciplines (formal theory).

The attempt to 'found' the study of adult education in conventional disciplines has not served us well and I suspect this is due, in the end, to the problematic nature of the notion of 'foundations'. The problem of rigour and relevance, discussed in my chapter, stems from the concern to found adult education in the disciplines and the consequent blindness to the importance of the practical.

Now in my chapter I quite deliberately did not deal with epistemological questions. As Bright rightly points out, this was not because of a failure to recognize their significance but because it seemed to me that the traditional debate about epistemology is one which should not be entered if one's purpose is to put forward an alternative theorization. The framework in which the debate is cast is such that one is inevitably placed in the role of an 'absolutist' or a 'relativist'. I would not wish to be cast in either role, because both assume that knowledge is problematic and argue about the possibility of secure foundations.

All this, however, presupposes knowing subjects who are spectators or observers of a world of knowable objects, separate and external to themselves. Here I would want to take the arguments put forward by Heidegger (1967) that we can make these distinctions between subjects and objects, the knower and the knowable, only because we are already in and of the world. We are not subjects encountering independent objects but in a world within which we are immersed or 'thrown' and where 'objects' are encountered in terms of everyday practices of coping (Heidegger calls this the 'ready to hand'). Separating knowing subjects from knowable objects is thus a second-order activity which presupposes the immersion in the world where there is no such separation. Our dealings with 'objects' are, in the first instance, in terms of how we use them through our practices. The question of how we know them and whether the basis for our claims to know are justified simply does not arise.

Heidegger also refers to other kinds of practices which are related but at the same time crucially different. One is the 'unready to hand', concerned with coping when things go wrong or when there is a problem. Here coping (acting in the world) and conscious thought are both present and mutually interactive in the resolution of the problem. In the unready to hand the world and our practices are no longer 'transparent' but through the encounter with a problem are suddenly disclosed or revealed.

The other is the 'present at hand', which is a practice concerned not with coping but with contemplating and examining 'objects' in the world with a view to figuring out their properties and characteristics. This, of course, is the practice of formal theorizing concerned with 'knowing' the world through observation and the consequent formulation of universal and context-free 'laws' about it. The significant thing here is that the practice of formal theorizing and its validity as a practice are not being denied. But it has to be seen as a <u>practice</u>, one of a <u>number</u> of practices and certainly not in any sense as a <u>basic paradigm</u> of practice. This means that its epistemology need not be privileged nor its methodology set up as a universal standard.

With the present at hand subjects and objects are separated and therefore the traditional epistemological concerns become appropriate. On the other hand our knowledge of the world is not primarily through the present at hand. In the first instance it is through our situatedness in a network of practices, our 'everyday meaningful world of significance' (Palmer, 1969), in the second instance it is through the breakdown of part of that everyday meaningful world and only in the third instance through its analytical contemplation and detached observation. This third-level knowledge is thus unlikely to be of much help in .directly understanding the first level.

The practice of formal theorizing is thus not to be privileged over the practice of coping, since if we were not already 'thrown' or situated in the world we would not be in a position to theorize anyway. This is a powerful argument against the technical-rationality model, discussed at length in my chapter, which sees acting in the world as subsidiary to and derivative from theorizing. Equally it is a powerful argument against conventional disciplines as epistemological foundations.

Heidegger's analysis is an important source of illumination because in stressing the primacy of practical activity and situatedness in the world it allows a redirecting of attention away from traditional epistemological questions, which from the viewpoint of the adult eduator are dead-ends, to more fruitful questions concerning the nature of the practical and the hermeneutic understanding associated with that. We are thrown into the world as beings who understand, and understanding underlies all our activities. We project meaning (interpret) and these interpretive projections are rooted in situatedness. To interpret anything, however, is to have already placed it within a certain context and approached it with a certain perspective - in other words, with the 'prejudice' or prejudgement inevitably given to us through situatedness.

A discipline is itself a practice which is situated. It has its own 'prejudices' and 'tradition' or historically evolving interpretive culture. To say this is to conventionalize disciplines although not necessarily to reject their 'truth' root-and-branch on the grounds, for example, that they are hopelessly 'ideological'. Other than as a statement of an abstract and in itself ideological position I cannot see what 'rejecting' disciplines means in concrete terms. Furthermore unless we are to fall into reflexive paradox the recognition of the influence of ideology must imply that we are not helpless to counter that influence.

This 'conventionalizing' of disciplines necessarily leads to a questioning of the very notion of 'foundations'. It is not simply a question of whether disciplines such as psychology are legitimately foundations of adult education but of the foundations of disciplines themselves in certain epistemological conceptions. In other words, it is necessary to question the <u>foundations of foundations,</u> a process which has led me to conclude that the worry about whether there are or are not secure foundations of knowledge is misplaced.

All disciplines are ultimately founded on an epistemology or theory of knowledge. For a belief to be accepted as knowledge and an interpretation to be judged as valid there must, it is thought, be some ultimate foundation which itself does not need justification and which thus provides universal criteria of validity.

Knowledge is deemed to be knowledge only if it is <u>true</u> in the sense that it <u>corresponds</u> to the way the world <u>really</u>

is. But as we have seen, this assumes a knowable world external to knowing subjects. Rather, because we are in the world, in the very act of understanding (knowing) the world we have already interpreted and appropriated it through our situatedness in society and culture. If, following Rorty (1980), we question the notion that knowledge somehow 'mirrors' or represents reality, then its foundational character is undermined.

The emphasis now switches to the shared meanings in shared practices as the essential framework within which conceptions of knowledge and truth are located and developed. Gadamer (1975) reminds us that our situatedness defines our 'horizons' which are not limits but the possibility of a continual process of openness to experience and thus the very condition of knowledge.

Rorty maintains that since knowledge does not mirror 'reality' it is not therefore concerned with a pursuit of truth which unequivocally and finally settles claims to knowledge. Rather, claims to knowledge are settled conventionally within social practices and shared meanings. Their justification is pragmatic, not foundational. In other words, do they allow us to cope more effectively with the world and do they allow us to understand and change?

This process of edification is concerned with knowledge in terms of coping and personal development rather than knowledge as foundationally justified. According to Rorty we should stop worrying about epistemology and instead engage in critical dialogue. Edification is therefore about being creative through dialogue rather than experimentation and the application of scientific method. Truth is about disclosing the world rather than accurately representing it. The emphasis is on understanding rather than 'finding out', on development rather than certainty.

Edification also has implications for what we take rationality to be. Standards of rationality do not stand outside history and social practices. We must, therefore, have a concept of rationality which is implicated within rather than outside these.

The same is the case with 'scientific method'. It is not some universal algorithm without the application of which secure knowledge would be impossible as if mechanically going through a set of universal procedures will make knowledge more secure in all circumstances. For explaining, predicting, and controlling (i.e. the present at hand) 'scientific method' will likely do the job. But it is unlikely to do so if the concern is with understanding and interacting with others. The kind of inquiry as defined by its purpose is thus the crucial consideration. In any particular inquiry one has to be rational in terms of practice within that inquiry (Rorty, 1982). Being rational is to act in certain ways appropriate to the particular situation. It is part of practical knowledge and hermeneutic understanding.

This, then, is the idea of a dialogical rationality within particular practices and inquiry. Claims are justified through dialogue involving interpretation, deliberation, and choice. We argue for or against a belief but do so not in terms of whether it has a secure foundation in a universal rationality but pragmatically in terms of the concrete advantages and disadvantages of the belief. Similarly 'objectivity' can be seen as an expression of consensus and 'truth' as that which can be dialogically validated by those 'who share the same world at a given time in history' (Rowan and Reason, 1981: 133).

It follows from this that dialogue may reach a temporary end-point but by its nature is never permanently terminated. Gadamer refers to the 'fusion of horizons' which leaves open the possibility of simultaneously changing one's 'prejudices' and deepening understanding of the unfamiliar and the problematic. The same is the case for standards of rationality. Warnke (1987) makes the point that rationality is 'a willingness to admit the existence of better options' and to be open to 'future defeat' (p. 173). In passing, one notes the significance of this in terms of the notion of 'dialectical logic'. According to Bright, I am supposed to uphold this as against formal logic whilst apparently unaware that it is parasitic on the latter. But what is so special about formal logic that we should privilege it thus? That one should recognize the partiality and contingency of one's knowledge and the possibility that it could become more comprehensive in dialogue through the synthesis of opposing viewpoints thus leading to 'better' knowledge strikes me as a perfectly coherent and unparasitical position.

Furthermore, to emphasize dialogue is to recognize that our existing beliefs, claims, and practices are seen to be inadequate only through being confronted by other beliefs, claims, and practices. Conventional disciplines may in certain circumstances fulfil the role of this 'other'. However, they can do so only if they are genuinely part of the dialogue - in other words, if they are no longer seen as a foundation.

Rejoinders and further comments

In effect, it is unnecessary to see disciplines as foundations of anything. The very notion of 'foundations' is something which philosophers have invented in their obsessive search for a counter to the 'Cartesian anxiety' - if there are no ultimate foundations, then there can only be chaos (Bernstein, 1983: 42). But is chaos the only alternative?

One need not say that knowledge claims can never be justified or that it is impossible to decide between the true and the false. All we need to accept is that in evaluating claims to knowledge and in deciding the true from the false we cannot 'step out' of history and the social practices located in history. Forms of knowledge (disciplines) are conventional and justified not by universal and ahistorical criteria of truth and rationality but pragmatically within the arena of dialogue and through practice. Thus the alternative to 'chaos' is dialogue.

Dialogue, however, may not be genuine and unconstrained, openness to learning may be limited by ideology, and knowledge is always co-implicated with power. Disciplines, as Foucault (1972) has pointed out, are not just neutral bodies of knowledge but have constitutive and regulative power. For educational practitioners, disciplines and the notion of foundations are inevitably part of their prejudices and traditions. At the same time, however, these are not fixed and immune to change. We can 'step out' of particular prejudices although not out of prejudices as such. Our interpretive horizons change as our understandings change. Being situated does not imply being determined or hopelessly constrained. Our horizons are continually developing through the engagement of our 'prejudices' with the unfamiliar and problematic.

The significance of a hermeneutic viewpoint is that understandings start from ourselves but as we change so things which had an apparently fixed and unchanging meaning no longer do. If we are able to surface our prejudices and thus reveal the influence of tradition and the nature of our situatedness this critical process of self- and situational-awareness can allow us to cope with the limitations and constraints of ideology and power. It is precisely because it recognizes the potential multiplicity and often submerged dimensions of meanings that hermeneutic understanding is capable of revealing ideological constraints.

Through theorizing the practical, therefore, the nature

of hermeneutic understanding is revealed. I take this to be particularly important because it reminds us of the relationship between the study of adult education and the objects of its study. The idea of the 'double hermeneutic' (Giddens, 1976) where both the subject and the object of study in the social sciences inhabit 'pre-interpreted' worlds is also useful in thinking about adult education.

The task of the social scientist is to effect hermeneutically a 'fusion of horizons' of differing pre-interpreted worlds. Clearly the theorist and the practitioner in adult education are situated in 'pre-interpreted' worlds. This has vital implications both for the nature of knowledge in adult education and for the issue of what is an appropriate curriculum. Adult education is perhaps even more complex, with a triple hermeneutic involving the theorist, the practitioner, and the 'clients' of the latter. It is therefore perhaps not surprising that the study of adult education is gradually revealing itself to be a highly complex matter and that it has so easily fallen prey to simplistic theorizing.

Theorizing the 'practical' stresses the hermeneutic, interpretive dimension. The study of adult education by relating itself to the practical necessarily incorporates this dimension in its own theorizing and curriculum practice. Consequently the purpose of theory in adult education is essentially pragmatic. The concern is not with practitioners imbibing bodies of formal knowledge culled from the conventional disciplines in the vain hope that they might be able to 'apply' this to their practice but to help them problematize and refine their situated understandings and practices.

As Bright rightly points out, my quarrel, such as it is, with the conventional disciplines is not to deny their legitimacy or 'truth' as theoretical activities which attempt to explain the world but with the notion that they are in any sense 'foundations' and that therefore their content and methodology should be privileged. I have tried, in this discussion, to indicate why this is unhelpful and in so doing one of my aims, implicit up to now, has been to 'reconstruct' and in a sense 'resurrect' the pragmatic.

The latter has clearly accumulated something of a bad press through its association with certain kinds of practice aimed at giving 'consumers' of adult education what they want regardless of what it may be. It follows from what I have been saying that merely criticizing these practices from some kind of a priori position is inappropriate. The task is more to understand them within the situated understandings and contexts of practitioners. Having problematized them, theorists and practitioners may then dialogically reach a deeper understanding of both the possibilities and the limits of these kinds of practice.

In this enterprise we may well be aided by understanding the philosophical implications of 'being pragmatic'. Here again I turn to Rorty, who points out that to be pragmatic is to be located in the practical rather than in 'universal' theory. It is to have a 'vocabulary' of situational action where truth is related not to foundations, accurate representation, and algorithmic method but to the consequences of beliefs and claims in terms of their contribution to understanding and edification. Being pragmatic, therefore, is not to have a theory of knowledge and truth but to be willing to participate in dialogue. Dialogue seeks knowledge and truth but recognizes that since the quest is not constrained by the search for foundations it is both situationally oriented and action-led yet potentially endless. The traditional epistemological concerns thus need not cause anxiety except in so far as they constitute an obscuring ideology which must be problematized within the dialogue.

It is clear also that being pragmatic in this sense is an integral part of the hermeneutic project which I have outlined and is therefore particularly appropriate to adult education both as a field of study and as practice. Consequently this has implications for the relationship between adult education and philosophy. The latter is itself a practice situated in history and culture. We need to see philosophy not as 'an ongoing timeless debate but as the setting up of projects responsive to the demands of differing historical situations' (Wain, 1987: 9). It is part of history and culture rather than the external universal touchstone of knowledge claims.

Given this, therefore, I find it hard to accept Paterson's claims for the role of philosophy as 'logical analysis'. This seems to me to construe philosophy as an instrument of the 'pure reasoner' who is detached from the 'social and cultural context by the adoption of methodologically secured sets of rules and enquiry' (Anderson et al., 1986: 72). But surely the philosopher is also situated? For a situated inquiry such as adult education whose object is situated practices and understandings philosophy's traditional role of 'guardian' of knowledge claims and methodology is frankly not very edifying. Philosophy must be a participant in the dialogue, not an epistemological policeman outside it.

References

Anderson, R. J., Hughes, J. A., and Sharrock, W. W. (1986) Philosophy and the Human Sciences, Beckenham: Croom Helm.

Bernstein, R. J. (1983) Beyond Objectivism and Relativism, Oxford: Blackwell.

Foucault, M. (1972) The Archaeology of Knowledge, London: Tavistock.

Gadamer, H-G. (1975) Truth and Method, New York: Seabury Press.

Giddens, A. (1976) New Rules of Sociological Method, London: Hutchinson.

Heidegger, M. (1967) Being and Time, Oxford: Blackwell.

Palmer, R. E. (1969) Hermeneutics, Evanston: Northwestern University Press.

Rorty, R. (1980) Philosophy and the Mirror of Nature, Oxford: Blackwell.

—— (1982) Consequences of Pragmatism, Brighton: Harvester Press.

Rowan, J., and Reason, P. (1981) 'On making sense', in P. Reason and J. Rowan (eds.), Human Inquiry: Sourcebook of New Paradigm Research, Chichester: Wiley.

Wain, K. (1987) Philosophy of Lifelong Education, Beckenham: Croom Helm.

Warnke, G. (1987) Gadamer: Hermeneutics, Tradition and Reason, Oxford: Polity Press.

Index

Index

United States of America
(USA), adult education
11-12, 141-66; definition
143-4; epistemology 141-
2, 164-6; functional
analysis 144-7;
historicity 155-6;
philosophy 159-62; and
politics 147-8, 150-2,
156-9; and UK 148-52,
154-5
Usher, Robin S. vii, 9-10,
40, 42, 55, 57, 59, 65-92,
174-217 passim, 233-41

values, 14, 20, 26-8
vandalism 35-6
Vandenberg, D. 91
Verduin, J.R. 142
Verner, C. 143

Wain, K. 241
Wallace, K. 149, 156, 162
Wallace, R.K. 155
Warnke, G. 76, 78, 237
Weber, Max 134-5
Westland, G. 44